DANCE

a projection
for the future

THE DEVELOPMENTAL CONFERENCE ON DANCE   November 24 – December 3, 1966
University of California, Los Angeles, California   and May 28 – June 3, 1967

ALMA M. HAWKINS, Project Director

The work reported herein was performed pursuant to a contract with the United States Department of Health, Education, and Welfare, Office of Education, Arts and Humanities Program, Contract OEC 4-5-062061-0966. Contractors undertaking such projects under Government sponsorship are encouraged to express freely their professional judgment in the conduct of the project. Points of view or opinions stated do not, therefore, necessarily represent official Office of Education position or policy.

Preface

In this twentieth year of publication of IMPULSE — The Annual of Contemporary Dance, we are honored to present the Report of the Developmental Conference on Dance, sponsored by the United States Office of Education, Arts and Humanities Program. The contents of this volume are in direct accord with the consistent and reiterated commitment of IMPULSE: to enlarge the frame of reference of dancers, teachers, and interested laymen; to consider dance in relation to the individual and society; to contribute to the literature of dance by publishing essays by qualified persons directed to the chosen topic of each issue. The subjects have been varied and vast. Lest anybody conclude that IMPULSE has been making "cosmic legislations," to use Korzybski's term, we have dated each year's book and have pointed out that at this time this is what these individuals have thought about this particular subject. In retrospect, it is both interesting and reassuring to note how many of the essays have become "classics" or collector's items. Of course, we are talking about only twenty years!

In an evanescent art, such as dance, even with the great strides that are being made in notation and in film, much of the "time-binding" must be done by the printed word. Words, indeed, have evocative power in our verbal culture. But our very over-verbalization has contributed to some of our present difficulties. The current rather desperate search for "sensory awareness," on the part of adults from 18-60 and beyond, the yearning of adolescents and young adults to "turn on," and the deep disappointment and unease of parents on seeing their children "turned off" in school all give evidence that the people have been cheated or have lost something very early in life — an important part of their individual human heritage.

What can dance do about it? That is what this book is about. Forty-five persons from the fields of dance, education, music, notation, criticism, psychology, philosophy, and biological science worked long and devotedly for a total of seventeen days wrestling with this problem. I was privileged to be there and see it happen.

IMPULSE 1968 is addressed to the future — a projection of potential. It is our hope that these "more" words about the art that disappears into thin air will serve as an architectural blueprint for action.

Marian Van Tuyl

San Francisco, March 1968

Contents

Introduction

The professional dance artist, artist-teacher, and administrator now have the opportunity to bring about major changes in education that could have profound influence on the growth of dance as a performing art and the aesthetic education of students. New major curricula are being established, more theatre dance productions are available to students, and colleges and universities have a closer relationship with professional artists than in any previous period. Innovations will lead to significant and lasting developments only as they are based on a vision of dance as a performing art and of dance as a medium for education.

The idea of a developmental conference on dance was born out of the recognition that, in this period of rapid change, dance educators who must make critical decisions that affect the future of dance needed an opportunity to discuss basic issues. The leaders in the Arts and Humanities Program, Office of Education had been engaged in developmental projects in music, art, and theatre. They were also concerned about the unique needs of dance, so, with the support and assistance of Kathryn Bloom, Director, and Jack Morrison, Theatre Education Specialist and Acting Dance Specialist, the developmental conference on dance became a reality.

The primary goal of the project was to bring together a representative group of experienced and knowledgeable artists, scholars, and educators to explore together the role of dance in education, and to evolve a point of view that would give direction to the immediate as well as the long-range curricular and research developments in dance.

The conference was carried out in two phases — first, November 24 — December 3, 1966, and second, May 28 — June 3, 1967. The specific purpose of Phase I was to consider the role and nature of the dance experience in education and to develop curricular guidelines. The program began with speakers on dance, philosophy, creativity, movement, and music, who presented ideas from their special fields having implications for dance, and then led discussions. The participants were divided into small work groups which assumed the responsibility for preparing reports on the topics: Dance as a Four - Dimensional Art, Movement, Form, Artistic Growth, and Intellectual Growth. General discussions, including the entire conference group, were an important part of the proceedings.

Phase II was concerned with the construction of a blueprint for the twenty-five year projection of undergraduate and graduate major curricula. The relationship of the professional artist and performer to education was a central issue, discussed at length after four statements by dance artists.

The task was a large one and the time was short. Our work was directed, primarily, toward thinking through basic philosophic issues which determine policy, and sketching out implications for curricular developments, teaching, and research.

This report reflects a deep concern about the quality of the dance experience, a determination to make the creative dance experience available to students at all levels of education, a sincere desire to find effective means of relating dance in education to the mainstream of dance as a performing art in our society, and a commitment to dance as an academic discipline which provides varied patterns of graduate study supported by artistic and research achievements.

While participants dreamed of the ideal, they were aware of existing problems. Educators are expected to initiate new curricula, further creative and research endeavors, and establish functional relationships with professional artists. New dance departments must pioneer unexplored paths in a complex academic world, despite the shortage of qualified faculty, inadequate budgets, insufficient space, and lack of appropriate theatre facilities. Nevertheless, the building of a dance program in keeping with the dream was the primary concern of the participants, and to that end we worked.

As a result of being deeply involved in a common task, something important happened to each of us, and to the group. Our understanding grew and our skill in working together improved. These human intangibles may not be apparent in a printed report, but I suspect that they will be reflected in our leadership during the coming years.

As coordinator of the conference, I want to express our deep gratitude to the Arts and Humanities Program for making the project possible; to Kathryn Bloom and Jack Morrison for their support during the planning stages and throughout the project; and to Irving Brown, successor to Jack Morrison, for his generous assistance in program planning, and guiding the project to completion.

I wish to acknowledge the splendid contributions of all the participants who gave so freely of their

wisdom, experience, and aspirations, and made our work together a success. They came ready to share ideas and to plan for the future. Throughout the conference there was an openness to ideas and a dedication that was truly remarkable.

My sincere appreciation to the Advisory Committee — William Bales, Jean Erdman, Dorothy Madden, and Ruth Murray — for their constant support and wise counsel.

My thanks to Tamara Comstock for the many hours spent in transcribing conference tapes and for assistance with the shaping and editing of the final manuscript.

And lastly, my sincere thanks to Marian Van Tuyl, Editor of IMPULSE, for assisting in the editing, and for publishing this report as a special issue of IMPULSE.

ALMA M. HAWKINS

Manifesto

The purpose of education is the full realization of the total man and his understanding and communication with others.

Art experience is an ingredient of that total realization.

This ingredient in dance is a unique, non-verbal revelation of an aspect of living.

Incisive and specific information from the behavioral, medical, psychological, and social sciences is providing us with the strongest evidence that dance as a basic art is vital to the development of the whole individual. In our period of rapid change and fragmented experience, the development of the whole person becomes increasingly difficult. The education of the senses and the objectification of feeling through the arts provide one way by which man is able to know himself, and to shape and bring order to his world.

Most educational systems at the present time do not afford an opportunity for growth in these areas. For that reason, we, the participants in the Developmental Conference on Dance, believe that dance should become an increasingly integral part of society and, therefore, of education.

There should be:

The opportunity for every child, male and female, to have a dance experience.

A skilled dance teacher in every school at every level.

Space and time and the financial support necessary to dance education.

Available resources such as films, books, recordings, and notation.

Exposure to the best of all types of live dance performances.

An honors program for the gifted individual.

The climate and conditions that will interest men in dance as an avocation and profession.

Representatives of dance in education on all councils, boards, and faculties dealing with the education of our people.

AN EXPANDED FRAME OF REFERENCE

Left to right: Selma Jeanne Cohen, Alma Hawkins, Shirley Wimmer, Thomas Watson, Joan Woodbury, Jack Morrison

FOR DANCE

Dance in Perspective

JOHN MARTIN

The dance is so newly arrived among the respectable arts that when you undertake to talk about it, it becomes necessary to make clear at the start just what it is you are talking about. There are passionate advocates of classic dance, modern, ethnic, social, folk, religious, ritual, tap, jazz, rock 'n' roll, each with its own technical concentrations, vocabularies of movement, and so on; and much blood and venom are expended in exalting each of them severally and denouncing the rest of them collectively. What is ironic about the situation is that they are all the same thing; or at least manifestations — or perhaps specialized corruptions — of the same thing.

It is that "same thing" that I am going to talk about; let us call it simply basic dance. It is not new or old, pretty or ugly, uplifting or demoralizing; it has no standard technique and no vocabulary. It is not even itself an art, though it is the basis of all art; it is an animal function, comparable loosely to digestion, and just as vital. Even in its manifestations as art it has no history; catalogues of artifacts do not constitute histories. Like digestion, it operates in relation to immediate circumstances, and any historical approach to it would necessarily be in effect the history of the circumstances that have caused it to function. The dance has no independent life that can be isolated and examined under the microscope, dissected and analyzed. It does not grow; it simply rises to the occasion in times of necessity.

In a "developmental" conference on dance, such as this, then, it is not any development of dance that can be discussed since it is incapable of development; the development must concern the ways and means of making this uniquely valuable animal function more easily recognized, better understood in all its art aspects, and more widely and skillfully applied. It is only in the last generation or two, since the universities have championed it, that it has begun to acquire status, and I am confident that ultimately it will attain a rank of respectability equal even to that of digestion. My only proviso is that the universities become increasingly the

sponsors of the creative practice — let me repeat, PRACTICE — of the dance.

Do not misunderstand me; I am not advocating academic-mindedness toward an activity that is in its very nature non-intellectual, spontaneously experimental, irrational (if you will) and altogether "psychosomatic." The universities, indeed, have no monopoly on academic-mindedness; neither do they demand it as a prerequisite by any means, in spite of their reputation to the contrary. In no other field of public activity has there been any comparable recognition of the essential nature of the dance. I am speaking now of the best of them, the freest, those with the greatest sensitivity to contemporary creativeness. By divinely ordained fortuitousness, dancing came in by the back door — the Physical Education Department. Where else could it have escaped the Pauline interdiction of the body as "vile"? For it is an art of the body — the whole body, including the instrumentalities by which it acts. Because of the increasing perception of its nature and potentialities, it has gradually managed to work its way upward from Physical Education into a sphere of its own. If it had been invited into the academic community in one of the more highbrow departments — music, for example, which is the most predacious of all the arts — it might never have been able to work its way down to its own medium, the body, and it would almost certainly not have a department of its own by now.

As a matter of fact, the university offers deliverance to the dance from its own kind of academic-mindedness, which is not to be underestimated. There is a whole school of thought that threatens the dance from within on these lines. It considers that no type of human activity has entity until it is codified. Once this is done, it can be "understood," and filed away neatly for future reference, when, as and if necessary. It has become a part of "knowledge." Check. Attention can then be turned to new fields of activity to be reduced similarly to impotence but acceptableness in the filing cabinet.

The so-called "classic" ballet — more accurately,

10

the academic ballet, or, if you are a real balleto-mane, the "danse d'école" — is the form that falls most obviously into this category. Every truly creative choreographer within its ranks who has dared to approach it from an unorthodox angle — from Noverre to Fokine to Balanchine — has been incarcerated in the doghouse — pending, of course, the day of his eventual deification upon the accept-ance of his once intolerable heresies as, in turn, standard. One hears often and often (sometimes under surprising circumstances, including a recent session in a UCLA Extension series of lecture-demonstrations, when nobody could rise and shout "No! No!") that the ballet is the true and exclusive foundation of all the art dance of the Western World, including the modern dance.

Now, the earliest date claimed for the ballet is 1489 (and that was merely an elaborate banquet at which courses were introduced and dramatized, if you will, by superficially appropriate entrées of dancers — Jason of the Golden Fleece with the roast lamb, sea deities with the fish, Hebe with the wine, etc. It was perhaps the first more or less formal-ized approach to the practice that had grown fairly common on a smaller scale throughout the Middle Ages.) Anyhow, taking it at its face value, that estimate of priority is pretty tough on contributions of earlier centuries, including the Greeks' efforts some 2000 years before.

Such a claim, however, is just an example of what we might call Renaissance-itis. You will recall that the Renaissance did not start until 1453, when Constantinople fell and all the scholars who had taken all the books about the ancient civilizations of Greece and Rome to the Eastern capital with Constantine, now moved them back to Italy. This happened, I believe, on a Tuesday in August at about 11:30 A.M. Obviously the foundational dance of the Western World could not have been started before then.

Actually the Renaissance, THE Renaissance, was never heard of as such until 1840, when for the first time on record the word was used by Jules Michelet. (Did you ever wonder how the Italian Renaissance came to be referred to almost univer-sally by a French name?) Twenty years later the Swiss Jakob Burckhardt wrote a book in German on the subject under Michelet's name for it, and some years later John Addington Symonds wrote an even more exhaustive work in English — and we were all set with THE Renaissance. It had all been codified for us; we had a Fact to file away — along with

those other Facts, such as that the Puritans were against sex, though not one of them who had not died in infancy ever had less than eighteen children.

But facts are so much more objective than experi-ence; end-results are so much more file-able than process. Yet life itself is process, and not facts, and its end-result is inevitably nothing more nor less than death. And that is really the theme of my sermon this evening.

The very concept of THE Renaissance is a curious one, beyond the possible point of accepting the imagery of the word as referring to what we have come to call humanism, or the rebirth of antiquity — a distinctly questionable attitude in itself. If the concept means rather the flourishing and progress-ive awareness of peoples, we must accept also this ever-expanding creativeness as the natural state of man; those periods of catastrophe, such as the Hundred Years War or the Black Death or those long and disintegrating centuries in the West when Rome was yielding to the so-called barbarians, which we call the Dark Ages, must be seen as merely interruptions of this state and this process. And it is worth remembering that even these Dark Ages were the very centuries when in China painting rose to new heights in the T'ang Dynasty, when printing began to evolve, when the brilliance of the Sung Dynasty was dawning.

Such interruptions as occur throughout our history, dark as they are, are more than compensated for in the resumption of the natural progression by those periods of heightened activity and produc-tivity, which make up a normal cycle of recurring renaissances. We are either too close to it or too susceptible to Renaissance-itis to realize that for the last hundred years we have been in the midst of a renaissance of perhaps unprecedented richness — and are at this moment in the full swing of it. (And I don't mean the "cultural explosion" and the real-estate-sponsored supermarkets of the arts going up everywhere.)

But Renaissance-itis is not the only aspect of this passion for codification, and the danse d'école is not the only field that suffers from it. The so-called modern dance itself is in the throes of embalming itself in the filing cabinet. Its two incomparable revolutionary figures, Isadora Duncan and Mary Wigman, have been reduced to a slogan or two, and nobody seems aware at all of what they did; while the personal creativeness of its most potent performing and choreographing artists is being codified into systems and vocabularies to be substituted for creative compulsion, passion and productiveness. If the movement of the modern dance is not creative in itself, no possible arrangement of it can make it so. Its original and fairly world-shaking concern with the otherwise inexpressible realization of the individual's specific relationships to his environment has been diverted into synthetically reconstituting and re-arranging the ashes of codified movements while the flame and the fuel of the doing are allowed to go up the chimney. There is a great difference between movement, the substance of the dance, and movements, its residues. Modern dance has begun to look with horror at personal commitment, at the idea of transfer of experience. It is yielding to the contemporary trend of denial of the body, which has become more and more merely the servant, the executant of ideas — a development which would no doubt have made St. Paul extremely happy.

Here is an academic-mindedness from which only the universities can deliver us by their commitment to the understanding and practice — again let me repeat, PRACTICE — of basic dance, which includes, indeed consists of, experience of the body.

Let me explain, with great over-simplification, a little more of what I mean by basic dance in this sense.

For all our concern with what we call the "higher" life — intellectual, philosophical, artistic and what you will — we are nevertheless animals, and as such have evolved all these so-called spiritual activities quite functionally for our own preservation and advancement as animals.

The pattern was set in the dateless darkness of the "primordial slime" by a little hunk of highly tonic protoplasm, activated by the twin drives of maintaining and increasing itself. When, if ever, we understand where that tonicity came from, we shall understand what life is. (Better not wait.) What is important is that by its existence and persistence in obeying the built-in urgencies of survival and mastery, it and its progeny down the ages have evolved bit by bit a remarkable series of mechanisms and instrumentalities which we take quite for granted — levers, periscopes, reachers, graspers, smiters, biters, flee-ers; senses, nerves, brains, coordinators — by means of which it is possible to exist in an environment and conquer it. In our advanced, cultivated, refined and sophisticated era, it has become accepted practice to denigrate this

miraculous thing called the body — to treat it simply as an instrument to serve our pleasures and perform certain other rather vulgar and nasty functions not to be talked about in polite society. But pretend as much as we choose, the exact reverse is true; the body is not the servant but the master who gives the orders, and all our precious "higher" life exists as the result of our visceral demands and for the sole purpose of protecting and aggrandizing us as animals.

When these demands are for any reason not to be satisfied in the immediate environment by this wonderful superstructure we have evolved for the purpose — and most of them, to be sure, can — the result is a psychosomatic malaise, which is a fancy way of saying a stirred-up state commonly known as emotion. To allow it to continue unassuaged would be to deny the vital animal drives of maintenance and increase, to imperil our very existence and what might be called its teleological justification. It becomes necessary, therefore, if the actual environment does not yield, to supply a synthetic environment which will, so that the malaise can be quieted, the emotion resolved. And this is how art comes into the picture. Art is simply the providing of a temporary, appropriate, synthetic environment in which harmonious functioning can be restored — an objectification, as it were, of the ideal solution of a particular frustration.

The greater the pressures of our complex society, the greater the frustrations of the basic drives, hence the greater the need for art, the greater its frequency of manifestation, its breadth of acceptance, its range and depth of quality and effectiveness — in short, its inevitability.

Movement, which is the very essence of the primordial protoplasmic tonicity, in which alone it finds itself in function, remains the first natural agency of response, and is the medium in which this rectifying process called art first manifests itself. In the hierarchy of the arts, then, dance rises first to the occasion in times of necessity.

When it rises to the immediate personal necessity — to an individual's especially focused psychosomatic malaise — it results in personal art; when a great period of dance occurs, it is the rising to the pressing occasion of the times.

A striking illustration of this occasion-at-large is the Renaissance. (If we accept the concept of THE Renaissance for the sake of discussion, we may as well accept other over-simplified concepts that grow out of it, for their convenient, if by no means literal, truth.) Actually the dancing of the Renaissance did not take on the form of art until it quit being play — that is, self-entertainment; until the amateurs of the courts quit amusing themselves and began to practice it for the pleasure, edification, enlightenment — what you will — of the spectators. The qualifying difference between play and art is that play is satisfied with the experience itself, while art requires a spectator for the projection of the experience before it is complete.

The urgings of the amateur court dancers — ballroom dancers, we would call them — were deeper, however, than mere self-amusement. They had realized (no doubt on that Tuesday morning in August, 1453) that they were no longer browbeaten wretches, constantly being branded as miserable sinners whom an angry God would inevitably punish; who had no minds of their own and whose vile bodies should be treated with contempt, denied and scourged. Suddenly under the impact of humanism, they were able to see themselves as essentially noble, free-minded individuals entitled to assert and enjoy their individuality without penalty. The only trouble was that what they saw when they turned from these visionary truths to physical reality was not encouraging. Though the princes among them — largely condottieri and the like — had sumptuous palaces and rich apparel, they did not have the requisite nobility of person, the manners, the elegance to match them. To rectify this situation they very logically called in dancing masters to remove their loutishness — to teach them how to move in their shoes with points three feet long, their gowns with twelve-yard trains, their panniers, their swords, their headdresses weighing pounds upon pounds. The urge beneath their dancing, in short, was a vital one — to find and declare their innate elegance and authority, and rise above their state of fear-ridden animals.

It is perhaps significant that in every great revolutionary period of the sort, man has been moved thus to find his real nature and redeem it from captivity to enslaving practices of whatever sort. The Romantic Revolution turned its back on these hard crystalizations which the 18th century — the Age of Reason — through its encyclopedists and academies had made of the polished and elegant practices which had seemed so liberating in the Renaissance. Inevitably it turned now to a nostalgic desire for the age that the Renaissance had destroyed, and went all out for a neo-Gothicism, full

of mystery, fantasy, adventure, even religiosity, in terms not of the Latin and the formalities that prevailed in both church and court but of the simple speech and feeling of the people, with their undisciplined extravagances. It was here that the ballet reached its greatest heights. Make no mistake, it was no desire for acrobatics that drove the ballerinas to dance for the first time on the tips of their toes; it was a natural yearning for the body to rise to the "spiritual" purity of the unearthly realm inhabited by airy sylphides and wilis, and altogether suitable to those idealized (and generally foully mistreated) young maidens who were the epitome of the art.

The Industrial Revolution brought about a revolt not against the petrifactions of academism, but against the even more stultifying effects of the machine: men, women and children transformed into machine-tenders in order to make possible the mass production of hideous "conveniences"; urbanization and the overturning of proven concepts of the home, women in business and in politics, and so on.

So we find weight put into the other side of the balance: William Morris and his passionate revival of handicrafts; art nouveau (which was not as foolish as its present upsurge would lead us to believe); the theatre of Craig and Appia and Stanislavsky; the architecture of Sullivan and Wright; the revival of folk dancing in Sweden and England and Hungary; the revival of the Olympic Games; dress reform for women; Delsarte investigating with meticulous care the relation of gesture to experience; and so through all the arts.

In Isadora Duncan came the glorious climax — a stripping away, actually and metaphorically, of bustles and corsets, shoes and stockings; the revealing of woman as woman, bodily and spiritually; no ethereal wili inhabiting graveyards and heavenly spaces, no grossly traduced maiden dying of heartbreak; a return in essence if not in intent to Rousseau and the long line of philosophers dating back to the Reformation who had been the prophets of the great political overturnings at the close of the 18th century; a "natural" woman to match a "natural" man of Whitman; a complete abandonment of prescribed systems of moving and vocabularies of movement, in favor of what has been called "natural" movement (somewhat erroneously, since we do not go about skipping and tripping and waving the arms in life), but at least movement that was not alien to the body's totality and was not plastered upon it from the outside.

On the basis of this revolution, the whole modern dance was evolved, responding consistently to the changing forces about it, and having expended its magnificent energies to the fulfillment of its own ends, died. It is futile to try, as we are now doing, to extend its life arbitrarily by allowing its once vital practices to become classicisms — by cherishing residues and attempting to manipulate them. We might as well attempt to create in terms of sylphides and wilis without the urgency that once gave them validity.

Already, indeed, we are in the thick of a new revolution, the Electronic Revolution, and what will shape the dance of the new era will be the instinctive reactions of the body to these new pressures. That it will be a vital era is beyond doubt, for the battle will inevitably be a fierce one.

The problem that faces us is exactly the opposite of that which faced the men of the Renaissance. Theirs was to become nobler men; ours is to become better animals. For the computer is here and the computer is the enemy of the body. Its function is to by-pass process and arrive at end-results. But life is process, and is not concerned with end-results; indeed, its end-result can be nothing but death.

A year or so ago there was a picture in the paper of a little girl dialing in on a computer which would give her the answers to her school problems. In the learning process, however, it is not the correct answers that are educational but the process of discovering them. Similarly, we do not live simply for the purpose of dying; if so, we do not need a computer to bring it about.

It is the body ultimately that has created the computer, an instrumentality quite outside itself; and this it has done for exactly the same purpose that has led to the evolving of all its superb personal superstructure through the ages; namely, to serve its basic drives to live ever more fully and commandingly. Now having created this new and detached handiwork, the body must assert its authority over it, just as it must assert its authority endlessly over its self-integrated personal superstructure.

The fact of the computer's detachment is crucial; for it is designed to take over much of the process of the self-integrated superstructure of the body itself and without paying anything back. Since it is by process that the body, the human entity, lives and grows, it is inevitable that with the removal of this process to an outside agency, the body, the human entity, will cease to grow, and indeed, through disuse it will gradually atrophy.

It is possible to envision, in a combination of science fiction and horror story, the ultimate shriveling up and disappearance of the entire superstructure of muscles, nerves, brain, bony levers, graspers, walkers, periscopes, until the body, the human entity, has become simply a hunk of tonic protoplasm existing like a kind of oyster on the half-shell, with no mechanisms left but flippers to turn switches to activate computers.

Already, without the computer, we have arrived at perilous crises of "progress." Ever since I have lived in Los Angeles it has been frighteningly apparent to me that sooner or later people would be born without feet or legs, because the environment will have rendered them superfluous. We already live in a machine called a house, with everything built in and electrically operated, and with wall-to-wall-carpet apparently growing out of the concrete floors like fungus. From there we step into a movable cell called a car, press a button or two and pass into a limbo of absolute nothingness but noise, speed and confusion called a freeway, until we arrive at another machine called an office, where we perform certain largely mechanical and electronic routines before reversing the process and returning to the home machine. If you try to walk, you may actually be arrested; at best, the warm-hearted Angelenos will consider you slightly mad and insist on transporting you in their cell to wherever you want to go, even if it is only across the street. (Whether this is to keep you from having to go to jail or to protect you from being such a "square" as to persist in the use of those obsolescent feet and legs, is not clear; but at any rate, it is kind.)

There is no community; only an aggregation of isolated individuals who do little more than see each other out of car windows en passant. Naturally, nothing of what we call euphemistically a cultural life can come into existence, for culture is a racial, a tribal, a communal development. We seem quite content to satisfy our cultural hungers in solitude by means of radio and television, usually while we are reading or washing dishes. Obviously we are on the road to the oyster-on-the-half-shell state, and with the computer now in the picture, it need not be long. Perhaps, to be sure, all this is actually progress, and resistance to it is only inertia — a disquieting thought.

But to snap out of this ghoulish romanticizing, the problem is a real one. I am not advocating the sabotaging of the computer, by any means, for it is a remarkable invention of yet unrealized potentialities. Also, since it is the product of our own animal drives, it is not to be rejected lightly. And it is of manifest practical value even in these early stages in abolishing the wasteful ordeal of meaningless mental and physical drudgery, much of which we have outgrown and cannot profit by further.

But if we cannot and must not wipe out the computer, neither can we yield to its automatic assumption of the role of our synthetic mind. As in all the practices of living, we must find a balance, for harmonious and creative living demands the achievement of equipoise — the recognition and acceptance of all forces, playing them constantly against each other so that oppositions are neutralized in what amounts to positive collaboration. It is as if we were consciously a ball in a fountain, pushed upward by the water and pulled downward by gravity, so that we remain substantially in the same place, without either defying gravity or turning off the water, and in action rather than with the inertness of non-participation. It is a state not incomparable to that tonicity of the viscera which is the root of life.

Since the computer is designed to take over from the body and deprive it of process, only the body, which is its creator and master, can oppose its usurpation. To the degree that it is beneficial in removing drudgery it must be embraced, but the point of equipoise must be recognized and established.

The pressing occasion to which the dance must now arise, then, is the preservation of the body, the re-assertion of its primacy as the instrument of living, the making of ourselves not more detached, introverted and metaphysical, but better animals with awareness and pride. Art is not whipped cream on the bread pudding; it is a function of living. It is concerned not with beautiful thoughts but with animal drives.

Drawing by Alwin Nikolais

The Expression of Feeling in Dance

SUSANNE K. LANGER

I don't think that dances should be made by first thinking about what you are trying to do and what you are trying to make, in words. That isn't the way artistic thinking works. That is what I am going to talk about. There are a few concepts that I would like to make clear: feeling, projection, subjective and objective, and intuition. I don't think you gain very much by having one person's definition of concepts of such importance in words which have meaning for that person, for then you have to have all those other words defined. Concepts should be defined more or less as you come upon them and need them.

Expression of feeling in dance: I think everybody, at times, talks about "expression of feeling." Certainly John Martin did last night, without telling us what "expression" meant and what "feeling" meant. If I hadn't thought about this for a great many years and read about it, I would have had a wrong impression of what he meant.

Havelock Ellis called his anthropology book THE DANCE OF LIFE. I noticed that Mr. Martin talked about this and that kind of dance, and, of course, "the dance of life." There is a reason why Havelock Ellis called his book THE DANCE OF LIFE. Somehow life seemed to him like a dance. Now, I would like to raise the question: in what way can life seem to a person like a dance? Or why can it? What is there in history that seems like a dance? Obviously, movements of history are not like human movements. History does not consist essentially of motions which make a pattern. It consists of changes, and those changes are very largely not physical motion at all. Natural history, I think, would not appear to anybody as a dance. It is only human history that has this quality of being a moving, dynamic pattern, an entity. And what is the reason? Human history, or human life, which is human history, is a pattern of tensions and release of tensions. These tensions exist only for feeling. It is what Henry James once very nicely called "felt life," using the term for that which a literary work of art has to convey. "Felt life" is an excellent term because it sums up the human version of what might

be called "biological existence," "biological history." It takes in rather more than just one's own body feeling, or self-consciousness, because it is more complicated than that. So it is not natural history, but only human history, which is a pattern of feeling, of "felt life."

We come to the first vague, and very vaguely used term, "feeling." When people speak of expressing feeling they will use the synonym "emotion." By emotion they usually mean something they can name: fear, anger, love, hope, etc. Some of these are not even feelings, are not even emotions. For instance, strange as it may seem, "love" is not an emotion. Love is an emotional relationship. You can love a person all of your life; you cannot have an emotion all your life. Love is a relationship which constantly and quickly gives rise to a lot of emotions; that is, it heightens the emotional level in certain relationships that we have with human beings. It is a play of emotions; it is not an emotion.

This is one of the cases where it is very hard to make people realize the importance of words. Many people resent that kind of distinction, say it is hair-splitting. Well, let's say I am doing sloyd, as you do in high schools, and I am supposed to join a little picture frame. The teacher says, "But that is not joined. That corner is gaping and irregular; it makes a wrong angle entirely." It wouldn't do very well to say impatiently, "Well, the pieces touch each other, don't they?" That is about the degree of exactness that most people are willing to give their words. They kind of mean "a little bit — something like that," don't they? Or, "If you know what I mean." The answer is, "How should I know unless you say it?" In philosophy we have to be hair-splitters; we have to be exact.

By "feeling" I mean something broader than the customary technical usage of the word. I think I come closer to the popular usage here. I mean anything that can be felt: the table under my hand; the digestion Mr. Martin was talking so much about, which we hope we don't always feel, but which we often do; everything that impinges on the body and registers in our awareness. We have a way of feeling the impingement of light in what we call vision. We feel the impingement of tones in a very specialized way. With tones it is a little easier to see how hearing derives from feeling, because when you hear the deepest notes of an organ it feels more like enjoying a vibrator, let's say, than like hearing. You no longer have accurate pitch. You go a little below that, and it really appears as vibration which you feel, more than as a tone with pitch and tonal quality. Yet there is a perfect gradation into sound, into hearing. Also, with both light and sound, and even with an overwhelming smell, there is a line where it breaks over into pain. There are very many sounds on the radio that hurt my ears. It isn't just that they are unpleasant as sounds, but the special senses are highly developed ways of feeling impacts from outside.

On the other hand, we feel our own activity, we feel our motions, not only by coming into contact with different things. You make a gesture which you don't see or feel by touch at all; you feel the whole set-up of your muscles when you are going into action, so you have a very deep bodily feeling of being set for action. You also feel emotion, and you have a great many feelings that don't rise to emotion, but which are emotive feelings. For instance, you can't speak of an emotion when something annoys you just a little bit. Say a fly annoys you; you may get cross if it comes too many times, but the first time you are hardly aware of it. You notice it, but it is just a little bit unpleasant. So pleasure and displeasure are included in what I call feeling. On the whole I would say that I am using "feeling" to mean anything that can be felt.

There is an advantage, philosophically, in using the term that way. When you take "feeling" in this way, you can run it back into natural history, as far back as you can be sure there is any feeling, so you connect with all biology, and you can take that right back into biochemistry. Thus you make one subject out of life. You can take it the other way and derive all the activities of the human mind from feeling. All intellectuality can be derived that way, especially from one of the most insistent feelings we have, the feeling of conviction, when something looks logical or illogical to us. It is not a simple feeling. It arises out of a tremendous play of mental activities, and it is one of the greatest topics of all human psychology. It is one of the great topics of all psychology, how this develops in human beings, and probably not in any other creatures. But that would take us too far afield. I want simply to point

out that that is the reason why I adopt this rather unusual usage, letting feeling mean anything that can be felt, whereas psychologists today for the most part are restricting it to pleasure and displeasure. In ordinary parlance we really have only two meanings which don't fit together. One is having "feelings," emotions, getting your feelings hurt, or something like that. The other is simply external feelings; you feel in your pocket; you feel a coin in the hem of your coat; you feel a hole in your pocket. Now, that is another sense of feeling, tactile, or cutaneous feeling; and we feel pain. I think, popularly, we don't realize how these things belong together.

There are good physiological reasons why feeling, probably in a very early stage, can be divided into two main classes. One, I would call "sensibility," and the other "emotivity." I am using "emotivity" instead of "emotion" because it takes in so many things that are below the threshold, the limen of emotion, but of the same cloth. Sensibility is what we might call the peripheral feeling of the organism. Every organism is structured in such a way that its periphery (its skin, or even in a single cell, the cell membrane) is geared for emergency action. It is always exposed to uncontrolled, and uncontrollable impingements, and is always structured so that it has very complicated filtering actions. It will let some influences through, but usually it processes them along the way, before they ever get to the inside of the organism. Therefore, its responses are quick. The whole realm of sensibility has this character of quickness about it.

So by "feeling" I mean anything that can be felt. We cannot hold anything for contemplation without projecting it by means of a symbol of some sort. All our thinking requires some kind of symbolization. We can think only what we can conceive. Now conception is something that animals probably do not have. I think it is a human specialty, intimately connected with the use of symbols, which is something animals do not do. These are all big subjects; they can be challenged; they can all be threshed out. But I will have to ask you to take my word for it — I have been threshing them out for twenty years.

A symbol does not serve to indicate that something is here or is there, the way a sign of that thing, or that condition, would do. An ordinary verbal symbol represents or projects an idea. What does it mean to project an idea? First of all, let's look at the literal meaning of "project." Project means to stick out from a level surface. We say, for instance, a bracket projects from a wall, a horn projects from a creature's head. In so doing, a projecting object, or part, or item of any kind stands out noticeably, presenting itself more readily to perception. I think that is the circumstance that gives the concept "projection" its metaphorical value. In our ordinary speech, at least in modern life, we use it metaphorically much more often than literally. For instance, we project a plan of action; we project a picture on the screen. I think it is safe to say that in all metaphorical senses a projection is a principle of presentation.

A logical form is simply a pattern of relationships. It can be quite simple; it can be very elaborate. In dealing with languages and codes, you have to have some sort of key which tells you how to translate one kind of relation into another. Of course the most familiar ones are writing, labanotation, and musical notation. You have to learn what means what, and there you have a projection either of language or of a dance pattern, but only a pattern. It is a very abstract projection. Equally abstract is a projection of music, musical pattern. There you have made a fairly simple, consistent, and coherent abstraction by which you can make a translation of one code into another. You really have equivalent statements. Everyone knows that no two languages can be translated exactly into each other, but you can certainly make such a statement as, "The length of this table is so-and-so many feet," in any language to people who understand what you mean by "foot" and who use foot measure. Say "centimeters" or "meters" and more people will understand you. There you have a code, and you make an abstraction.

Your statement in two languages, your written and your spoken statement, your dance figure and the notation of it, each pair of statements has one item in common which is what I call the "logical form." You can call it the structure, a structure where you leave the thing structured open. In the one case it is a structure of sounds, in another it is a structure of motion, in a third it may be a structure of sounds which have meanings. In language it is not the sounds that translate from one language into another, but the concepts. There you have a pattern of concepts which you can express in a great many different ways.

So the process of symbolic projection rests on the recognition of one and the same logical form in two different things which are, therefore, two exemplifications of the same form. We sometimes say they are two expressions of it. It is in that sense that I am using "expression." You will find, if you go into it and think about it, that it takes in the ordinary sense of expression, too, but we will leave that out at present because what I mean is what you might call "logical expression," or projection of the idea of the thing. That is what we negotiate with a symbol. We express the logical form which is exemplified by two different things. One is very easy to get, and the other is very hard to get, so we exemplify the easy thing.

All human consciousness is shot through and through with symbol making and symbol using. Most of it is not nearly as simple as, for instance, the visual projection of temperature by a thermometer. When you look at the human mind and the things it does, you will find such radical differences between mental processes, for instance, between religious worship and planning the hours of the day, planning what you ought to do next, or planning a meal. Or such differences as between inventing a dance, composing any work of art, composing music, composing a poem or a prose piece of literature, and doing arithmetic. There is an enormous difference there. You get an entirely different set, an entirely different feeling, and you know very well that somehow you are doing it by a radically different process.

Now we come to that process. The whole so-called discursive mode which you use in reading a thermometer, in doing arithmetic, in planning a dinner, all that is done, perhaps, below the level of speech, but in word-governed types of thought. You may do it only with catch words, or you may think you do it without words, but the influence of language, even on thinking that is largely just little images, is there. It doesn't matter how you think about such things. It is all in a pattern that could be translated into words. "Could be translated" is the important thing here. It isn't that we use words, necessarily. It isn't that we ever translate it, but we could. The acme of this kind of discursive symbolism is certainly mathematics because, fortunately, the pattern of physical facts, the pattern of things that one studies in a laboratory, is very much like the pattern of mathematics. We have stumbled upon the pattern of physical relations in our mathematics. Bertrand Russell remarked that, once, and very characteristically and truly said: "Perhaps that is why we know so much physics and so little of anything else." He is exactly right. We know enough physics to blow up the moon, but very little of anything else. Actually any thinking which departs from the factual mode where you can use discursive symbolism requires a different kind of symbolic projection.

Symbol and sense must share a logical form, but one thing we can't put into any projective literal form, any discursive form, is the life of feeling. It is the whole realm of what you might call "subjectivity," inward experience, taking in every little twinge of any little ache, taking in every simplest physical pleasure, such as a ray of sunlight on your shoulder, taking in every bit of emotive life and every movement of pleasure, displeasure, and so on. That is what we are helpless to put across in discursive terms. We can name the big emotions and that is why people who speak of the expression of feeling always think, "Oh, you ought to be able to say this is love, this is anger, this is joy, this is so-and-so," whereas I don't know of any single passage of music that expresses one such lump of emotion.

We say, "She is mad at you," and that is all we need to know. We don't need to know how she feels, what she feels, and how being mad at somebody originates, how it builds up, how it grows, how it is sometimes kept up on purpose, and all of those things. You cannot put over the actual dynamic pattern of a feeling by saying, "She is mad at you." The obvious answer to such a statement is, "Why?" Then you mention a fact of some sort: "Oh, she thinks you did this-and-that." Why does she think so? "Oh, somebody told her so." Now that is really pretty crude when you compare it with our intimate knowledge of physical facts. For instance, when you look at a physicist's equation that covers three blackboards, the statement, "she is mad at you because somebody told her so-and-so," is very, very simple.

There is no reason to think that our inner life is so much simpler than physical facts outside, that anybody can do psychology who can't learn physics. We have, however, a means of expressing not only that somebody has an emotion, but what we know about feeling, and not only emotive feeling, but what we know about our direct experience, our body feeling, our so-called "self feeling," which is the level of awareness. I think the only symbolism for that is in the arts, all the arts. What you do when you make a work of art is to create, not a straight symbol, because a symbol can be translated, but an expressive form. That is why I can't say that a work of art has "meaning," for that is very confusing, especially in an art like dance, where you think it must mean doing this-and-that — it must mean something that has nothing to do with dance at all, either something dramatic or psychological. I say a work of art has import, and use that word simply because semanticists are annoyed and confused to have another meaning of "meaning." The word "import" has another virtue, because with "meaning" you can abstract the meaning, you can express it in another symbol, and then you can interpret your symbol in other terms, as with a dictionary. If we don't know what a word means we go to the dictionary; we get a complex of other words that mean the same thing; then we get the meaning by comparing those two. You can't do that with a work of art. You cannot interpret it. You can interpret it in performance. That is, you can interpret by finding an idea, not necessarily the idea, in a piece of choreography, or in a piece of music. Usually it is what psychologists would call "over-determined," it has more than one possible import, and you stress this, or you stress that, and one import or another will come out of it, so that it is very much, in that way, like a real organism. Therefore, the work of art has not meaning but import. It is a good word because the meaning can never be taken out and held up to view and identified. It stays in the symbol.

The interesting thing is that when you make a work of art that expresses the mode of feeling, it does so because its elements are structured the way the life of feeling is structured. Musicologist and psychologist Harold Pratt put it succinctly, though naïvely, when he said: "Music sounds the way feelings feel." That sums it up. Dance looks, sounds, and feels like feelings feel. But notice that what is the symbol there is not composed of little sub-symbols. Everything has to flow into it. It is a single symbol which has the import. It is articulated, but you can only articulate aspects in it. You can't take them out and put them together. An artistic element does not keep its character when you take it out of one work and put it into another. It doesn't even keep its character if you take it away from one place and put it in another. It does something else. You may have an element which is, for instance, a spot of very intense color such as red or blue in a picture. On the palette that color doesn't have the same sort of meaning. If you take it away from one place in the picture and put it in another, you are doing so because you want that element to do something else, and it becomes another element in the other place.

I want to make the point that when you get an expression of feeling in a work of art you are making a very high abstraction. You even abstract from what is known as a "color value" to some value that different colors can have in common. Homer, for instance, always refers to the "wine dark sea." Now, Greek wine is red, the Mediterranean is very blue, but the depth and the transluscence of the blue in the curl of the breaking wave, and the glow of the red in a glass of wine are somehow the same. That is what Homer abstracted. That is what, to him, made it a perfect metaphor that everybody would understand. The "wine dark sea." It is dark with a glow, just as wine is with sun shining through it. In art you make those abstractions without feeling that you have to account for the fact that you let red stand for blue, or blue stand for red. That is a higher abstraction than the abstraction "this is red," "this is blue," "this is green," that is, of color values. You have a value there which these colors, in their places, have in common. That doesn't mean that red can stand for blue somewhere else. Not at all. You have actually transcended the physical abstraction for something that can be symbolized in more than one physical way, even more than a sensuous way, in this case. So what can stand for what in a work of art? Nobody can tell you. In language we have a dictionary which tells us items of meaning. In art there is no such thing. There is no rule for expressiveness, for making an expressive form. There is no rule for interpreting it, but it is directly given to intuition. It is made by the intuition of import, the idea.

From beginning to end a work of art has to be an expressive form. Every element that goes into it has to enhance that expressiveness, but it doesn't have to have emotive significance in itself, because in a work of art something happens. Instead of seeming to see an expression of feeling, you perceive a quality. The import of art, the feeling in the work of art, appears as quality. It is what we call an emotive quality, a living quality or a dead quality, but it has the semblance of being a characteristic of the work, and something that belongs to the work, because it can't be taken out. In art there is a symbolic transformation of feeling values into quality. I think one way you can see how the elements in a work all combine to make the work, is that each element exists only functionally. You cannot take it with you when you take it out, for the meaning runs out of it.

The elements are all articulations within a single form. I think in dance it is particularly difficult to see that all of the elements are virtual; they are

virtual gestures. The value of the gesture in dance is to make the dance, not to express a feeling at the moment. That may be at a high point. It may be all concentrated in one gesture, the way the meaning of a poem sometimes just comes together and comes clear in one word, but you don't have to have a poetic meaning in every word that you use, by any means. The dance is made out of actual gesture, but what has to get across is a virtual gesture, the appearance of a spontaneous expression, and not every gesture has to have that. It is the whole that has to produce that. That is, everything has to have the quality of that dance, so that a tremendously expressive gesture will mean nothing at all if it isn't toned to the whole. That is why I say a gesture coming from inside is only virtually a gesture. It would have no such character if it were a perfectly genuine and direct expression. It all has to be toned to the work, and within that work some gesture becomes tremendously telling, even the pose becomes immensely telling, very much the way something, let's say, like a little decorative scallop such as the Renaissance painters like to put into their pictures at the top, becomes very important because it hangs over a figure. If it didn't hang over a figure it would be just something you could see in any department store advertisement. By hanging over a figure, that shape takes on a new meaning altogether, as lights do in pictures. You can throw them all out and you can make a picture on a different principle. It can be very nearly as expressive, if you have really reached the thing you are driving at in the painting.

So the work as a whole is made by articulations in a single form. The essential unity of the piece is a formal property which is required by its symbolic function to express "felt life." Our life, or feelings of life, all arise from a kind of ground line or groundwork of body feeling and sensuous orientation, and a sense of personal activity. In physiology that is simply muscle tonus — the autonomous activity of the nervous system which, for instance, does not need any stimulus to make a brain cell fire. It will fire anyway. You can get whole assemblies of cells going into action in the brain through a stimulus, but there are constant circuits of activity going on in the brain, and in the whole nervous system. After all, the nerves have to keep the muscles activated to keep the metabolism up all the time, at least in such complicated creatures as mammals. If you cut a major nerve to a limb, you can expect catastrophe by and by. It certainly won't function, and after a while it will lose its feeding power. Nerves feed the body, which means there is constant activity going on. That is below the limen of feeling, for the most part, and yet there is also a degree of activity which, in a healthy being, is felt all the time, though we have no name for it, and we are not aware of it. It is the difference between a person alive and a person dead. Even when we are asleep we keep a certain posture; we keep our postural tonus, for every posture has a minimal degree of contraction that it keeps all the time, or that it intermittently keeps reasserting.

So something in a work of art has the character of this basic life feeling. There has always got to be what I would call the matrix. I think that is what you create the minute you start a work of art, and it becomes something other than the objects on this table. That is the primary illusion. Upon this all the other things you do, all the other creative elements play, especially secondary illusions which give it its depth and perspective, which make it more than a kind of blank space.

If you create a virtual space in a picture, you will find that what you are really doing, in articulating it, is using and creating all kinds of secondary illusions such as substantiality, events, things going on, motion. Motion is the main one you use all the time. In a work of art, any work, all line is motion, and all motion is growth. All appearances that come into any work of art are in an artistic transformation, usually characteristic of another art. So that you have an immense play of secondary illusions, and they are secondary because they are not that groundwork, they are not there to stay, they come and go, they appear and disappear. In music you get a sudden sense of expansion which is, of course, the primary illusion of virtual space. It is secondary in music, it is tremendously strong, it is used all the time, it is created all the time. Musical space is something that many musicians themselves think is their primary illusion because they are so aware of it, but you are usually hardly aware of the primary illusion at all. That disappears. It is like your body feeling.

The main points that I want to sum up here are that in art you have what I would call "metaphorical symbolism." You present a single, untranslatable symbol directly to intuition, and in art all feeling is transmuted into the quality of the work. The great function of the work of art is to present a symbol, without which we cannot conceive our inner life. Art is the great revelation of the whole life of feeling of which we otherwise know so little, as Bertrand Russell said, ". . . we know so much

physics and so little of anything else." But we do, in fact, know a great deal through art.

The question that arises is this: If we really can't know our inner life, if we can't have ideas of subjectivity without art, which is the objectification of feeling for us, how does the artist who brings out something new know it before he has seen it? How can he know a feeling before he has seen it projected? I think the answer is that he has seen it. What he has seen is the quality that a work of art has when it gets across, when it is expressive. He has seen expressive form, and he has seen it in nature. You know there are days when everything has a special quality for you. I don't know whether everybody has had that experience, but I think probably very nearly so. There are days when everything composes itself, when everything has a quality of beauty. The creative, the original artist is a person who is very ready to see that. Naturally we get a great deal of education along those lines from all the art we have known. A person who has never seen a dance would probably not get very far in the composition of dance. In the case of a child, the spontaneous expression gets in the way of the dance. The child will compose something and think of how it appears. He will make an appearance, but it is always very short and scrappy, because he does not know how to give it continuity and shape. That is why there have been no great infant prodigies in choreography. This is rather remarkable, for there have been in music, and there are a few in the other arts, especially poetry. An occasional child makes real poetry, though not great poetry, usually, because there is not enough articulation of feeling in the world for the child yet. Music seems to be the readiest, but it occurs more frequently in the adolescent than the child. I think Mozart is the only case of a real prodigy in early childhood.

The real poet sees in nature that special quality, and that is what he tries to get. It isn't something that he very intimately knows as feeling. It is a quality from which he actually learns the nature of feeling. There is an example of that in Isadora's autobiography, where she tells about seeing the wind running along a palm frond. She says she spent hours and days getting that motion translated into her fingers, for she had seen it as an expressive element, something she could build in and use. She had seen it in nature, and it seemed to her to express a feeling. Now remember, feelings you see expressed in art are not things with names. She would never have thought of saying,

"It has such-and-such a feeling," "It feels like this," or "It feels like something," referring it to some events in life. It was just a pure, abstracted feeling that she saw in the quality of those moving palm fronds as the wind went through them.

It is not only the artist who sees thus. A very great morphologist and biologist, D'Arcy Thompson, remarks on the shape of a lily of the valley that is coming into bloom, the gradation, the curve and the expressiveness that that gives to it. He says we might call this "phase-beauty." I think that is a very apt word, but it was a scientist who expressed it. Then he said, "You get the same sort of thing in wind going over a corn field, in waves on the sea, and you get it, sometimes in reverse, in the kind of flower that opens at the top first, and then matures downward." It is the sense of a gradient. It was that gradient that the palm leaf created that gave Isadora her idea, and which, incidentally, was recognizable because all our feelings have a gradient. That is why it was an image of a way a feeling goes, the way a feeling grows, and the way it ends, and why she spotted it as an artistic element. Now, the palm wasn't expressing anything, and the wind wasn't expressing anything on purpose, but here was the quality, an emotive quality, something that reflected the life of feeling. I think it is that that a creative artist gets directly from nature, or directly from human life, sometimes.

So art is not only the objectification of feeling. It is, conversely, for us, the subjectification of nature. We find our own inner life presented in nature. What the artist has to do, however, is to compose it, and that is another question entirely. Anyone might just see a little artistic element, or a momentary sense of the beauty of something. What we call beauty is expressiveness, and whatever is expressive for you becomes beautiful, even though it may not be at all in the Medieval or Renaissance canons of beauty. I would say that all art is a symbolic projection of human feeling, a symbolic negotiation, giving us knowledge of feeling, where we can have no knowledge without it. It is the objectification of feeling, and the subjectification of nature. That is what gives it that tremendous unifying feeling so that you always have a sense, when you are in the presence of a great work of art, of what is sometimes called identification with the world, a sense of expansion of yourself, so that the boundary between self and world seems to be transcended. It is that transcendent quality in art which is tremendous in some dancers.

Discussion

SUSANNE LANGER

Irving Brown: From whence comes the matrix?

The matrix doesn't come, it is made. It is made the minute you transform a canvas into a space, and that happens with the first line. The minute you step on the floor it becomes a dance floor and the matrix of a dance is established. Your matrix is set up with the first move, the first line, the very first element you produce. There is an excellent description of that in Hans Hoffman's SEARCH FOR THE REAL.

Irving Brown: Do you find it and then identify it?

Yes, it happens. Usually you don't identify it because you take it for granted, you are so aware of it. The fact is that the minute you are looking at even an empty stage, if you are a theatre person, it is a stage to you. Philip Barrie's TOMORROW AND TOMORROW begins with an empty stage, and Martha Graham's PRIMITIVE MYSTERIES begins with the stage in perfectly black darkness. It could be a play, it is still ambiguous at the moment the curtain goes up, but the very minute a dance figure comes in, the whole dance is established.

William Bales: Ben Belitt wrote a piece for Martha Graham many years ago, called "Dance Piece," and he says exactly that same thing. You put your foot on the floor and the stage becomes a maze. That is the dancer's errand in the maze, to make shape out of it.

SUSANNE LANGER

: The late Arch Lauterer talked so much about what happens the minute a human figure enters the space. You perceive space in relation to a human figure. You really don't know how deep, how wide, how high it is.

That is why one of the most dangerous things in the world is to let a play spill over the footlights. For a while it was the fashion to have an excursion leave the stage, go through the audience, and return to the stage. That was at a time when everybody thought that audience participation meant getting into the play and that the footlights should make no division. Of course, that completely ruins most pieces. I am not saying it can't be done; I would never say anything can't be done. All it takes is a genius.

Lucy Venable: I wonder if you could define quality?

It is very hard to define quality since quality is supposedly an indefinable impression. You see it or you don't. In the ordinary philosophical literature, for instance the British Empiricists, "quality" is used in the sense of red, blue, C-sharp, hard, soft — that which was, to them, a datum. All data, as we call them in science, were called "qualities." What I was trying to show here was that there are qualities which different data could have in common, not in the sense that different things can be red, and different things can be blue, but on a different level of abstraction, like the red wine and the blue wave which have a common quality. Also, there are relations. Freud, in his early writings, points out that qualities in the ordinary sense, like hot and its opposite, have an intimate relation. That is what I meant when I said all feeling, and everything that can symbolize feeling, has an element of gradient in it. School children will often say, "Oh, it's so hot it's cold." "It's so cold it's hot." Every gamut of quality has the two ends, and if you ask yourself what that expresses for "feeling," you discover all acceptable, discernible and meaningful quality lies between two extremes, too faint to be perceived, and too great to be borne. So it is always inbetween these, and the result is that every artist who works with any kind of ordinary color, or sound, or anything like that, is working with the possibilities of that whole gamut, one way or the other, so that you have this great fecundity, the great potentiality, in everything that you use. In every gesture, for instance, you are steering between what is trivial, too little, and what is exaggerated. Now the minute you exaggerate, you have to have a very good reason to do so, but you can go as far as you want, to the point where in a quality it can't be borne, or in an act it would break the form. We always work between what won't make the form, and what will break the form, in all art.

The thing that only a work of art can put over, and often in very abstruse symbolic transformation so that only a really artistic intuition will get it at all, is that the characteristic of everything biological, of all life, plants, animals, green scum has, besides its actual existence, a tremendous potentiality. Now in art that is where you get your potentiality, and it is always precarious; when you make an artistic element you are making it between the danger of not putting it over, of not enough, of too little and too late, and breaking the form. Between not making the form, and breaking the form. This balance, symmetry, is always at the bottom of it, and that expresses what, in life, we feel as potentiality.

There are many aspects of living, of life, and especially of "felt life" (and of course art deals only with "felt life"), from which the mind finally becomes articulated and formed.

SUSANNE LANGER

> Joan Woodbury: You made the statement about art being the subjectification of nature. From a dancer's point of view, would that be the subjectification of the nature of ourselves as animals?

I suppose it could. That would be a very interesting relationship, because you would really have a double process there. First of all, before you can subjectify something, it has got to be objective. Now your knowledge of yourself would have to be objectified, and resubjectified, which would be a very complicated epistemological process. When you take yourself as a part of nature, then certainly you would do exactly that.

> Thomas Watson: You used the phrase "virtual gesture." I wonder if you might talk about the word "virtual" for a moment.

When you create a work of art, that work of art is not the physical thing that you are using your hands to make. It is always in the nature of an apparition. That is, what you are doing is simply abstracting an appearance.

Now what I mean by "virtual" is an image. You can make the image which will be a real physical thing sitting there, but the image you are creating for perception exists only for perception. A picture, of course, is the easiest thing to see. Actually, what is a picture?. It is a surface smeared with colors. What you see are volumes, forms, so-called "space tensions." I talked about "virtual space," which is most easily seen in a picture. It is not the space of the room you are in; it is a space which exists only for vision. You know perfectly well that, if you go up to even the most realistic picture, what you will feel is canvas, more or less sticky, more or less roughened with paint. Certainly, it is not the thing you see, not the space you see. The space you see is "virtual space." That is a perfectly good term in physics. Physicists talk about the space that you see behind a mirror as a "virtual space." They will even measure it. In the picture, even if you are painting a non-representational picture, you are making a space which is not a space in the room. In music you create virtual time, and the time of a piece may vary greatly. Music is an organization of time, not an organization of the time that we measure with clocks, but the organization of a created dimension of time, and that is "virtual time." The reason for always making a virtual entity in art — and it always is, everything in art has to be virtual — is to make that abstraction of the conceptual. You abstract the appearance because the appearance, which has absolutely no value in its own right, will take on the symbolic value in a way that a real object, which has value of its own, cannot.

> Thomas Watson: Then, using the word "gesture" in connection with "virtual"...

In dance, you are making an actual movement, but the gestic value of that movement is different in dance from what it would be if you made it by chance, spontaneously, because in dance you are building up a whole virtual realm of interacting power, purely apparent — it is really not there. When you see a visible tension between two dance partners, there isn't really any such tension between them at all. It is an appearance. That is what I meant by "virtual gesture." Virtual gesture has to be made in such a way that this appearance is governed by the level, the pace, the type of movement, the style of the dance as a whole. It is

SUSANNE LANGER

not a spontaneous gesture, yet it looks like one. So it is an abstraction, from an actual gesture, of a dance element. If you see the actual gesture, it just breaks the image wide open.

> Dorothy Madden: In other words, you are talking about the illusion that is created by a movement, or a series of movements?

Yes, but it isn't usually created by one movement. The illusion is created by the dance as a whole. Where you have only one dancer in a solo dance, the illusion can be created by one moving body perfectly well. It takes awfully little to create a work of art. I sometimes wonder what is the minimum for any work of art. Think of what marvelously big music was created in the Middle Ages without tone color changing, without harmony, just in "plain song" where you had not even chordal music, nothing but men's and boys' voices. If you take that music and play it on a stringed instrument or on a piano, it is nothing. They had to use something which is not usually musical material. They used the Latin words, the big words. If you tried to sing "plain song" with other words I think it would fall flat as a pancake. The bigness of the Latin words took the place of what we would do with, let's say, chordal harmony. It filled the form. It is an interesting thing that here you have a really non-musical material which becomes entirely musical when it is used.

> Participant: You mentioned a person getting the feeling of what he expresses from his sensitivity to nature, to certain qualities of light, etc. Is this not also a factor in aesthetic appreciation — this sensitivity? How can we make people more sensitive to these things?

Exposure, that is all. I think as soon as you try to take children by the hand and lead them to it and make them feel it, you only get a reaction of falsity, or they feel they ought to feel a certain way about it. They don't really like it. That is where you get that false aesthetic in so-called educated society. People feel that they should have a critic tell them what they ought to like. That is very widespread. I can't think of anything sillier than to believe someone should tell you what you ought to like, because you see it, or you don't. You like it, or you don't. Sometimes you can appreciate something without liking it.

From the point of view of the teacher, I think judicious exposure is the only way to sensitize people to anything. Sometimes you can show something to a child by simply calling its attention, simply expressing the fact that you notice it yourself. Children will, occasionally, make the weirdest remarks — have the weirdest reactions to things. I remember, one time when my children were little, we were driving and the wind was blowing leaves on the trees. Suddenly, one of the children said, in the most vehement way, "I hate the under-side of poplar leaves." I never knew why, but it was a very strong aesthetic impression.

Much more exposure, I think, is the answer to the "insensitivity" problem. When I went to school, right around three sides of the room ran an excellent copy of the Parthenon frieze. I loved those ten minutes of being able to look at the frieze every single morning. I knew that frieze by heart, and I realized, when I saw it in the British Museum, that we had a very good copy there. I knew every figure and, what is more, I knew the feeling of those figures, the rhythm of that frieze, and what made the rhythm. I knew every fold of the dresses. I realized I had

SUSANNE LANGER

known from childhood why it was beautiful, and if you asked me why, I would say: "Because of that and that and that." I wish we could have much more exposure — good pictures in school where the children see them all the time, in a place that is not cluttered by having a thermostat at one side on the same wall, and some kind of ornate and meaningless chair. Rather, find a good niche, or wall, and put one good thing on it, and perhaps never mention it.

Irving Brown: Is that what you mean by "judicious exposure"?

Yes. I should say injudicious exposure is dragging children around to see too many things for too short a time. Judicious exposure, for a child, is seeing one thing many times or for a long time, because a child's perception of a thing grows, and it only grows by constant exposure to the point of familiarity. Our children are usually shown so many things that they "ought" to see that they haven't taken in any of them. It doesn't mean anything to them. They have their noses rubbed on it, and you can't see a picture by flattening your nose against it.

Participant: In speaking of rhythm this afternoon, you mentioned a theory of rhythm which you felt came from artistic form. Would you talk more about that?

I will give you the doctors' problem. They have been working with so-called "circadian rhythms," meaning approximately around the clock, but not exactly, i.e., the biological rhythms of our breathing, metabolism, circulation, the kidneys, the digestive organs, etc., which all go in cycles, and all come out approximately even with the rhythm of the day, the twenty-four hour rhythm. They have been operating entirely with a definition of rhythm in terms of periodicity. A rhythm is usually a recurrence of some kind of event in exact periods of time.

What is surprising is that, although the events recur roughly diurnally, none of them has any particularly exact periodicity, and when you line them up your periodicities don't come out right, so that it is very hard to say, "This is really a rhythm." What puzzled me in working from art — no longer with art, though it is illustrated in all art — was that in watching the motions of any beautiful animal, or a tennis player, you see they never repeat a motion exactly, or even approximately. The tennis player does nothing you could call cyclic in the sense you speak of the cycles of the heartbeat — nowhere nearly as close as to periodicities, or to recurrence. Every motion of a tennis player is rhythmic, so what is rhythm? You can see it immediately in all of the arts. You find it in a Parthenon frieze, but most of all, of course, you find it in music and poetry.

In biology, I think the fundamental unit is the displacement of matter, or motion in the sense of displacement of matter within a certain length of time; the basic unit in biology is the act. By the act I mean this unit that you can find even in a metabolic cycle. What I refer to as a biological activity is a series of acts which are concatenated in this way — every act has a build-up, it has a typical form. An act is a natural event; it is not something that you have to add to nature in order to get life. You have a prototype of it below the level of life, in a great many chemical reactions. Test it yourself. Take a glass of lemonade and

SUSANNE LANGER

put a teaspoon full of soda in it, and what happens? It fizzes, then it comes to rest. You have put an alkali into an acid and you get an air stop. All right, that is the end of that. It does illustrate, however, something that starts way down in the lowest forms of life, right down at the biochemical level where you begin to have what I call, not real acts, but a "proto-act," something that is on the way to forming acts. All acts are of this basic form, of impulse, rise, consummation, and what I can only designate with the good musical word "cadence." Every musical phrase builds up that way; every element in art builds up very much like an act. Now the cadence is the most interesting part, because it is extremely variable. It may simply come to rest so that the act gets lost — it is finished. It goes only so far and then it runs out the way water runs out when you spill it. You don't know just how far — it is seepage. It may be taken up before it is entirely exhausted and be drawn into another act. It may also do another thing. The cadence of one act may prove to be the uptake of another, and then you have rhythm. Rhythm is a relation among acts, a relation between two acts, for instance, but not always just two. Let's take a very simple case, where you have two acts of such a structure that the cadence of one is already the uptake of the next, so you can't make any clean line between them at all. I think the most perfect example of that in biological acts is breathing. The minute you start to exhale, the need for oxygen begins way down in your toes, in your shoulders, in every part, every tissue in your body. It builds up, and very quickly gets to the point where it simply has to turn over into inspiration. You have to inhale when the exhalation gets to a critical point. Now the exhalation is the cadence of the previous act, but it also, though you may not know it, (you think the act starts from inhalation, but it doesn't) starts with the body's need, the crying for oxygen and, in that way, human beings, who use speech and song, control their inhalation, as a singer does. It can be very irregular, but it is always rhythmic. It is one of the deep natural rhythms of the body, and you can't go too far in monkeying with it before it becomes commanding — you have to take a breath. So there is an example of rhythm which is by no means repetitious.

When you look at a tennis player or a dancer who is not dancing a set figure, but changing from one figure to another, every relaxation is already the build-up of the next tension, and this measure of tensions and relaxations is highly variable. You can build up a tension so that you really feel its breaking point; it has to break somehow but, as it breaks in a living body, or in a work of art, it already has started the next element, the next act. It was out of art elements that I got this. That is, in many ways, a more usable notion of rhythm than the notion of periodicities. I mean scientifically more usable, and it was derived from art. I am using it now quite far away from art. Other people are, too.

> Alma Hawkins: It sounds to me as if that is the basis of what we often speak of as "continuity."

Yes. It is what makes continuity, and what keeps the drive going. You don't get continuity just by putting one thing after another. It is real continuity because it drives itself all the time. When it is done, you get acts piled on acts, acts made out of acts, and in the end the whole work

SUSANNE LANGER

has the form of a single act. Incidentally, one very great biologist, Paul Weiss, said: "In a way you can regard a life as one act, like one great billow of the ocean, undisturbed by the ripples that play over it. It has a basic form." Every work of art has to have that basic form which, again, is like the form of an act with an initial impulse that can be fed from all sides. There is nothing simple about that impulse. It builds up. It has its consummation and cadence.

Participant: Is this, perhaps, where we get our sense of what we call "dynamics"?

Yes, this is the dynamic theory of biology which comes out of art. That is what I meant when I said that art is a dynamic image. A dynamic image is very hard to make in discursive terms. Every item of feeling, everything you can symbolize at all of the life of feeling, requires this dynamic form. I think you can carry it over into science, but you will never get it out of physics. It may be the image with which you have to operate in biology.

There is a very great difference between a model and an image. In biology you can borrow a great many models from physics, from all kinds of sciences. It was the computer that suggested some wonderful theories of neurology, of what goes on, of so-called circulating memories, etc. They probably have revealed mechanisms of the nervous system. That is fine. But what you must not borrow from physics is the image. An image shows you how something appears. It gives you an idea of what it is that you are trying to analyze and describe. If you haven't got an image, you are just groping around and picking up anything you can analyze, and it may be absolutely unimportant. The image gives you the idea of the phenomenon, and nothing else.

A model doesn't show you what something looks like. It does not need to look like the thing it means, at all. It shows you how something works, and that is a different story. It is a different abstraction. In a model you always make a discursive abstraction. You can say it in words. A model will be accurate to a degree. An image is a very different thing. An image doesn't show you how something works, at all. That is why in art an image is something virtual; it is pure appearance, and it is not put together in the way a living organism is put together, and yet it always has to seem organic. A work of art isn't actually a living thing. It has what we would call "livingness" rather than life. It is not a biological object. You cannot analyze it like an organism, and yet it has to be organic. It is an image, not a model.

Thomas Watson: Going back to your discussion on rhythm again, and your mention of a series of acts, the body's organic rise and fall, isn't a rhythm a result of a kind of emotional compulsion, a necessity, a drive?

I don't think so. I think it is the form which compulsion takes. That is, the existence of any actual rhythm somewhere has a biological cause. but rhythm is a form. It isn't a result of a drive. Every act begins with an impulse. When you are making a dance, you are performing an actual act, not something virtual. You are making something virtual, but what you are doing, yourself, is physiological, biological, actual. I would distinguish between "virtual" and "actual," the actual being the realm of our act.

Left to right: William Bales, Joan Woodbury, Jack Morrison

Creativity

FRANK BARRON

My subject today is "Creativity." As I started to compose my thoughts on the subject for this conference, I was reminded of the fact that as recently as 1959 at a National Science Foundation Conference on the topic of "The Identification of Creative Scientific Talent," I realized suddenly, in the midst of the discussion, that the word "creativity" had never occurred spontaneously in my mind. I never had thought the word although I have spoken it often enough and have even put it in the title of a book. Even today I don't think the word, and probably for a good reason; it is an abstraction, in an area or a universe of discourse where precisely what is of interest is "underlying process." There may be some good reason for not finding any use in thinking the word "creativity," if you are considering the matter with which it deals. It is also, by the way, a recent arrival in language, just as the word "unconscious" is. These words did not occur in our accepted lexicons until fairly recently.

Having said this much already about "creativity," I will now continue to use the term.

The very great increase in interest in creativity can, I think, be traced to two social forces far more massive than mere psychological research. For a time, in psychology itself, it was fashionable to say "all this research on creativity is just a fad which will soon pass." It hasn't passed. I think the reason is that it doesn't arise within professional psychology, at all.

The first source that I see for the interest on the part of people in general in human creativity is what was signaled by the explosion of an atomic bomb over Hiroshima. What was signaled, I feel, was the enormous capacity for destruction that resides in the human intellect, and, withal, the fact that this awesome power of intellect can be turned to constructive ends if man should will it so. The role of Albert Einstein in this extraordinary development is especially interesting. Some of you may know the little book called WHY WAR? in which an exchange of letters between Einstein and Freud is published. Einstein wrote Freud at the invitation

of the ill-destined League of Nations, and Freud replied. The questions put by Einstein were: "Why do men have to go to war? Will it ever change?" Freud gave no answer to cheer those who need cheering; the best he could say was: "Well, at least there are people like you and me, who are in correspondence with one another, and talking about this matter." But a decade later when Einstein looked Hitler in the eye and read there a genocidal intent directed against the Jewish people, he then made explicit a possibility that he, and others, had realized. He set out then and took a significant step in the development of a weapon to destroy many other human beings. In the face of threat to the continuing life of his people and his nation, he went to war.

This relationship of the most constructive to the most destructive potentialities of human intellect is, I think, part of the setting for the general increase of interest in human creativity. Often this consideration is merely in the background of consciousness, but it is there nonetheless, a sort of cosmic optimism tinged with dread.

The other source for interest in creativity is the really fantastic increase in the acceleration of the rate of change itself. Here, sometimes, simple numbers can tell you the story that you don't notice much even though you see it happening all around you, and within you, too. The rate of change could be described as rapid between 1945 and 1950, but there is really a radical increase in it since that time. The major developments are ones that we all read about in the newspapers. One is the population explosion. In 1850 the population of the world was about half a billion, and in 75 years (by 1925) it was one billion. In 37 years (by 1962) it had become two billion. It is estimated that by 1975 it will be about three billion. Seven years after that it will be four billion. So a child born in 1962 will by the age of twenty have seen the world's population double, and if he lives in California he may seem to see it quadruple. And since there will be more people there also will be more brains. There may be as a result more of the same thoughts, but as we know from experiments in group problem solving and word association tests, when you increase the number of people, the absolute number of rare solutions or associations increases also. Of course, you get an obvious increase of common response, but you also get a large increase in the absolute number of rare responses. It may well be, therefore, that we are also seeing a great increase in the absolute number of original thoughts as a function of the increase of the number of brains. Perhaps other by-products of this are with us, too, although it is not that simple, certainly. Population statistics on the number of scientists among us are quite arresting. For example, it is estimated that about 90% of the scientists who have ever lived are alive today, and the amount of technical information is doubling every ten years. So just the problem of information storage and retrieval is a very considerable one.

With this has occurred, too, a vast increase in the power available to man; e.g., the step-by-step development of things like the steam engine, the gasoline combustion engine, the electric generator, and now the nuclear reactor. There has also been a rapid increase, since 1850 particularly, in the discovery of natural elements, and the control of natural forces. There is also vast increase in our perceptual power through developments in photography linked to the telescope and radio, including perception of the very small through the increasing power of microscopes. The efficiency of computers, in turn, is in part a function of the increased efficiency of miniaturization procedures.

All of these things mean that right now something is happening that is different from what has happened previously in the history of this species. This offers a tremendous challenge, or perhaps threat, which it seems as though human wisdom may not be able to meet. Look, for example, at the central problem in nuclear weapons proliferation, the so-called "n-th country problem"; as more and more countries gain control of the capacity to use nuclear weapons, the danger increases of their setting off a conflagration, whether by accident or miscalculation. Little headway has been made on this problem because of the human relationship factors involved. In the face of these facts it seems to me we are justified in saying that a crowning crisis in the evolution of man is at hand.

I believe that what the U.S. Office of Education is doing right now is a response, however bureaucratically limited (inevitably), to the need for creative leadership in education. We must accent that aspect of human nature which offers some hope that we may meet the challenge, in brief, the creative aspect of our nature. This, I believe, is the admittedly cosmic background of the problem and the reason for our engagement in it.

As we turn from these considerations to techniques of study in psychology we are going to drop down several thousand feet from the cosmic to the very mundane, so hold on to your hats. In psychology, we are working still with essentially simple enumeration, and the kinds of ways of finding out what is going on in the human mind (or human minds) are not very different from what would have been available in Sir Francis Galton's time, some 100 years ago. In fact, many of our techniques are derived from ideas of Galton's. But let me describe something about the research program that I am myself involved in.

The group of psychologists, with whom I work at the Institute of Personality Assessment and Research in Berkeley, decided in studying creativity to seek the cooperation of persons of a very high order of creative ability, and to ask them to come to Berkeley and be studied by means of interviews and experiments and tests. We have now studied several hundred people in a variety of fields. We tried to get enough individuals in a given field so that we could do some simple statistical analysis within that field.

A typical study was our study of creative architects. We set up a panel of five experts on architecture, and we asked them to name individually for us the forty architects whom they considered the most creative in the United States. It turned out that there was a fair amount of agreement, so that only 66 names in all were produced by these 200 nominations. We then invited all 66 to come and be studied. Forty of them accepted. In similar fashion we studied creative writers, mathematicians, and research scientists.

Question: Have you studied any of the particular performing arts or visual arts yet?

Barron: Some painters, but it wasn't a large enough group to make the kind of comparison that we made with the other group, and we used only interviews, not tests. We are planning an extensive study of painters if we can get the support for it.

Question: When the groups were selected as being the most creative, was the selection on the basis of quantity of product, or quality of product, or originality of product, or what?

Barron: We put it rather simply. We said to the nominating panels, "We want those people who are distinguished for their creative contributions to the field." The emphasis was on "creativity," though we used other words in the definition, like "originality" and "freshness of approach." All the people we studied were highly productive. I was quite surprised at the volume of productivity, in fact.

What, then, are the relevant findings that are consistent from group to group and that can be considered to be well established "core characteristics" of the creative person?

In relation to creativity and intelligence, two statements must be made here, which at first may seem mutually incompatible:

a. Persons of a high order of creative ability are usually in the upper 10%, or perhaps upper 5% of the general population in terms of I.Q.

b. Within groups of such persons, and even when highly creative persons are compared with merely representative persons in a profession which calls intrinsically for creative ability, there is usually zero correlation between creativity and measured I.Q.

A clearcut example of these findings is provided by the study of creative architects, carried out by Donald W. MacKinnon, director of the Institute, and Wallace B. Hall. MacKinnon and Hall compared 40 architects (who were drawn from the sample of 66 architects judged by the panel of experts to be the most creative) with two control groups: one selected at random from the Directory of American Architects, and the other selected so as to match the highly creative group in certain characteristics, such as age, geographical location of their offices, and similarity of background in training and professional experience. They found that the high-level test of general intelligence we had employed because it is considered to provide accurately differential measurement in the high I.Q. ranges (the Terman Concept Mastery Test) failed to differentiate among the three groups. In order to counter objections that the test was too limited to verbal reasoning, and that it was perhaps subject to errors of measurement because its administration was not individually monitored, they called upon their subjects some time after the original study to take another test, the Wechsler Adult Intelligence Scale,

which is the most widely used, and generally considered the most valid, factorially variegated, and comprehensive individually administered intelligence test. Again, the group averages proved to be virtually identical, all within one point of 130 I.Q. While similar re-testing has not yet been completed for other groups studied, the findings with the Terman Concept Mastery Test for those groups have been quite similar. Creative writers score significantly higher than architects, and their estimated average I.Q. is greater than 140. So too with mathematicians and scientists, and only in the mathematicians sampled is there a positive relationship between rated creativity and measured general intelligence. That relationship is small though significant. Among student painters who took part in one of our research projects at the Rhode Island School of Design, the correlation between their Scholastic Aptitude Test scores and faculty ratings of their creativity at the end of three years was -.09.

The generalization suggested by these findings is that for certain activities a specifiable minimum I.Q. is probably necessary in order to engage in the activity at all, but that beyond the minimum, which often is surprisingly low, creativity is uncorrelated with I.Q.

If creativity is not a function of I.Q., what then is it a function of?

First of all, our findings suggest, it is a function of style or modes of experiencing, or stylistic ways of using the mind. These include modes drawn from C.G. Jung's theory of psychological types, and the polar opposition between preference for phenomenal complexity versus simplicity that some of my own work has pointed to.

a. The perceptual versus the judgmental attitude.

According to Jung, whenever a person uses his mind for any purpose, he performs either an act of perception (i.e., he becomes aware of something) or an act of judgment (i.e., he comes to a conclusion, often an evaluative conclusion, about something). If one of these attitudes is strong in a person, the other is correspondingly weak. The judging attitude is said to lead to an orderly, carefully planned life based on relatively closed principles and categories, whereas the perceptual attitude leads to more openness to experience, including experience of the inner world or self as well as experience from without. The perceptual attitude facilitates spontaneity and flexibility.

In our studies, every group but scientists is predominantly perceptual rather than judging, and in every group, including scientists, the more creative individuals are more perceptually oriented and the less creative are more judgmentally oriented.

b. The intuitive attitude versus the sense-perceptive.

The act of perception itself, according to Jung, may be of two kinds: sense-perceptive, or intuitive. The sense-perceptive attitude emphasizes simple realism, and is a direct awareness of things as they most objectively are in terms of the evidence of the senses. Intuition, by contrast, is an indirect awareness of deeper meanings and possibilities. Creative individuals are characteristically intuitive.

c. Complexity versus simplicity.

One of our main findings, probably the most solidly supported by diverse kinds of evidence, has to do with the relationship of complexity to simplicity, or order to disorder. We noted that the individuals identified as more highly creative seemed to be able to discern and to prefer more complexity in whatever it was that they were attending to, if it was not readily ordered, or if it seemed to involve contradictions that were perplexing, or that could not be resolved at the time. On the Rorschach Inkblot Test, for example, creative individuals show a marked tendency to synthesize, to find a single synthesizing image in the ink blot which brings together many elements. In other words, they pay attention to more of the possible determinants of response. Color, shading, and form, e.g., as well as content such as human or animal forms.

Another test we made up ourselves is called "Symbol Equivalence." We present a stimulus image such as leaves being blown along in the wind. Then we ask the respondent to create other images somehow equivalent to the stimulus. For example, leaves in the wind could be. . .well, one response actually offered was "clothes in a Bendix dryer, being tossed up and down, and seen through the window." Another was "a civilian population fleeing before armed aggression." We scored the responses just as you might score an essay examination, giving points for the extent to which the suggested image reproduced aspects of the original stimulus image.

Another test that we developed, not intended to be a measurement of this factor, but relevant to it, is called the Barron-Welsh Art Scale. This consisted originally of 400 line drawings in black ink on 3" x 5" white cards. We asked some 80 painters throughout the United States to take this test. We asked them to say which ones they liked and which ones they disliked. We compared their likes and dislikes with those of people in general and then we picked out those figures which showed a big percentage difference of like and dislike between painters and others. Those were cast into a scale to yield a score representing one's degree of resemblance to painters in such preferences. Now, it turned out that the painters were selecting figures that were more challenging, in the sense that they were more complex than the other figures, and less obviously balanced. The kinds of figures disliked by artists were generally static rather than dynamic. They were constructed by a geometric principle that was easily deduced at a glance. They were generally cleaner. The other figures were frequently described as messy, or even chaotic, in some cases. Creative scientists are very much like artists in these preferences.

I have interpreted these and related findings in my book CREATIVITY AND PSYCHOLOGICAL HEALTH (New York: D. Van Nostrand Co., 1963) as follows:

"We are dealing with two types of perceptual preferences, one of them being a choice of what is stable, regular, balanced, predictable, clear-cut, traditional, and following some general abstract principle; the other a choice of what is unstable, asymmetrical, unbalanced, whimsical, rebellious against tradition, and at times seemingly irrational, disordered, and chaotic.

"We suggest that the types of perceptual preference we have observed are related basically to a choice of what to attend to in the complex of phenomena which make up the world we experience; for the world is both stable and unstable, predictable and unpredictable, ordered and chaotic. To see it predominantly as one or the other is a sort of perceptual decision; one may attend to its ordered aspect, to regular sequences of events, to a stable center of the universe (the sun, the church, the state, the home, the parent, God, eternity, etc.), or one may instead attend primarily to the eccentric, the relative, and the arbitrary aspect of the world (the briefness of the individual life, the blind uncaringness of matter, the sometime hypocrisy of authority, accidents of circumstance, the presence of evil, tragic fate, the impossibility of freedom for the only organism capable of conceiving freedom, and so on).

"Either of these alternative perceptual decisions may be associated with a high degree of personal effectiveness. It is as though there is an effective and an ineffective aspect of each alternative. Our thinking about these various aspects is as yet based only upon clinical impressions of our subjects, but it is perhaps worth recording while we go on with the business of gathering more objective evidence.

"At its best, the decision in favor of order makes for personal stability and balance, a sort of easy-going optimism combined with religious faith, a friendliness towards tradition, custom, and ceremony, and respect for authority without subservience to it. This sort of decision will be made by persons who from an early age had good reason to trust the stability and equilibrium of the world and who derived an inner sense of comfort and balance from their perception of an outer certainty.

"At its worst, the decision in favor of order makes for categorical rejection of all that threatens disorder, a fear of anything which might bring disequilibrium. Optimism becomes a matter of policy, religion a prescription and a ritual. Such a decision is associated with stereotyped thinking, rigid and compulsive morality, and hatred of instinctual aggressive and erotic forces which might upset the precariously maintained balance. Equilibrium depends essentially upon exclusion, a kind of perceptual distortion which consists in refusing to see parts of reality which cannot be assimilated to some preconceived system.

"The decision in favor of complexity, at its best, makes for originality and creativeness, a greater tolerance for unusual ideas and formulations. The sometimes disordered and unstable world has its counterpart in the person's inner discord, but the crucial ameliorative factor is a constant effort to integrate the inner and outer complexity in a higher-order synthesis. The goal is to achieve the psychological analogue of mathematical elegance: to allow into the perceptual system the greatest possible richness of experience, while yet finding in this complexity some over-all pattern. Such a person is not immobilized by anxiety in the face of great uncertainty, but is at once perturbed and

challenged. For such an individual, optimism is impossible, but pessimism is lifted from the personal to the tragic level, resulting not in apathy but in participation in the business of life.

"At its worst, such a perceptual attitude leads to grossly disorganized behavior, to a surrender to chaos. It results in nihilism, despair, and disintegration. The personal life itself becomes simply an acting out of the meaninglessness of the universe, a bitter joke directed against its own maker. The individual is overwhelmed by the apparent insolubility of the problem, and finds the disorder of life disgusting and hateful. His essential world-view is thus depreciative and hostile.

"We have not hesitated to refer here to perceptual decision, to an act of choice on the part of the individual. That is to say, we conceive this as a matter not simply of capacity, but of preference. Such a choice does of course involve perceptual capacity, but beyond capacity it is a matter of orientation towards experience in a sense, perceptual attitude. In their important theoretical article (in search of the perceiver in perceptual theory) Klein and Schlesinger have emphasized that their empirically found patterns of modes of perceptual response (to which they give the name syndrome) are to be thought of as 'preferred styles of expression rather than required ones' (italics theirs). In search of the perceiver, they came inevitably upon choice rather than capacity or necessity as the determiner of observed response.

"This very perceptual decision, of course, is itself determined; and it is to the search for the determinants that the next step in this line of research will be devoted."

I have given here a somewhat sketchy overview of some of our best-established results. Those who are interested in a much fuller picture may find it in my forthcoming (Fall, 1967) book, CREATIVITY AND PERSONAL FREEDOM, to be published by D. Van Nostrand Co., and in CREATIVITY: Its Diversity and Development, to be published in the Spring of 1968 by Holt, Rinehart, and Winston.

34

Discussion

FRANK BARRON

Participant: In the life history of the individuals studied, was there a time of recognition of themselves?

There was. We asked when it had begun, knowing what they were – writer, mathematician, architect. Mathematicians knew earliest. One man worked in a canning factory. A glimpse of sunshine caught his eye. It was like a mystical experience; he knew he had it in him to be something besides a worker in a canning factory. Another man suffered a grievous loss; a dear friend committed suicide. First, he wept. Then it occurred to him he could either step back or step forward. If he stepped forward he would have a life of creation. He stepped forward and felt he was one with the universe, identified with the cosmic order. While in college, Theodore Roethke wrote an essay lamenting the fact he never got "A's" in writing, for he knew he was going to be a great writer.

Bonnie Bird: I wonder if we don't have some confusion about creativity. Creativity in dance has become a very specific "thing" to some people, namely, how you teach composition. We need to discuss what we mean by "creative" in the teaching of dance. I think it is many things, from different points of view. For you, as teacher, it is being able to help a student. Why is it important in the education system? We have to be able to answer in words that have some meaning, as John Martin says, "in the viscera — the guts," and hit in terms of people's experience.

Marian Van Tuyl: I think we have to go behind dance, and discover what the power is that we have in our hands. That will lead to recognizing that dance is an art which deals primarily with the kinesthetic sense.

Joan Woodbury: Is it a process we are talking about — a process of growth in an individual from one stage to another? Is it a commodity? In your experimentations, discussions and discoveries, have you decided anything about it?

As I said, I never thought the word "creativity" in some nine years' work on aspects of the problem, and I even wonder whether I still ever think it, except as it is now part of discussions that occur. Probably one of the reasons for this is that I think of different aspects of activities that play a part in creative process. Indeed, much of our measurement effort has been devoted to different aspects of this process. Originality, for example, is a thing distinct from spontaneous flexibility, which, in turn, is different from adaptive flexibility, which, in turn, is different from associational fluency. All of these things play a part, for instance, in writing. Take the question: Is not all writing creative? If you have a group of people, all of whom write poetry, I would say that the activity they are engaging in is intrinsically creative. There are different orders of merit within what they do and what they produce. Further, if you read their poetry and think about it in these other terms, you can generally say, "This poet is very original in his ideas." "This one hops around very rapidly in terms of images." Then you can begin differentiating this big "i-t-y" part of it and, in fact, when you do get down to brass tacks about any creative product or particular process leading to a product, you don't talk about creativity, you talk about these particulars.

FRANK BARRON

In talking about architecture, you only say a problem solution is creative when it has these other qualities: the originality, and various other hallmarks of what you call creativity. What I am saying is that some activities can be ordered in terms of the degree of intrinsic creation called for in them, then, beyond that within the given activity, you can discern orders of originality. Part of the discomfort one may feel is that the term "creativity" has been popularized; another part of the discomfort that I feel is that there is some sort of halo around the term — or an occasional dollar sign.

There is also a tendency to forget that there are unpleasant aspects of creation; it almost always involves destruction. In relation to the education process itself, the very first thing is to think of a child in school. Before he goes to school, he moves around very freely. In school he sits unmoving at his little desk for a large part of the day. That image conveys one important contribution dance might make to education in regard to the creative potential of children. There is a tendency towards overemphasis of the verbal in education. The healthy thing about an interest in creativity of movement is that it may help restore balance, giving full scope to the child's potentialities. There could be real reform in educational practice in the elementary grades if those things that the arts are primarily concerned with were brought back into the setting. I think your point, Marian, was very important about what this power is that we have in our hands, and the step behind dance to the kinesthetic.

Jack Morrison: If we think of research as discovery, then research applies to us all of the time. One of the things we haven't done in the arts is to include research. It has always been classes and take care of the students. Nothing is wrong with that, unless you fail to work at discovering new ways of doing things. I think we know what dance is, and that we have to accept it and see how we can do it better. The best way to begin is to do, in various places, what you people can do very well and could do better under different conditions. What are those different conditions? Let's say we want the kind of dancer Alvin talks about. We've all known such youngsters unless they have already dropped out in a fourth grade slump. So what are we going to do about that? What are the kinesthetic actions we want to encourage. That is part of our research at every level. We will have different ways, but let's get at this kind of discovery.

Eugene Loring: One of the most important things is to make people aware of themselves as human beings, aware of human relationships, and aware of nature around them. Increasingly, in teaching choreography, I find students totally unaware of themselves and life. I believe they will learn awareness through movement, and be able to express it in movement. Even little children are not aware; they don't recall what they see in nature, they are not aware of touch, smell, hearing. It is terribly important that we make them aware, because what else is there to create about but life itself, and human problems?

Participant: One of the problems in choreography classes is finding your own way as a student, or as a teacher helping the student find his way when he is blocked by habits, stereotypes and imitations. In the complete works of a writer, could you spot in his development a time when he might, consciously or unconsciously, have been imitative in certain early books, then gradually begin to see his individual characteristics come to the fore and ultimately come into full bloom?

FRANK BARRON

Oh, yes. I think you get a high degree of imitativeness, even among people who are basically quite original. Yeats is an example. He is certainly a poet of tremendous power and originality, and yet his early work is highly imitative. I was startled, on reading a letter from Yeats to his father, to discover that his prose completely imitated his father's style However, that is to be expected; that is how you learn, to start with.

I think we try too hard. I think we should take it a little easy on this creativity implication. If there is any, it will emerge.

> Vera Embree: So far, at this conference a key word has been "exposure." We have to use all of the methods we know, which puts a great responsibility on us, as teachers. In a given class you may reach one student if he attends a concert. You might reach another by saying, "Try to move, restricting one hand to the hip, one hand to the head. What can move?" When trying to get my high school students to make a dance, I have found that I have to make them aware of their bodies, and that it is all right to use them, because many of them are restricted by the disciplines that have been imposed upon them in our society. They have to be released first, and I find that invariably this comes from teaching them something about technique. Usually, it starts at a very elementary level, and then it develops. Sometimes, experience with other arts provides the stimulus. It may evolve out of listening and moving to music. In my school, there are many children from deprived backgrounds, where they just don't even know these things exist. I let them realize that they are there, and that they can be fun; it is just that elementary, before somebody can finally come out with a dance.

> Elizabeth Hayes: What do you feel are the values and dangers of apprenticeship in the arts: Do you think it helps or hinders growth as artists?

I don't think I could say anything about it beyond that; naturally, everyone learns somewhere. What do you all think about it?

> William Bales: We were visiting Grant Wood in Iowa. He taught everyone to paint the way he did. I said, "Don't they all turn out to be little Grant Woods?" "Um-hmm." "That's abominable, isn't it?" He replied, "Well, if they have any talent, they won't be happy going on painting like Grant Wood, and they will go their own way. If they don't have any talent, they will at least have learned one discipline."

Even the great geniuses are certainly not un-derived, and you have Stevenson's recommendation, "Play the sedulous ape," and so on. All the greatest artists have served apprenticeships. They break it some place, split from the master, and go out on their own. Picasso did, making the break by doing some symbolic thing like taking his mother's name. You learn where you can, and if you can learn from someone who is great in his own right, you would be wise to do it, I suppose, unless it interferes with something in you that would be lost if you did. I don't think there is any general prescription.

> Martha Hill: Alvin, how did you start to become a choreographer?

> Alvin Ailey: I always wanted to make dances, but for a long while it wasn't practical. I couldn't do ballet — boys just didn't dance like that — it was impossible. Once I was going to write music and the Great American Novel. I imitated all the poets from Baudelaire to Eberhardt. Then I found Lester Horton, and he was making the kind of dances I thought

FRANK BARRON

were important and meaningful, bringing together some pretty wild elements — modern dance. It had everything in it, the writing, the poetry, the art, the paintings I wanted to do, and from there I started to make dances, feeling my way slowly, because you have to find out if you can make a living doing that, and I'm still not sure you can. It is something you do because you have to do it.

Lester Horton never taught any courses; he didn't make you do exercises of any kind. He simply opened things, presented things to you. There was music, there was painting, there was great taste and imagination, all there for you to see. It was just the atmosphere of that man — what he radiated — his whole personality — his marvelous creating, the way he lived, what he was, that touched anybody who was sensitive.

Selma Jeanne Cohen: Eugene, do you feel it would have been easier for you, getting started, if you had had courses in composition?

Eugene Loring: Oh, positively.

Martha Hill: Do you think all dancers should be required to study choreography?

Eugene Loring: Yes.

Martha Hill: To make original work?

Eugene Loring: No. That is not necessary. I think you should study choreography just as a musician, even if he is not going to be a composer, studies harmony and counterpoint to understand the structure of the music he is playing. If students understand how things are put together they will advance more intelligently, and they will understand a choreographer more readily. As we all know, in the professional field, the problem of economics is constantly greater, so the choreographer needs people who can respond immediately.

Lucy Venable: How do we give students the broadest kind of exposure to choreography, if our location does not provide it? Musicians have scores to read, painters have paintings to look at, but what do the dancers have to see, except their own teacher?

"Dances vanish into thin air" is one of the generalizations I keep thinking about.

Eleanor Lauer: It seems to me that a person who has worked really creatively in any of the arts will tend to carry this attitude into many other aspects of his life and thus, automatically, to shun the banal, the rigid, the fraudulent, etc. As dance teachers, we work with large numbers of students, only a few of whom will go on to become dancers in the professional sense. With the many others, we try to help them find in dance a means of expression and growth within themselves as well as a source of pleasure in seeing dance performances. But, beyond that, I would hope that if we could help develop their creative capacities, their attitudes toward everything they encounter in the world as they grow up would be affected. They would not insist on simplified solutions to complex problems, they would not join "hate groups," they would not be likely victims of demagogues, etc. The broad benefits of involvement in creative activities from childhood could be reflected in every phase of life.

Jack Morrison: I think that is where the stakes are for education.

Drawings by Alwin Nikolais

Music and Dance

BETTY WALBERG

I am going to speak of some of the ways in which I think we can enrich dance music, no matter where it is used — in the studio, in college, profession-ally — and then tell you of some of the devices and techniques I have found helpful.

I find there is great lack of musicality in the studio, in the childrens' school, in the high school, in the college — wherever technique is being taught. Usu-ally, music has a stagnant and dull sound in the classroom. There are two reasons for this. One is that, many times, the musician does not under-stand dance or does not like dance. The other is that the teacher really does not like music, and does not have a knowledge of music and its fasci-nating complexities. There is rarely a two-way discussion between the teacher and musician. This is harmful to the students, because they may end up with a separation in their musical education.

There are several areas to consider in how to use music for dance. I began to think about this on Sunday afternoon when Mr. Jackson played for "Improvisation." We all kept saying, "Come on, Jack, enter in and play. Do some music." What we were actually saying was, "Will you please un-derscore the movement." We weren't really asking him to make music. There is nothing wrong with that, but we should be aware of it — of what we really want.

The following five things apply to dance music: un-derscoring the dance, supporting the dance, keep-ing the dancers together, accompanying the dance, and, finally, dance and music together — that im-portant area where the dance and music are such integral parts of each other that they are like voices in a string quartet. I don't think we do any of these five things with awareness, variety or imagination, so I am going to discuss some practical ideas, which might expand the use of music, academically and professionally.

Music education in relation to dance, wherever it is found — in school, in a performance, or in a company — is divided into six categories: music for childrens' classes, for technique classes, for composition classes, for choreography, how to use and perform that music in a performance, and the

music course that is taught for the dancer. I don't like this sort of distinct separation, for it lacks a kind of continuity in growth and development, so I am going to begin with the technique class, and say what I think can be done in it to further the total picture from the start.

There are many scales (the tonal materials of mu-sic) which possess various tone textures and feelings of space. These are never explored, but could be, even while the dancers are just doing a plié. In addition to the "regular" major and minor scales, there are the whole-tone, pentatonic, twelve tone scale, and the modes. A twelve tone scale is a very complicated one in which to improvise suc-cessfully, but one can take what might be called a "tone series," and develop that series. If, in a class, you start thinking of just tone sounds, it might help the invention that takes place, making more of a play between the dance and the music. I feel there is a great lack of wit in the use of music in the dance class.

Often, you will find a redundancy of tone color or tone center in a class. There is a reason for this. It is easier to improvise in some keys than in others, and it becomes a habit. I think the teacher and the dance musician should have much more dis-cussion with each other, before and during class. The teacher can say, "Let's try modes today," or, "I would like to try a whole-tone scale today, while we do pliés," and hope the musician knows. It is important that it comes from the teacher. Often, he may be after a certain quality. If the musician starts experimenting on his own, the teacher may say, "That doesn't feel good." Actually, what he is saying is that it is not comfortable. I find it very dangerous to have it always comfortable in class.

A comment about keys; none of this, I feel, is at all mystical. Keys can affect the way you move; you do react to keys. If the minor scale is played a lot in the class, it does something to the feeling of the room. It can make a heavy atmosphere. The key of "C" can have a different space feeling from the key of "G". You can only become aware of this through discussion and experimentation. The flat keys have a different texture from the sharp keys, and some keys are better than others for certain instruments. It is important to sense and know this, because, when you begin choreographing and selecting music, or having music composed and, eventually, orchestrated, the key you choose, or the tone center that is chosen, will greatly affect the dance work. I think you must see that this awareness begins in the technique class.

When you start experimenting with key relations or scales, the student will start listening and, by that listening, his posture changes. It might just change in the ear area; it might change in the back of the head; it might change in the way he descends or ascends. I find it very exciting, and I think we should all try it much more.

Moving on from the tonal relations of keys or the scales selected, we come to that strange thing called "meter." This is a fascinating and mysterious thing when it comes to dance. I, personally, don't think of meter in relationship to the rhythmic structure. The rhythmic content of the movement, or rhythmic pattern of the movement, suggests the structure of what I am going to compose, but not the meter. Often, with children, if I beat out a certain rhythm and then say, "What did I do?" they will answer, "Oh, that is a tango." But, if I say "Three-four," and ask what that reminds them of, they will say, "A waltz." Now, they really didn't think of a meter from that rhythmic pattern. To me, a meter has a content, and by content I mean a quality of space, recall, and even, perhaps, form. That is because, as a musician, I see bar lines.

On one occasion, a choreographer said to me, "I want a basic pulse, or a basic pattern, Betty, of ..." and he demonstrated, because he couldn't verbalize what he wanted. I said, "Do you want a gallop or a jig?" A gallop is in two-four and, for me, visually, it is much more condensed than a six-eight, and the choice may affect the movement. I bring this up because, often, in the dance class there is no exploration of meters. You do a plié, or you do something across the floor, in exactly the same meter every day. Who is to say you can't try a plié in a five-four? By meter, I also mean the starting of an exercise with an up-beat or a down-beat. That affects meter and phrasing. I've been watching "down-up-up-down-up-up" for years. I don't know why it can't sometimes start with "up-up-down-up-up" or "down-down-up-up-down."

There are no set rules involving meters, except in regard to notating. The technique class can have much more exploration in meter. It will help the dancer in composition or choreography, so that he will not always use the same meter he has had in technique class for a movement pattern.

Think about how you might expand your use of meter in the classes. Meter sets up "main" accents and "secondary" accents, but the dancer is also involved with "impulses." That is why the musician, writing for dance, has to look at movement to find out how long it takes, where the impulses lie, where the main and secondary accents lie. If the musician keeps on playing the same thing, the impulse will remain the same no matter what is the emotional or content use of that movement pattern.

There should be more experimentation with the dancer as the "melody" and the piano as the rhythmic structure, and then a reversal, in which the pianist just plays the melody, and the dancer thinks of himself as the rhythmic accompaniment or harmonic structure. This builds up a sensitivity to rhythm and harmony, and it can be very exciting.

There is not enough exploration of what I call the basso-ostinato use of music. It is usually a little motif, two bars or four bars, which continues, and repeats itself, and repeats itself. It has an exciting rhythmic content with, in its own way, a beginning of a melody, and it makes the dancer aware of a new energy. I enjoy using the basso-ostinato with sustained movement or an adagio, because it puts another kind of pulse inside the legato movement of the dancer with its rapid, agitato feeling.

It would be very inventive to have the pianist sing to his own accompaniment. No one ever uses the voice in class. Try using the voice as well as the piano, or use the texture of the piano, the wood, etc. I am not terribly fond of isolated sounds of wood, then playing, and then inside the piano for an effect, but I think it is fun, if the pianist is agile enough, to play the keys and then add a sound on the structure of the piano.

Now we enter another area of music for the class — the use of dynamics and expression: legato, staccato, accent, stress, marcato, phrasing, tempo. All of these affect timing and the musicality of the dancer. Many times, a teacher or choreographer will say, "I would like an accent there." What he really means is a stress. A stress exaggerates the time; an accent is something that is more exact, and we all know what legato and staccato are. I have not been to too many studios lately, but, usually, the music all sounds the same to me, because it never has any variations in quality and dynamics. If you are using a concept of staccato for an exercise, I think you should ask the pianist to stop using the pedal. Too much pedal can make the studio murky with sound. I don't believe any musician would be hurt if you said, "Let's don't use the pedal today, let's try the class without the pedal and see what we find."

The accent and stress will affect the class in the leap and the jump. Are you going to catch the stress of the movement or the stress of the music; when the dancer is up, when the dancer lands, when the dancer takes off, in the middle? Too often, the dancer marks the accent, and the music mimes the accent. Eventually, it becomes like two people talking at the same time; they are saying the same words, but you don't hear either one of them.

This brings up the whole problem of training dance musicians and dancers; I call it the contrapuntal device. Awareness, and the use of dynamics, will strengthen the rhythmic sense, but it is that matter of comfort, again. I think it is very important to bring into the class a much stronger use of counterpoint between the music and the dancer. It can become, in a sense, like a music course without being pedantic. By the time the student begins composition or choreography, he may have a vocabulary and knowledge of music that just seemed to sneak up on him and, most important, a physical awareness of music.

I think, also, there should be more jazz in the classes. By jazz, I mean good jazz, and by "good jazz" I mean jazz that satisfies my taste! I think that is about all it amounts to — one's own personal taste. We seem to be frightened that if we play jazz, it might seem a little ordinary, mundane, and not very intelligent, but I don't care what age you are, you do respond to jazz. You respond to it because it has a very strong rhythmic drive.

I see nothing wrong with young people exploring the so-called "Beatle" music. I have analyzed it, and I have worked with it. I did some "Hullabaloo" shows just to find out what it is about. It is really built on the madrigal tonality, especially the kind called English "Rock and Roll." It actually centers around a tonal center. This music is here. Why ignore it?

I have found that I enjoy improvising for ballet more than for modern, if we are going to make a separation between the two. I enjoy it more, because a sequence of movement is set up. It is not always rhythmically varied, so it gives me a marvelous chance to be really creative. With modern, sometimes, it is so complicated with impulses and accents that it leaves me little room for experimentation, usually ending up with my simply making sound effects. Once in a while, the teacher could devise a simple pattern, and then the dancer could experience something more musically complex.

We sometimes say a person is a born dancer, because he is rhythmically so good. I have done no research on this, but I do think there probably are people born with a natural sense of rhythm. One of the places to make students aware of whether they are listening and really rhythmic is in the technique class. I find, many times, that the class is very sloppy. The teacher says, "Go over in the corner and feed out in fours." The pianist sits down and he doesn't have a phrase. The dancers don't know when to come in on the beat, and it goes on and on.

Often, we think of rhythm as something constant. That is what you call "pulse," though the expression is not in the musical dictionary. What we have been talking about here is not pulse. Pulse really means what the heart and the blood stream of the person are doing. That is why you will frequently find that a dancer will say, "You played that too quickly for me today." Usually not — it is just that he is feeling different that day; his energy is different. We confuse rhythm with pulse. When I speak of rhythm, I mean the "whole thing," which includes accelerando, retard, rubato — they are all different. I don't mean "twice as slow, twice as fast," which is the way to become more proficient in using movement more quickly, more slowly, and hanging on to the pulse. There are exercises to cultivate pulse, and others to develop rhythmic awareness. I often use the "Goldberg Variations," played by Glenn Gould, as an example of the difference between rhythm and pulse. The dancer will believe it has a constant beat. Then I will say, "All right, let's try clapping to it." It is terribly inconsistent, but that is how Gould interpreted the whole range of the composition; how he used the notes rhythmically.

You should seriously consider the means by which you arrive at both pulse and rhythmic training. Rhythmic training develops the sense of phrasing. To me, the phrase in dance is not like the phrase in music. I consider a phrase in dance to be what melody is to music. There is a subtle difference. Phrasing in music is the way in which I might stress a note, slur a note, how I might interpret; but a melody in music is the rhythmic structure of highs and lows in tone. Therefore, when I think of phrasing in dance, I am more apt to think melodically — what a melody is like. Most dancers, when they get into choreography, have difficulty creating a phrase, because we stress the pulse rather than the phrase.

To increase sensitivity to phrasing, pulse, or rhythm, the pianist should be given more opportunity to set the tempo in class. A teacher will often have one pulse, and the whole class is conducted with that same pulse. When the student leaves the classroom, he is aware of only one tempo for a movement pattern.

Sometimes I ask the dancers to visualize the notation. A musician is greatly affected in his interpretation of a piece by the way it is notated. A dotted half note looks and feels different from a dotted quarter. I find I am more conscious of the look of the note when I am working with dance. It is fun to say, "Let's have absolute silence in the class for a moment. Let's think about a plié, visualizing a dotted half descending, and ascending to six eighth notes. Don't click your tongue, just see it." Then set the pulse. It is amazing to see what happens — the change of body movement, when they start thinking about it. Or say, "Let's try eighth-quarter, eighth-quarter, down, and then move up with a half note or two quarters" — something like that. Marvellous things can happen. I think it is worth investigating on your own.

Silence is very important. It is hard to hold still — the quietness worries you. After the dancers have the experience of visualizing the notations a few times, subconsciously, they begin to sense overtones; they are not as fearful of just standing still or having little music while moving. It can help them to be aware that there are overtones in the body as well as in music.

There is a strong tendency toward too much musical support in technique classes. By support, I mean the amount of music (notes and dynamics) within the meter or tempo. I believe that is why many choreographers rebel against music, when they finally start choreographing for themselves. An effort should be made to make the music more sparse and clean.

I am not in favor of all composition being done without music; that is, first composing the dance and then putting music on the framework of the dance.

I think you have to work both ways, but in the learning experience it is important that the dancer composes to an already written piece of music, so that he will sense music as form, not just structure. Form and structure are different. Form, for me, is the harmony, the melody, the structure, the tonal structure, the rhythmic structure. Structure is like the blueprint the architect uses to build a building. Seeing the building only through that blueprint, can be a little dull and hard to imagine. You need to see the actual building. Too often, we teach music as structure and not as form.

There should be much more working together between the students and the musician; trying ideas. With a written composition, the musician can help tremendously in analyzing the dance. More important, I see no reason why things can't be "said" within some kind of preconceived form. At least, try it, so that it isn't such a haphazard sequence of movement. The musician can supply a helpful "distance" between the dancer and his work and, with this distance, the dance becomes less self-indulgent. The musician can become an editor. I am assuming you have a good musician when I say this. I think you must do this, because otherwise we are going to lose the people in dance music, for they don't have a chance to be as creative as the choreographer.

You must work with all areas of music with dance: Webern, Beethoven, Schubert, Bach, and so on. There is a gamut of musical material; short, beautiful pieces that can be used in composition class. Try these in the technique class; use much more music in composition, and what happens is that, during the entire time, the dance student is listening to music in an active way. You can listen to music all of your life, understanding a rondo, a sonata, a symphony, structurally, and it doesn't mean that you know how to use it compositionally. For a dancer to sit in a room with earphones on listening to music over and over again must be a strange experience for him. I think it alienates him from the music. It is more sensible to have him listen at home. If he wants to get up and move to it, he can. It is not a separate thing to listen to music, to understand its form, and move to it. He must do all three. He has to listen and use the music. I work with dancers who can only dance by counting. They have to go on counting, constantly, because they don't know how to listen, and how to use the music when they move. A professional must have dexterity in both realms.

Susanne Langer used the word "cadences." I often have students attempt to choreograph a cadence. In music, there are various types of cadences, which can help along new ideas in movement. We have the perfect cadence, imperfect cadence, mixed cadence, half cadence, deceptive cadence. "Deceptive cadence," to me, is crossing a phrase in a movement of a dance — you think it is going to resolve itself, and then it moves on. I don't have students do a cadence exercise musically; I have them do it in movement. Then, I put music to it, so it becomes a movement and musical cadence. I play many cadences, and I say, hopefully, "Try for that in movement." It can be done; it is not anything that takes magic. Actually, it is hard, hard work; doing, doing, doing, and more redoing.

Then there is a motif. A motif in music may be a little two-bar sequence that has a certain character. It can be used when a dancer is depicting a character. The contraction of the old lady's shoulder in THE COACH WITH THE SIX INSIDES is a motif, Bill's boxing movement in the "Champion," and Jane Dudley's movement in "The Harmonica Breakdown," which I remember so vividly, are motifs.

A motif, a melody, and a theme are all different, but many times we think of them as the same, and, worse yet, treat them in the same way. One should start making distinctions, and this should take place in the composition class. A theme speaks for itself. It is different from a phrase, or a melody, or a motif. It announces the tone color of the piece. The most common use, of course, is the theme and variations. It has no special distinction until it is varied, when suddenly the original theme takes on another color. Usually, the theme is very simple so that you can make variations on it.

In teaching rhythmic analysis, I am against constantly putting notation on the board, and having dancers simply stand up and walk or clap the rhythmic pattern, for it doesn't accomplish very much. Many times, I can have my dancers clap a pattern beautifully, walk it beautifully, but move or choreograph to it, they cannot. The hardest thing for the student is to recognize the inner pulse of a rhythmic pattern. He may be able to devise highly complicated things, but, if he can't relate to the inner pulse of that pattern, he never seems to be what I call a really good, rhythmically aware dancer.

Learning syncopation is complicated, and much more investigation in the manner of teaching it should be done, isolating the different areas of the body; syncopating in that fashion, rather than syncopating only in the sound of the feet.

There is an area in music called grace notes and trills. I will say, "Try a grace note in the port de bras on the beat. I don't care what you use, the finger, or anything. Try a movement like a grace note anticipating the beat. Try it in the trill." It calls for subtle timing, but, also, the imaginative use of movement. You would have to find your own way of doing it, but I have tried it and wonderful things happen. I always relate it to the vocabulary of music, so that students feel it is not separate.

One more illustration on choice of meter: a choreographer will say, "I am going to do about this tempo." I'll say, "Do you want it 3/4, 6/8, 3/8, or 4/4?" These look different; they are different, and they should feel different. They should affect the movement. Unfortunately, many people who work with dance don't know the possibilities. They think 6/8 — moderate tempo; 3/8 — a little faster; 3/4 — medium; and 4/4 — a sort of march tempo. There is a tremendous range of tempo in 6/8, 3/8, and 4/4. If you have strength in movement, your tempo really communicates.

If, in the training of a dancer, you use these devices I have been discussing, it can't help but affect his attitude and feeling towards music when he starts to choreograph.

Choreographers use music in very different ways, because they instinctively respond differently to music. I am going to pick four, who are quite different. One man I have worked with, and know very well, Jerry Robbins. He is very aware of the horizontal structure of music, and he is moved by what he calls the "rhythm" of the piece. That is why he chooses Stravinsky; that is why he feels a kinship to jazz. He calls it the "organic" quality of music. Mr. Balanchine delights in the analytical part of the music. He is involved with how intricately something is composed, the melodic structure, the contrapuntal and harmonic structure. He is what I call the "linear aware" man. Anna Sokolow and Martha Graham use music in such a fashion that they don't necessarily dance measure by measure. There is a movement pattern, perhaps 20 counts, and maybe the music and dance start together and end up together at a certain point, but what happens in between is quite separate. Miss Sokolow uses it more, I feel, as an underscoring of movement mood or effect.

44

I haven't touched on electronics at all, because I have not worked with it. I believe in it, but I don't necessarily believe in the way it is being used. It has often been used more in a pretentious manner than a sincere, emotional manner. It is an excuse. The composer and choreographer didn't know what to do, musically, in the first place, so they brought in little "beeps," which have nothing to do with the content of the dance. Does all movement lend itself to electronics? Do all ideas? These are serious considerations, which do not appear to matter to many, who seem to believe all ideas work with electronic music. I do not think they do. There are very good composers working in this medium. Students should listen to their music. It takes a good deal of thought to compose, because they do have a form. The dance should not have a haphazard form just because the music seems to be haphazard.

I liked the idea of Joan Woodbury's using vocal sounds in the demonstration of improvisation the other day. I think more of that can be incorporated in the experience of the dancer — not necessarily in performance, however, because you have to be careful as to what vocal sound means. It is difficult to have a vocal sound on stage and then bring in music and have a meaningful relationship between the two.

You must realize that these are all just my own personal feelings and personal experiences. I am concerned that there are very few musicians becoming involved in music for dance. They are leaving it. Very few musicians will play for dance anymore.

Discussion

BETTY WALBERG

Joan Woodbury: I have been thinking about what has been said. Possibly I should have said to Jack (the musician for the Improvisation Demonstration), "You set yourself some musical problems which are related, somehow, to what we are doing, so that in your improvisation you also have stops, which are of various lengths, that have to do with — well, balance on one leg — something that might have to do with balance of tones." But I was not asking him to watch what he saw.

You must see dance if you are going to play for it.

Joan Woodbury: Couldn't there be some correlation between co-existing at the moment — as a player?

What is the point of it, Joan?

Joan Woodbury: I think it's to sense some relationships between. . .

But you are asking him to be on his own, and the dance to be on its own, so I don't see what the relationship is. I think you were making it much too separate from what was happening physically. What would have happened, Jack, if she had said, "Improvise in the style of Webern — his 'Six Short Pieces'" — What would you have done?

Jack Jackson: Just that, I think.

What would have happened musically? It would have had stops, right?

Joan Woodbury: I would have had to be a little more explicit.

That is what I am talking about, Joan. You must be specific with a musician.

BETTY WALBERG

>Jack Jackson: I wouldn't overlook the possibility of a preliminary discussion. I think, if I had had a clear understanding of what the objectives and problems were, I could then have edited and interpreted. The question was, whether or not I was to be impelled by what I was seeing, or whether I was to act independently.

>Dorothy Madden: I set a certain study in which I asked the students to illustrate in movement, tensions, silence and negative space, with reference to modern concepts in many of the arts. I asked the musician if he would please do something rather linear, perhaps in the feeling of a madrigal. He said, "I don't see it that way."

Well, I would just tell him to do it. You are not in error, and he is not. Just tell him to work and do it. Now, he may not, but he might find something by doing it.

>Dorothy Madden: We had a long discussion on this.

Well, you have to understand that musicians like to discuss things, and it is good to give them a chance, but there is a point where you say, "Please do it; I am after something here." Now, what do you mean by "negative space"? You see, that would throw me, as a musician.

>Dorothy Madden: Silence is really what I meant. In painting, the space you haven't used is called "negative space."

What would you think that relates to in music? If you have a rest, you don't have negative space. If you have silence, you don't have negative space. What were you after?

>Dorothy Madden: I was after that linear feeling, that "drawing" feeling you get from not too much harmony.

My reaction to "negative space" is that I might play something à la Scarlatti, and I would leave that for a moment and go into something with a completely different musical texture, and the space between those would be, to me, "negative space." That's how I would treat it as a musician. But, really, if you said "negative space" to me, I wouldn't know what to do. I am cross-examining you. You brought up a problem. You should just tell him to try it.

>Bonnie Bird: What do you think about the possibility of using the tape recorder constructively? It is rapidly becoming the worst enemy of live music, and yet it is going to be used.

You mean recording something and then using it for a performance?

>Bonnie Bird: Yes, and for class work, too.

Sometimes, I think if you have a very bad musician, it is better to have good music on tape, but I think it is terribly limited. It is a hard question to answer, Bonnie, because it certainly is not ideal. Soundwise, there is a big danger in working with "canned" music all the time, because it does feel and sound very different from live music.

BETTY WALBERG

The tempo, energy and "presence" are different. You can play exactly the same tempo on a record as you do with an orchestra, but it is going to feel different in tempo. The musician and dancer should be aware of this.

> Dorothy Madden: What do you feel about a teacher who uses a drum for accompaniment?

It depends on how inventive the person is with the drums. Sometimes the sound of drums will do the work, and the dancer is doing nothing. That is the danger. They get so emotional about the sound that, actually, nothing is happening in the body. I think it can be done with great excitement if there is a relationship between the two.

> Ruth Murray: I do feel that the modern student of dance doesn't think of the music, necessarily, as something that is too important.

If the teachers and the students feel the need of this person, usually the administration will adjust, financially. If you make him a necessary part, and he is so valuable and so good, they will often pay more.

> Joseph Gifford: If you get a decent enough salary for your accompanist, you can ask more of him. This is not someone you hire by the hour. This is a faculty position. As soon as you get it on that basis, it gives a certain dignity to the position.

I think you have to look at it both ways. You could bring in someone who is very good, perhaps for only three times a week, and pay him well enough. He doesn't have to be part of the whole organization.

I think we can start by eliminating the word "accompanist," and really have that person be a creative part of the class. There are times when one accompanies — as an example, for a square dance. We have to be careful how we use the term, and think of accompanying as in the "Lieder" of Schubert, where the accompaniment makes its own melodic line.

> Alma Hawkins: We have had a tendency to think that the teacher is the one who is bringing insight and understanding to the class, but you have been showing us how the musician can also contribute in this way.

You have to open up a chance for him to do that. I think the only way you can get involved in dance and love dance as a musician is to participate in the technique class as well as the composition class. I can't stress that enough. That is where I got my inspiration for my life's work — playing for dance classes. I didn't just jump into composing for dance. You can get people excited if you involve the dance musician so that he is participating in a compositional way. As he improvises, he is really writing, composing music. Most musicians don't realize how valuable it is, professionally, to understand dance. Your imagination opens up when you start relating movement with music. What usually happens, because of my dance experience, is that I end up doing all of the arrangements for a show, because what we do in dance and music is so exciting on screen in comparison with someone standing up and doing nothing. If a person like Mr. Robbins does scene changes, I relate to them movement-wise — when does the set move around, what is the feeling when the set moves around, what will result, what happens to the stage? I end up doing all of the underscoring, because of my dance experience.

Jack Morrison: Betty started out by describing a situation in which technique and music were presented together, rather than music over here and technique there. I think there are many implications for all of the performing arts — pedagogical ones, which have to do with the use of time. For example, in theatre we have been looking at the English. Duncan Ross, at the University of Washington, says, "We will only teach acting in a room that is at least two stories high, like a theatre, with voice and movement and acting all at once, never, ever apart again." This process is, I think, absolutely sound. These things work together, organically, all of the time. It is a lot of malarkey if you just say "voice." You can't just say "voice" or "music" or "movement"! You are suggesting the same thing in dance, and I suspect this is cutting across the borders so that we could have a working situation such as you describe, where, in a room, at a regular time, there would be composers and choreographers and dancers working together. You could also cut out three courses and do the same thing; only really do it.

I don't think you can separate the craft from the art. There is too much separation. For instance, in the teaching of rhythmic analysis there should be more movement. Sometimes, the music teacher doesn't know anything about movement, so that two people are really needed to teach this necessary course.

Alma Hawkins: Jean Erdman, at our last meeting, stressed the importance of having a theatre and a stage for dancers as a laboratory for learning.

Nik Krevitsky: I think that what Jack said has the strongest implications for the curriculum in dance and music. The person he was talking about, who wants this theatre for an acting class, instead of one room where you would just concern yourself with voice, is a person who is hard to find. Betty Walbergs are pretty hard to find, too. Thirty years ago, at Bennington, there was a course called "Experimental Production." Nothing of that kind has happened since. To do "team teaching" in the dance curriculum, you have to get people of equal stature, who respect each other and can work together — like Martha Hill, Norman Lloyd and Arch Lauterer, who gave the course at Bennington. Arch would present a problem in composition that would deal with space and light; Martha would present a compositional problem in movement; and Norman would present a problem dealing with music. The students were really learning dance in relation to music, space, color and light. This is not happening now. It is of the greatest importance in the curriculum that people in theatre, music and dance work together so that, from the very beginning, students can have this experience, instead of waiting for a graduate course. No one person can do it all. None of us should have the arrogance to assume that he can be the total Renaissance man and do the whole works.

When Jack Morrison was speaking of the English theatre, I was reminded of the time I saw THE FLEA IN THE EAR, a production by the National Repertory Theatre, which is one of the best repertory companies in the world. It is a farce and, as I watched it, I said, "Everyone is really dancing up there on the stage." Afterward, when I

BETTY WALBERG

talked with the director, he said, "They are always involved with dance. When they start a play, they often dance the role, choreographing the movement." I think it would help dancers to have some acting to bring another dimension of movement for them. That could be part of the laboratory. The terminology the director uses is very different from that of a choreographer. The image is entirely different.

> Participant: It is interesting that when Jean Erdman auditioned, in a period of two weeks, 168 actors for THE COACH WITH THE SIX INSIDES, a large factor in her choice was in terms of how they moved in the scene where they had to go around in the little, imaginary "flivver." They all apparently had a good range of speaking, etc., but that was the determining factor.

> William Bales: There is one problem that I don't think we have recognized. There are very few places that are training musicians for dance. I think this is crucial to our problem.

> Alma Hawkins: It seems to me that in the universities we can do much more than we are doing in some kind of cross-fertilization with the music department — possibly offering courses for musicians in dance.

A lab course just to improvise with dance could attract people, I know. I don't think there is enough improvisation in the musician's training. You can only do this by a lot of hard work and practice.

> Allegra Fuller Snyder: There is a whole group of musicians — jazz musicians — who are oriented to improvisation. I think this kind of work would excite the young jazz musician.

Jerry Mulligan is a person who really loves doing this kind of work. He is a very well-trained musician and vitally interested in improvisation. I would think that some of you could get him to come and try improvisation with the dancers.

As a dancer, you have to start very, very early to learn about music. It is interesting, if you go through a musical dictionary, most of the descriptions are in terms of movement. "Rhythm is the motion of . . ." "Melody is the motion of . . . " "A melody has a content, a quality of space . . . "

> Martha Hill: And "Andante is like walking."

It is a little separate education that you should put yourself through. I think a musical dictionary should be in the classroom for students to refer to, so that they can acquaint themselves with musical terminology.

> Allegra Fuller Snyder: We do have to know how to talk about music. On the other hand, I don't know whether it is exactly the same thing as learning music in the way a musician learns music. I felt that Betty was saying that there is a different kind of understanding about music for dancers. So I was a little bit worried about it being said that,"It's just a question of dancers getting more fundamental music education." I'm not sure it is that simple. I think it is music education for dancers, but again, I think it involves this special person — the person teaching us (like Betty) who understands both sides.

BETTY WALBERG

Martha Hill: I agree with Allegra that there should be special courses in music for dancers. On the other hand, I am going to be the "devil's advocate" and make a strong point on the other side. The ideal person in dance in the future would be equally as good a musician as he is a dancer. He would learn to read music when he was six or seven. Betty Walberg knows about dancing; she doesn't dance, but she knows our shop talk, she knows technical terms, she knows one movement from another. She knows dance better than a great many dancers, and I think dancers have to know music as well as most musicians or we are never going to get this thing meshing. This should be done in public schools. I am making a "court case" for getting the respect of the dancer for the art of music by not having it watered down — which, of course, Allegra did not mean.

William Bales: You are saying music as music, then?

Martha Hill: I am saying, ideally, you would learn music as music.

Eugene Loring: I am teaching a music course for dancers. I had a girl who could not learn to shift her weight, just one-two-three. She would do one-te-dum, one-te-dum; and after she had note values I said to her, "Laura, that is not a dotted quarter, an eighth note and a quarter note. That is three quarter notes." I never had any problem again. I think it is terribly important for us to know as much about music as possible; musicians do not respect us because we cannot talk their language. Every time I can talk with a musician in his language, his eyes open wide, and he is immediately ready to work with me. The problem is selling the need for music to the dancers.

If you make it exciting, they will like it.

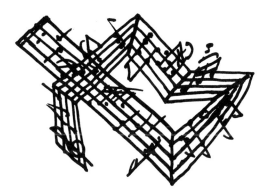

Carl Wolz: I would like to suggest that some knowledge of movement notation by the dancers would not only increase their musicality but would give them some prestige in equalizing the role of the teacher of dance and the musician in the situation.

Ruth Murray: This is really another whole discussion, because it is just seeing this total thing in reverse. I think it is extremely important that musicians get courses in movement early in their careers because, now, the music teacher is teaching much of whatever dance is given in the early grades. If you look at music textbooks for the primary grades, you will find that a great deal of the teaching material is movement, and yet they know nothing about it. The movement that is produced is the most stilted, stereotyped kind of thing. It is all very well for us to talk about increasing the musicians' respect for us by being able to talk their language, but we've got to say to them, "You have to understand what we are doing, and you have to provide for your musicians some movement experiences, because it is not only going to help them in their craft, but it will help them in their teaching." Music students are beginning to come in. They don't like it, because they don't move — they are embarrassed — but before they finish, they begin to get this relationship we have been talking about.

William Bales: We have all said it — dancers should be trained as musicians and vice versa!

Alma Hawkins: We have been saying things in many different ways. We started with the specific of music as one of the areas that we have to think about; the importance of our having more respect for it, greater knowledge and understanding in relating music to dance. Then we moved on to say that we have to bring the specifics together for a more functional use of all the elements of theatre.

William Bales: I have an anecdote that behooves us to learn terminology: Vivian Fine, the composer, said, "I left modern dance years ago. I used to get fifty cents a lesson to accompany dance, but I left it when one of the girls I was working for said to me one day, 'Vivian, play me some sideways music.' Then she said, 'Now play me some standing still music.' That is when I left."

Alma Hawkins: Thank goodness we have a Betty Walberg!

Left to right: Allegra Snyder, Elizabeth Hayes, Ruth Murray, Bonnie Bird, Thomas Watson

The Biological Organization of Man to Move

VALERIE HUNT

It is interesting that you have gone to other fields for stimulation. I think of Dr. Langer and the tremendous message, the ideas she brought us. Here is a philosopher whose breadth is vast, particularly in the field of aesthetics and the arts. To hear her say she has been studying science for ten years, and is coming out with a book on "mind and feeling"[1] — here is an individual who, to increase her insights, has gone to another field. We reach a point where the areas in which we have been spending most of our time really do not answer some of the more profound questions we raise. This has been my problem, too. I started in the area of pure science, and I stayed in it for a long time, trying to answer many of the questions which I raised about movement. I came to cul-de-sacs where the information was not available and, I am sure, in many instances will never be available from pure science. Therefore, I reached out into the areas of psychology, psychiatry and philosophy for answers which could fit into the area of science.

I have listened to your group discussions, and this is what I have heard: a need for technical preparation of the dancer to dance, to express; the possibility of codifying various techniques and arriving at better ones; the need for viewing man with a total view; the need for more knowledge and training of the instrument of expression. I do not know the answers, but one of the problems that you seem to struggle with is that you view the moving organism as an instrument, and you look at it as somewhat disparate from its expression, its communication, its symbolizing. I sometimes feel that this is an easy view. Do you see the human body as an instrument, a tool? I heard this word many, many times, and without a doubt, I have used it, too — a tool, like a garden hoe, that we become very skillful with, that we can do something with, such as gardening, farming; or as an intrinsic thing, like pigment, for example, that we can mix and eventually come out with something creative. If we take that view, we see movement as something quite distinct from behavior; a person would behave one way, and he would move another way, quite unrelated to his conceptuallizing, to his symbolizing, to his creating, or to his perceiving. Or, do you have this other view, which I think is a more ideal one, that the human body is a matrix? It isn't all, or everything, you have been talking about during this conference, but the living body is the start, and a part of everything that happens in dance. The moving body is not just a tool or an instrument. It is dynamically involved in all behavior. If we can take such a view, then the other specific concerns fall into a much better perspective.

Let me tell you what I believe at this time, and I would like you to date it "today," because I am quite sure that it will be altered as I gain more insight. I believe that the moving body is the center of man's experience. As the center it is intimately involved in perception, and it is intimately involved in conception. But the body is more than the center of experience; it is also the basis of further responses. Body movements show what has been conceptualized and what has been perceived. The body is not only part and parcel of perceiving and conceptualizing, but it, in turn, reflects what has been perceived and what has been conceptualized. In other words, it is the center of man's experience, what has happened to him in the experience, and what he does with it.

Let me clarify further. Such things as sensations, percepts and concepts that have been experienced show up in body expression, and even alter biological functions. What we have perceived is permanently recorded in neural and tissue cells, and as such enters into all ensuing expression. In fact, what has been experienced will cause functional and structural tissue change. Because of such facts I am unable to see the body as separate from experience. Therefore, I believe that the biological facts and experiences of the body are all that we have to work with in education, and that by educating the body through movement we can develop the entire level of the human's expression.

---

[1]· Susanne K. Langer, MIND: AN ESSAY ON HUMAN FEELING, Vol. 1 (Baltimore: The Johns Hopkins Press, 1967).

As a scientist, I would like to make some remarks about the living body, which, I think, have the greatest reference to movement. I see the living body as organized and directed energy or tension, and the manifestation of this living body is moving. You might reverse this and say that movement is organized energy or organized tension. But what determines the organization of this living body? First, we know there is a human biological organization for movement, which is not exactly like that of other animals. That takes us back to look at the nature of bones and ligaments, not just to describe them specifically, as hinged or arthrodial joints, but to look at them in terms of movement. Did you ever stop and think that the human body is built to go forward, and to go backward becomes somewhat more difficult? We can go backward, but all human joints are truly built to progress out toward the environment on a frontal plane. The upper part of the body is structurally built so that it not only goes forward, but it goes upward and outward to contact the environment. The range of movement in the upper part of the body is far greater frontwards and sidewards than it is backwards. The legs, more limited in all ranges, are structured to move primarily forward, or to hold the body stationary while standing. Such skeletomotor arrangement is compatible with major sensory equipment. The eyes are focused forward; we turn our body to see things to the side; rarely do we turn our eyes to their maximum location. The ears give us more information laterally. The areas that are in the greatest sensory contact with the environment are the upper part of the body, and the direction is up and out, and to the side.

Do you know that if a joint can't move in a certain direction there isn't any muscle there to move it? Movement specialists must learn basic anatomy this way. What is the shape of bones at the joint? What movements are therefore possible? Such determines where muscle is placed. Wherever, in the body, there is the greatest joint movement, there will be the greatest number of muscles organized to perform the numerous acts. Once, when I was first teaching kinesiology, I decided there ought to be a way to redesign the body to make it move better; so I made an attempt to alter it functionally and structurally. I failed, because every time I got a better movement in one part I created stability problems in another part. About all I gained from my mental exercise was to learn the tremendous movement advantages that result from the body's skeletomuscular organization.

Just a word about the nature of the organization of muscle. So often we and our students have named muscles and looked at their attachments, thinking this was a study of movement. It is not. This is a dead approach. We must realize that there are many static body positions, and from different positions there are different movements possible. We should remember that muscles are not the same, regardless of whether they look the same on the outside, or cross the joint in the same way, or lie in proximity to one another. Muscles are quite unique and individual in their functioning, as based on their structure. In those areas of the body where we must maintain stability against our primary force, the pull of gravity, we have a quality of muscle different from that in areas where we do not have to maintain this control.

We have muscles whose primary function is to maintain stability and fight against the pull of gravity to make possible additional movement through space. They are called the deep red muscles, and they are unique in that they are very slow responders. They create all of our flexibility problems because they get extremely tight. When they get a neural impulse, they respond slowly and they relax slowly; these are the ones that tear.

There is another type of muscle, commonly called pink muscle, that responds extremely rapidly and does not maintain muscle tonus for any period of time. We have to keep stimulating them constantly. These muscles give us the lovely ballistic, the fast, or free-flowing movement. In the spinal area are primarily red muscles, in the arms are primarily pink muscles, and in the legs there are paired red and pink muscles for both functions.

We have another kind of muscle that I think is important for us to consider. Eugene Loring brought this to my attention in talking about the value of the plié, the value of lowering of body weights by the contraction of leg muscles. There are several kinds of muscle contraction. One is a lengthening one, and one is a shortening. These are not the same. The lengthening contraction is a judgment of how much muscle contraction must occur to nearly, but not quite, overcome the resistance or the weight. The weight creates the movement and the muscle merely controls it. In a lengthening contraction, some resistance is overcoming this muscle contraction, but it is not overcoming it rapidly. A shortening contraction is the opposite; that is, the contraction is overcoming its resistance, either body weight, or body weight and object weight.

Here I should relate some new information about strength of muscle. Strength is a neural phenomenon. Recent research tells us that although a muscle will change — its connective tissue gets tougher, it gets more turgid, it has a greater amount of sarcoplasm — this does not constitute strength. It is the result of strength. Strength is an ability to stimulate the nervous system to its maximum and to fire many motor units all at one time. Strength is not the result of muscle change. It is true that when the muscle gets firmer, the person is able to perform certain feats that he was not able to perform before. But strength is primarily a neural facilitation.

In the biological organization for movement there is another big area dealing with the nature of connective tissue. Most anatomy books state that the structural architecture of the body is determined by connective tissue. The body is made up of protoplasm which is organized into such forms as bone, ligaments, muscle, skin and hair by the arrangement and form of the connective tissue. We are mostly connective tissue, with large areas of it in the body in the form of fascial planes and muscle coverings, which are primarily related to moving. The body areas having the greatest mechanical stress also contain more connective tissue for protection. Since the primary stress to the body is the stress of gravity, the strongest connective tissue lies over and adjacent to antigravity muscles. Likewise, the more we stress the body by moving, the heavier and heavier becomes the connective tissue in the stressed areas. Literally, connective tissue grows and serves as a guy wire. We lean on it, and we don't have to contract as many muscle fibers. Hence, in terms of just living, we need firm connective stability, but in terms of dancing, we sometimes think we have too much. Now the only places where the human body really gets tight, unless there is some pathology that affects overall connective tissue of the body, are in those areas under stress. We never get tight in the abdominal area; we only get loose there.

Another aspect in the biological organization of man to move is the nature of reflexes. I am not referring to all of the possible habit reflexes that can be established. I am talking about some very basic gross reflexes which operate or must be altered and controlled in all movement. These operate primarily on a spinal level, and they are extremely strong reflexes. Whenever one muscle group in these reflexes is used to a maximum, there is an overflow to all associated muscles. The reflex which is probably the most important is called the extensor reflex. I will ask the girls to demonstrate this. You have seen it a thousand times. It is nothing unusual, but it is one that organizes our movement.

Demonstration:

(To Students)   I want you to jump upward, extend your body just as high as you can extend it. I want you to turn sideways. Leap as high as you can leap.

(To Audience) Please note several things that are happening. When the students jumped, a combination of movements occurred simultaneously: their feet plantar flexed; knees, hip and back all extended as the result of the extensor reflex.

Let me demonstrate the same reflex in several other ways. Pam, I want you to lie down on the table on your stomach. Will you contract one of the muscles in the reflex?   Do it as hard as you can. Plantar flex your feet as hard as you can. I did not ask her to raise her legs off the table. I asked her to plantar flex her feet, but you will note that the stimulus overflowed to all extensor muscles.

(To Pam)   This time will you raise the upper part of your body and arch your back just as hard as you can without using your arms?

(To Audience)   I didn't ask her to plantar flex her feet, yet she did. I didn't ask her to raise her legs, or extend the hip joint. You can see the entire reflex operating as if it were extending the body against the pull of gravity. I could name the muscles, although the location is more important.

(To Pam)   Will you stand here, and slowly relax? Gravity will flex the hip joint, the spine, the knee joints, and dorsi-flex the foot. The extensor reflex operates against gravity flexion by extending these joints. We ought to use the entire reflex for strengthening any muscle within the reflex. If you want strength of the feet, or strength of the quadricep, you ought to use every muscle of the entire reflex.

Then we have another very basic reflex which is particularly strong in infants. It is called the flexor reflex or the reverse of the extensor, involving those muscles of the body which have to do with flexion.

Demonstration:

(To Students)   Pretend you have something in your hands. Will you push and crush that thing as powerfully as you can?

(To Audience)   Note what is happening to the body. Gail is going down toward a squat. If I had brought a hand demonstrator, it would have registered how much strength you can get in this hand, while standing erect, as contrasted to the greater strength when the entire flexor reflex is used and the body joints in the spine, shoulders, hips, knees, and elbows all flex simultaneously with hand flexion.

Haven't you seen the flexor reflex in the dance? One of the problems in our dance movements with some people is that we want them to do both, sometimes separately, and sometimes together, or a maximum flexion in one part of the body and at the same time a maximum extension in another part. This takes training or control of two powerful basic reflexes.

The next reflex I want to show you is the crossed extensor or crossed flexor reflex. It is the reflex that gives us balance during locomotion.

(To Students)   Will you jump and swing one arm forward and one arm back while your legs are doing the same thing in natural opposition? Note that all but one did natural opposition quite automatically.

Gail: I was choreographing.

That brings to mind another point. The crossed reflex is operative in walking and running and is so basic that, unless altered by higher neural centers, it will operate in all simultaneous flexion and extension of arms and legs. Many of the things you do in dance alter the most basic reflexes into movement that is more stylized and more interesting, but you should know that the basic locomotor pattern is a crossed reflex. Now, if you are working with beginners who are not skilled, you may find that when they are concentrating or are self-conscious they break the crossed extensor reflex, and walk, leap or run using the right arm and leg in flexion while the left arm and leg extend. Neurologically there are two animals hitched up this way, the bruin bear and the camel. These animals have a peculiar quality to their gait, a lumbering, swaying movement which gives them no balance problem only because they are four-footed.

Another neural phenomenon is called reciprocal innervation. I want to make it very practical because it is terribly important in movement. Actually, reciprocal innervation means that when one side of the body is in active muscular contraction there is corresponding relaxation of its opposite musculature. This is again one of the most dominant, most consistent reflexes operating on the spinal level. In a task-oriented movement geared to efficiency, the antagonist relaxes when the agonist contracts, but when the goal of movement is communication, expression of emotion rather than mechanical efficiency, the reciprocal action of muscles is thwarted. For example, when you do a restrained movement that has a great deal of power, you do not have reciprocal innervation. You are stimulating muscles on both sides of a limb at the same time. It is completely unfunctional, but it is expressive, and that is important for dance. It is dramatic, too, because it is unusual, and it is frequently more interesting than a simple efficient movement. It is difficult not to use reciprocal innervation. Its function is a free-flowing type of movement, or the efficient handling of an object. Many specific dance techniques have as a goal the control of normal reciprocal innervation. While this is desirable in producing interesting movement, it likewise increases residual muscle tension.

Let me divert our attention briefly to the problems of flexibility as related to muscle tension. Flexibility, like strength, is a neurological phenomenon and not just a connective tissue problem. Techniques that have been used by dancers to get flexibility are of two kinds; a bobbing or extreme jerking movement, or a static, held position in which the joint is stretched to its maximal range. I have just finished an electromyographic research on stretch which I will review for you, and then come back to practical application for dancers.

For a number of years I have had the feeling that techniques of stretch were inefficient, even doing damage to the body. My feeling was that we should devise methods of stretch that used reflexes to gain relaxation so that the body cooperated rather than fought back. My subjects were 150 college women. Some were dancers, some athletes. We affixed electromyographic electrodes to the hamstring muscle groups of each subject. We recorded the muscle tension produced from three types of stretches: the bobbing, the static, and what I named the reciprocal relaxation.

Briefly, the results showed that the jerk or bob caused the highest tension in the stretched muscle, and the static stretch next most. You all know that if you bounce and jerk there is a recoil or a stretch reflex, and if you stretch slowly you feel the pain of contraction. We also learned from this experiment that by using reciprocal innervation we got the greatest stretch and with the least discomfort. I will demonstrate this.

Demonstration:

(To Students) Stand, feet together, back flat. Bend at the hip joint into flexion.

(To Audience) We can measure how far they go by the position of the hands in relation to the floor. Although this is not a good criterion for hamstring flexibility, it is a relative measure from which to judge the effectiveness of an exercise.

If the students flex at the hip with a very slow stretch, they get immediate stretch on the hamstrings, which is quite painful. If they bob around a little bit, it doesn't hurt as much for the simple reason that there is not a constant pull or stretch reflex. But, on the other hand, with every down movement they do, they get a contraction which increases the tone. Here is an example of a reciprocal innervation type of stretch. Put your hands about at your knee level, right against your thighs, with your elbows extended, your knees extended, and your feet together. Everyone wants to spread the feet in order to take the pull away from the biceps which is the tightest muscle of the hamstring group.

In this starting position the hamstrings are not being stretched. Now, will you contract your abdominal and hip flexors as though you are going to pull your trunk and head down toward the ground? But don't let yourself get pulled down because your arms are holding you back. Pull very hard with your abdominals, with your flexors, but keep your elbows straight, hands on thighs just above the knees. Now, very slowly let your arms bend. Note how much more flexion occurred at the hip joint.

<u>Participant</u>: Oh, that feels good.

You see how much farther you went down? You should be able to get between 10 and 15 degrees on one stretch, no bobbing, no pain, no stretch reflex.

What we have done here is to contract flexor muscles, causing reciprocal relaxation in the extensor muscles, allowing them to lengthen, and thus putting a stretch on adjacent connective tissue. It can be done anywhere in the body where agonist and antagonist muscles are of somewhat comparable size and strength.

<u>Demonstration</u>:

Here is an example of the three types of stretches applied to the pectoral muscles.

(To Students)   Will you put your hands behind your neck? Pull your elbows back.

(To Audience)   They do not have a great deal of movement range. We could jerk the pectorals, increasing the tension, or pull the shoulders and the arms back, creating pain from the strong stretch reflex.

When using the principle of reciprocal innervation, we would start with the same position, hands behind neck, but this time the arms and shoulders will be only slightly drawn backward. I will stand behind the person, placing my hands on the back of the upper arm. (To Student) Will you push your arms and shoulders back against my resistance for about 10 seconds, until your pectorals reciprocally relax? Then I gradually decrease my resistance. Note how much farther backward her arms moved, and without pain.

The reciprocal stretch can also be effectively used to stretch tight hip or leg adductors.

<u>Demonstration</u>:

Sit with your legs spread apart about 45 degrees, knees extended. Place your hands on the floor close to the outside of your thighs. Now, contract your hip abductors, or try to spread your legs farther apart while you resist spreading with your arms. After about 10 seconds contraction, slowly take your hands from the floor, allowing your thighs to spread apart. You can now place the hands on the inside of the thighs and gently press outward. It is not unusual to get 10 to 15 degrees more stretch from one stretch. Not only does the reciprocal type of stretch increase the range rapidly and without pain, but the range will be maintained for a much longer time, and strength will be gained in the agonist muscle.

This type of stretch is now being used in the Dance Department at UCLA with far fewer injuries and muscle strains.

<u>Demonstration</u>:

Let me demonstrate this same type of stretch for the back muscles that get so tight. (To Student) Lie on your back with your knees bent and your feet flat on the floor. Place your hands against your knees, keeping your elbows extended. Contract your abdominals and hip flexors as though you were trying to do sit-ups. Keep your arms stiff, and work hard to flex your spine. You are contracting one side in the mid ranges, so as not to get a stretch reflex in the back. Now, after several seconds, grab hold of your knees and pull yourself into flexion. Note how much more spinal flexion you were able to get from this one simple exercise.

To continue our discussion on the nature of the body to move, let us consider the sequence of bodily movements. Movement always starts in the middle of the body. Whether movement terminates out away from the body or in close, it must start in the central part of the body, in the torso. If you are sitting down, and raise your little finger, the movement had to start in the center. You are not able to move any part of your body without first stabilizing the middle. Although you know it, sometimes you have forgotten that strong or stable movements of the legs and arms are only possible if the back and abdomen are equally strong. Sometimes I feel that dancers spend too much time conditioning the legs and not enough on the trunk.

Participant: How pervasive is that middle? Can you specify it?

It is the whole torso, the trunk and the hips. It is everything but the arms, legs and head. A dramatic example occurs with post-polio youngsters who have normal muscles in the arms and legs, but weakness in the trunk. They can hardly move their arms or legs. Remember that one end of all shoulder and hip muscles attaches to the body and unless this end is held firm, the other end attached to arm or leg cannot move strongly. Unless there is mobility and strength in the trunk, with the ability to contract by holding, lengthening and shortening, the entire movement of the body will be affected. If you watch the very excellent dancer, you can see that the movement starts in the middle. Often, students of dance prefer to exercise the periphery because the middle seems so unexciting. The middle is terribly emotional. Emotions first stimulate striated muscles in the trunk and at the proximal joints of arms and legs. While it is true that nuances of emotion are expressed in the periphery — hands, head and feet — the most powerful emotions primarily stimulate muscles attached to the trunk. For example, in the Oriental dance the center of the body is held firm; in the Balinese dance the center of the body moves a great deal laterally. In the Tahitian dance the center of the body moves anteriorly and posteriorly; the torso is held erect, but there is still movement in the center part. I want to stress that it isn't just these specifics about bones and muscles, or isolated information about physiology, which is important. It is the organization of bones, the organization of muscles, the organization of reflexes, the organization of connective tissue, which are very important factors in movement capabilities.

Today, the most exciting frontier in all science comes from the experiments of molecular biologists. They have discovered that each living cell contains structural forms of nucleic acid in molecules providing a genetic and experiential coding of each cell. The names DNA and RNA, derived from their chemicals, have been given to these substances. While the specific code whereby instruction is given and carried out in the development of new cells is not yet deciphered, it is known that memory in the form of coded information or stored learning is retained in some form within the DNA and RNA in each living cell.

Such molecular facts have profound implications for all disciplines concerned with human life and behavior. It seems tenable that human movement behavior is likewise genetically and experientially programmed in living cells. We who have worked with movement development and its expression in dance have believed, without proof, that we are dealing with a very basic level of human life — even cellular.

While verification of these ideas awaits future biological discoveries, consideration of the biological nature of man to move, would be incomplete without some reference to the discovery and function of DNA and RNA.

Let me summarize. I've tried to give you a very brief review of the biological organization of man to move. Such information tells us a bit about how the body knows how to move and defines our limitations and our base capacities. I think that is about all a biological approach can provide. I do not think that movement as directed energy can be understood from the biological nature of man to move.

All of the things which I have reviewed so far are common to all human beings and cannot describe adequately the great range of individual movement differences or the style of individuals. We know that basically humans are biologically similar, but their styles are extremely different. There is a kind of unique movement behavior. The interesting thing about movement style is that it is evident in all movement behavior, not just in dance. Whether the movement is task-oriented, or the purpose creatively or expressively directed, or a subconscious gesture, the person has continuity in his style, and he has variations. Some individuals display a higher continuity than they do a variation throughout their entire movements.

We have completed a study which established the reliability of certain aspects of style. Using a 7-point scale, we evaluated the movement of 40 youngsters by observation of the amount of time, the amount of space, the amount of force which they used during daily activities. Then we gave them some tasks, such as kicking and throwing balls, running and skipping. We asked them to perform these skills as big as they could, and as small as they could. Strangely enough, it didn't really make any difference what you asked them to do or how you asked them to do it; their style was consistent. It was as big as they could make it, but it wasn't like somebody else's big. We also found that the observers tended to rate movement on the scale, based upon their own movement styles. If their movement was small, they always graded smaller than a person who had large movement. If their movement was fast, they perceived fast movement in a greater range, and they would evaluate it as faster. We had to choose our observers from both those who had very fast movement and very slow movement; very big and very small movement; very strong and very weak movement.

By evaluating the movement in many tasks over several weeks, we could determine the movement style of individuals. From this study we found out that style is consistent with individuals.

We all know that style is a quality of movement. Although it is complex, we can discover those base reference points which underlie style. As dancers and movement specialists, we use numerous words to describe a style. Most words are neither accurate nor clear. We find no common nomenclature, because how we describe movement tells what it means to us. It has little to do with style, but more to do with what we get out of having seen that style. We tend to like the style that is our style, and dislike the style which is foreign to us. There is a study going on in the Dance Department at UCLA in which we are trying to arrive at, to evaluate, the style of dancers, and then assign dancers with certain styles to choreographers who have a similar style. We believe that the choreographer's ideas demand certain styles of his dancers, and if he has dancers who do not have this capacity, he has difficulty trying to lead and teach a particular dance. Movement style is an enduring sort of thing, because it is based on very basic concepts.

Demonstration:

I am going to ask the girls to do a number of movements, and I want you to watch them purely for style. I want you observers to look at such elements as the range of time, force, and space that each girl uses.

(To Students) Girls, will you warm up as though you were preparing for a dance class? Now, will you jump rope? We are not at all interested in your style of jumping rope, or your specific skill in jumping rope. We are interested in your movement behavior.

Will you improvise movement based on time? Will you change and improvise, based on force? Will you now move, based on space? Now, will you choose time, force or space — the one you enjoyed most — and continue improvising?

Joseph Gifford: It is a curious thing that first you asked for the emphasis on time, second on force, and last on space. But I was aware all the time that for me the emphasis was on force.

Valerie Hunt: Of course, all three exist in movement, but perhaps you are more perceptive of force. Did you notice that the girls did not change very much when I asked for the change from one emphasis to another?

I like to think of style as a central tendency from which you can deviate in both directions. But if you could watch their everyday movements, how they walk, how they eat, how they drive a car, you would find that there is a central tendency in how they perform simple skills, and it is based upon their range and proclivity in the use of force. They use what is most compatible and comfortable for them. Some individuals have a very limited range, and, regardless of the situation, they respond within this limited sphere. Others have a great range which allows them a more diverse style when needed. However, they too will return to a more comfortable style in everyday movement. You have taught students such as these, whose movements are in the upper ranges, on a continuum.

I want to bring to your attention the shape of movements in space as an individually expressive aspect of style. The movement shape in space has to do with the path one's limbs take. There are those who move primarily in circular paths. There are others who, in their gestures, in their handling of ordinary tasks, regardless of task demands, still follow straight lines and straight paths. Regarding direction, we have seen that we are biologically equipped to move forward, yet there are those who show strong style differences by backing up. This is fairly exciting, because it isn't common. Still other people move up, and don't appear to like to move down; then there are also the down movers. Some people do both. They move up if such is demanded, needed or felt, but can likewise accent the downward movement. This, of course, is ideal, but it is those with a very dominant and often limited style that we notice most.

Movement direction also contains a level of movement related to the ground. The extremes are those who walk on a high level, who gesture on a high level, as compared to those who, even though standing, move on a lower level.

Another element of movement style is manifested in individual rhythm. Rhythm, as I describe it, is rhythm within an act, and not rhythm between acts. The rhythm within the act is from beginning to end of the movement, or the flow of the movement. It is based upon patterns of neurological stimulation.

From electromyographic recordings of movement we have isolated four distinct patterns which we have named: burst flow, free flow, restrained flow, and sustained flow. Laban described two types of flow: bound flow and free flow. Our research

indicates that what he called bound flow is a combination of burst flow followed by restrained flow.

Burst flow can be described as a sudden burst of energy followed by relaxation. The total amount of neurological stimuli is given to the muscle at one time, with no aftercharge. The movement flows until the energy is spent. We often describe burst flow as a movement with a follow-through. The movement may be great or small but in every instance the time and force are equal — a great force produces a quick movement and a small force a slow one. Skill in striking, kicking, jumping, and throwing, essential in most sports activities, requires efficient burst flow rhythms. It is apparent also in ethnic and contemporary dance.

Free flow movements are characterized by their ballistic or smooth quality, with a gradual build-up of force and speed, followed by a gradual diminution of both. Neurologically, the amount of stimuli rises slowly and decreases slowly. Both burst and free flow are energy - conserving flow patterns. These are so prevalent in young children as to be called innate. In older life, and with increased levels of tension, these flow patterns are often lost.

The third pattern is a sustained flow. The movement appears to have a constancy in power and speed from its beginning to its end. What happens neurologically is a steady and even stimulation throughout the movement. Whether it is a fast one or a slow one, the force and speed do not alter. Many dancers use this rhythm quite exclusively. Perhaps, because it is less efficient or ordinary, it may have more communicative or dramatic import. I believe it is less innate and more learned.

The last type of flow in which the dancer is par excellence is what I call the resistance flow. The movement appears to be strong and restrained throughout. It gives a feeling of force or power, of something terribly dramatic, or of the struggle with human emotions. In restrained flow the neurological stimuli occur much as in the sustained flow, that is, as a steady stimulus. But it differs in that in sustained flow the stimulus is only to the agonist muscles, whereas in the restrained type both agonists and antagonists are stimulated together. This gives a drag or a hold - back quality to the movement.

From electromyographic recordings it appears that the bound flow, with which most of you are acquainted, is not a pure flow pattern. It is a combination of burst flow, a sudden explosive movement, followed by a restrained flow in which the movement is then held back by contraction of the antagonists. Such a flow has an explosive start followed by a suspension.

We could make some interesting observations about the flow aspect of individual styles. You have observed that persons who use one type of rhythm predominantly have difficulty when task demands require other types. I do not know that one flow is more or less communicative than another, but I do know that the sudden shift from one to another is dramatic. Probably dance teachers' techniques are based upon their preferred style of rhythm.

We have discovered that residual neuromuscular tension is patterned upon the preferred flows. For example, in the manual testing of tension of a person in a reclining position, the person will resist the movement of the testor (restrained flow), assist the testor's movement (free flow or burst flow), or hold the position (sustained flow). I have published a study concerning manual tension testing entitled "Validation of the Rathbone Manual Tension Test for Muscular Tension."[1]

Let me review my discussion so far. I described pertinent facts about the biological nature of man to move. I brought out the fact that despite the biological similarity of people, individuals possess a style in moving, namely, in the range and use of time, space, force and rhythm. I also stated that this uniqueness in individual movement was the result of experiences with the body, and percepts and concepts that had been developed as a result of such experience. I reminded us that memory of experience was recorded in the body, and in turn was reflected in ensuing movement experiences. But recorded memory does not remain in isolated fragments: information is fused, elaborated and abstracted into whole concepts. I have chosen those most important concepts which have their roots in movement experiences. The individual styles we have noted today stem from these concepts.

I want to talk about a concept of force. A concept of force is, first and foremost, a concept of weight, because force is nothing but an evaluation of an amount of energy used against weight. We cannot accurately judge force unless we have some judgment of the weights that this force has to work against. Our basic and our first weight is the weight

1. ARCHIVES OF PHYSICAL MEDICINE, Vol. 45: no. 10, pp. 525-29, October 1964.

of the human body as determined by the pull of gravity. All weight judgments are judgments of body weight plus object weight, or the weight of objects as compared with the body. For example, one of the problems we have in judging a thousand pounds of weight, and the amount of force necessary to move it, is that our reference point, body weight, is not comparable, neither is our force.

When we gain weight, as by falling down, our perception of weight becomes increased. When we lose weight, as by leaping up, or jumping in the air, our perception of weight is decreased. Elevators give us this same feeling of weight. Do you know where we feel weight most? Interestingly enough, in the middle of the body, right in the center of gravity, the core of the body. In fact, balance is really the perception of weight and its distribution around a central axis, a vertical and a horizontal axis. When we try to improve balance, we are working on the perception of weights, and the judgment of the power that it takes to control and handle these weights. Weight perception is one of the major aspects of kinesthetic awareness. Sensory nerve endings in the joints, muscles, tendons, ligaments, activated by gravitational pull on the mass and density of the body, give us information about the weight of this body. The kinesthetic awareness of the astronaut is confused because with the diminished gravitational pull his perception of weight is altered. He must be educated to counteract this perceptual distortion in body weight. Without re-education he misjudges the power necessary and is inaccurate in his movements.

We know that during the rapid stages of growth some youngsters display an adolescent clumsiness. Some of the causes are feelings about body in a social setting, but some of them are actually changes in body weight. If the weight changes, so must the concept of weight change. If you rapidly increase your own weight you have similar problems, and there is a lag in time before your concept of weight is altered so that you can accurately determine the power needed to control body weight.

We did a pilot study of the relationship of weight perception to the judgment of force. Our subjects, a group of young college women, were asked to lift an object a measured distance with the minimum amount of muscular contraction. We took electrical recordings of the muscle potentials. Then we blindfolded them and asked them to move the object the same distance again. We found they were not very accurate on the second trial. Following this initial testing we instigated a sensory re-education program lasting three months. We taught them to perceive the weight of their own bodies by being aware of joint and muscle sensations. In the training sessions we followed those procedures commonly used in techniques of relaxation classes. We had them handling objects of different shapes and weights. Our emphasis was constantly upon the recognition of muscle tension as a measure by which to discriminate weight. After one semester we retested the subjects according to the initial procedure, and found that their minimum muscular contraction to perform the same task was now about half that of the pre-test. When blindfolded, subjects were consistently more accurate in measurement of a predetermined distance. We believe that we had re-educated the concept of weight.

Additional evidence of the relation of weight discrimination to movement comes from a twelve-year-old clinical patient. He was referred to our lab with obvious coordination and balance problems. We found that he had a very poor concept of force. All force to him was either great force or no force. Instead of working on the difference between the feeling of strong force and light force, we worked on the perception of weights. We had him balancing in many positions, constantly stimulating him to recognize the difference in feelings of weights of the body in various positions. We would upset him slightly and let him feel his weight shift. Gradually he gained a concept of the vertical and the horizontal, which not only assisted his balance, but also gave him spatial reference points. As he developed a weight concept, a great deal of improvement occurred in the motor performance. He learned on his own to ride a bicycle and to swim, and became quite accurate in his judgment of force.

I doubt that an idea of "soft" or "hard" can be developed without a concept of weight, because power really is a judgment of the amount of force it takes to move a resistance.

Another young clinical patient's movement resembled a spastic cerebral palsied. We found excessively high tension in all areas of the body, with poor weight perception. Our procedure was again based upon the perception of body and object weights. We challenged his balance upside down and right side up. Too many times we think of balance as some form of upright stance. Actually, that is the perception of weight in one position. We started him, of course, on a low level, sitting, lying, kneeling, because his balance was so poor.

Later we had him balancing on tin cans, chairs, beams, as well as balancing objects. At the end of a semester, although I did not anticipate this, his residual tensions were too low to measure manually.

Let me go on to the concept of time. A concept of time, the sense of the relationship of events, or within events, we know is rooted in experiences with the body — those internal sequences such as breathing and heartbeat, behavioral series like sleep and hunger, also environmental rhythms of day and night, and seasons. A measure of the passage of time comes from how long it takes us to move from here to there. I have observed that youngsters who are restricted neuromuscularly, who cannot move rapidly, also develop a slow time concept. I am sure when automobiles first came into vogue there was a great distortion in the time sense, because one could travel faster. Most of us know how jet plane travel upsets our time sense. If our base inference point for time is how long it takes us to move somewhere, it is understandable why our fast machines confuse us.

In most forms of psychological disturbance or psychosis, we find a great disturbance in the concept of time. In fact, it may be one of the very first symptoms. It is my belief that we can only change the movement speed by changing the concept, because movement helps produce the concept of time, and becomes a reference for continued perception of time. If we really alter the time factor of movement we are altering a concept of time.

The concept of space I believe to be the most important concept that I will have discussed. I put it last because it is the most elaborate, and because it can only be developed along with, and following, a weight concept. Before ideas about space develop, there must be some concept of weight. Of course, we should say space-time concept, because space presupposes time, the factors that lie within space, the series of events that occur in space, the relationship of objects in space. The very first measure of space is the space that our own bodies occupy. We know nothing about space without a personal reference point: the space of my own body. I didn't get a chance to ask Dr. Langer, but my feeling is that we can't abstract "space" into "virtual space" without a pretty sound concept of "space," and primarily "the space of my own body." If you watch an infant develop a space concept you will note that by touching his own body he suddenly becomes aware of both the touched part and the touching part. He defines his limits of space on his body surface, not deep in the center like a weight concept, but the boundaries between his space and other space, which is outside space. We know that the periphery of the body is extremely sensitive to all environmental stimuli. Hands and feet give the greatest sense of body boundary or separateness from environment. In the sequence of body space development, children first define the erogenous zones which are connected with the environment. When they draw pictures of a human body it is a head. Later, they put a body on it. Arms and legs are last to be incorporated. We often find adults who know little about the space of arms and legs, and they move these poorly.

I have talked about the peripheral space of the body, but directional space is likewise body-oriented. Direction has to do with poles of space. We learn up and down body space, because head doesn't look like feet, and about back and front space, because we are equipped to go forward and not backward, and front doesn't look like back. The lateral aspect of the space concept is much more difficult because we are structurally identical; even the nervous system is identical. The ability to discriminate "sidedness," or side space of the body, must be learned. I don't mean dominance, such as right or left handedness. I mean the ability to discriminate the right from the left side of the body. If I gave some of you a right-left discrimination test today, you would be better than average, but some of you still don't know your right from your left. With some it would be a symbolic problem of identifying the word "right" and the word "left." Once one has developed the concept of sidedness of his own body this must be transferred to sidedness of other objects, and particularly sidedness of objects in reference to his body. Such skill has been called "mirror image." Do you know why some individuals cannot follow someone else in movement? One of the problems is a confused mirror image. Some women cannot do their hair while looking in the mirror, because the mirror reverses the image and they reach for the wrong side of their heads. Many motor problems can be traced to the inadequate development of body sidedness and its extension in mirror image. It is a problem in accident proneness. There are new studies on accident proneness and people who get confused by sudden turns of cars coming toward them, and mistakenly turn the wrong way. These people have an inability to transpose sidedness to other objects.

Let me move ahead to the final concept, which I think is the largest gestalt, and to which all of these other concepts are related. That is the concept of body image. While there are many other descriptive terms, I think the word "image" is the most correct and encompassing. Body image is the memory of experiences we have had with our bodies and the organization of these experiences into a kind of wholeness which gives us information about ourselves as living, moving organisms. Without it we cannot move purposefully. In psychopathology, when body image becomes grossly disturbed, all types of movement aberrations occur. The body image represents: the reality of the body as we know it; all of the sensations that come into the body; the defined body surfaces; the sense of the vertical and the horizontal; the feeling of body weight; the vision of body shape, size, color, and the sounds the body makes, all organized into a body wholeness which is "me."

The body image is all of the concepts I have talked about wrapped into a totality. In fact, you can't see anything without seeing a part of your body as a background. You may not consciously perceive your nose as you look at objects, but it is there and a part of what you view. You cannot recognize touch except by perceiving your body that touches or is touched, and you cannot perceive weight divorced from your own body weight. We know something about how body image develops and changes. Some time around the age of five or six we should have a fairly well integrated concept of body. It is flexible, changing with time and circumstances. Clothing temporarily alters a body image. Certain kinds of movement exaggerate the feeling of body; others diminish it. Many average people possess underdeveloped and poorly defined body images. The physically handicapped, who have been unable to use a limb, do not incorporate that part within their body image. They will draw pictures of limbless bodies. When a limb is amputated, the person experiences a phantom limb. Although the limb is absent, the memory of sensations still exists in the higher neural centers. Phantom limbs are painful long after the lesion has healed — the wailing of a starved sensorium for stimulation which no longer exists.

We know that body image is primarily "skin deep." It has nothing to do with viscera, or heart, or lungs. Since it develops from experiences with our body in its environment, those parts in closest contact with, or most affected by, environment, are more sensitive. When we elevate the body in a leap or twirl, we lose the feeling of body weight, diminishing the body image. I am thinking about some of the dervish dances, composed of extensive twirling, which are known to produce a trance-like effect. Probably, this feeling results from a dissolving of body image. Little children explore body image by twirling. The sudden gaining of weight, such as landing from a jump or an elevator stop, increases our feeling of body. A change in position, a change of axis, will heighten the body image. Leotards, for example, or any substance which comes in direct contact with the surface of the body as it moves, will heighten bodily sensations and sharpen an image. If you really want to learn to "hula," put on a grass skirt. The costumes which dancers use are not just used for the audience. They are used to heighten the sensation of the dancer about his own body, or particular part, and thus free his movement. I have even tried this with some youngsters who moved poorly in certain parts of their bodies. I have hung things on their limbs so that every time they moved, the tactile stimulus was increased. I was amazed at how their movement improved.

Participant: How much is the person his own body image?

He is distinctly his body image. He cannot be otherwise. There can be a problem between what we call the "ideal" and the "actual" body image. The ideal body image is that which you hold as a goal, and the actual body image is that which you really have accepted as you. If the two are not similar, stress results. Unless a person is comfortable with his body image, he doesn't like to move, because every time he moves he is exaggerating the body image he doesn't like. He isn't body-oriented and is not aware of his body. I think this accounts for some of our sitters.

A very sudden change in force, or in time, will heighten body image. Movements toward the body fortify it, and movements away from the body tend to diminish it. I found that average children who are struggling with the development of body image, and there are many of them, made more movements in toward their bodies than out away from them. It is almost as though they were seeking more body stimuli.

These are my speculations about body image, but there is more than just average evidence for them. We tend to choose those experiences which are compatible with our body image concept, and reject those foreign to it. Body image is not just sensations and perceptions; it contains a value scale of good and bad as developed in a social setting. I am sure the body image of people in very dissimilar cultures is not the same as ours, and ours surely has changed throughout the years. The activities and movements that we don't like to do accentuate sensations and feelings in the body which are not particularly comfortable. Perhaps this explains why many physical education majors do not like dance, even though they use comparable movement in sports activities, and why the dancer feels he has an albatross around his neck when he is asked to move with an object in his hand. The movement focus of the dancer is "introverted" to his own body, whereas the movement attention of the physical educator is "extraverted" to outside objects — balls, bats, etc. (diving, tumbling are exceptions).

Many participants of this conference have spoken about the value of working with dance experts, and what this does to the person, in his capacity to dance. I think that the various techniques and the personality of the master teacher help develop a flexible and comfortable body image which immeasurably enhances dancing capacity. When I work with children, I don't ask them to like different kinds of movement, I ask them only to experience them because I know if they will allow themselves to move differently, then something is going to happen to their body image. It isn't just something that happens to the muscle or nervous system as a result of technique. There is a change in the person's concept of himself as a result of his movement. There was one Master's thesis from UCLA which reported that the completeness of the body image of children in the fifth, sixth and seventh grades was positively related to the degree of motor skills.

We are all concerned with educating man to move, yet sometimes we lose track of the fact that it is education of the body, through the body, to move. By moving there are changes that happen biologically, there are changes that happen conceptually, and these are reflected in movement. In turn, they are basic to the kinds of choices people make in movement. I don't see an instrument as one thing, and the dance and concept development and experiencing and perceiving as dissimilar things. I think there is a great continuity within them. I have tried to pick out some facts about movement which I think are basic-basic, and to clarify pertinent aspects of individual movement style and, finally, to reiterate my belief that individual styles cannot be attributed to happenstance. They come from having perceived and used our bodies, developing basic body concepts which are so fundamentally strong that these become parts of many other concepts which we, as human people, operate upon.

Left to Right: William Bales and Irving Brown

Left to right: William Bales and Irving Brown

Left to right: Robert Lindgren, Dorothy Madden, Virginia Freeman Weil

DANCE IN EDUCATION—Four Statements

Jean Erdman

There are so many things one could talk about relating the dance to the dancer, and dance to the education of dancers. But, before everything else, let me say that in our country the sponsorship of the people teaching in the colleges has made it possible for dancers to exist at all by providing opportunities for special teaching and performances. Many of you at this conference table are the very people of whom I speak. Therefore, it is quite natural that creative dancers should develop an ever closer relationship to colleges.

We are gathered here, in fact, to define what this new relationship is to be. To start with, beyond developing an intelligent audience for dance, the college training programs are about to yield a wonderfully rich resource of new dancers. This does not mean that the studio life of individual dancers will not continue; it certainly will, for it serves a slightly different function in the dance picture as a whole. However, even those of us who have studios and are interested in seeing the dance develop in the way of our own aesthetic point of view, whether we look for new dance company members or go to a college to choreograph and teach a specific project, should be able to work with the dancers that have been trained in college. It is possible for college teaching to prepare young dancers properly because the body of techniques is well enough articulated to make the day of the studio-trained performers as the sole source of new dancers a thing of the past. The advantage of this broader base and wider range of points of view carries with it, however, one very real danger. If the training program becomes "academic" — organized so that: "This term we learn how to fall, this term we learn how to skip," and that sort of thing — it becomes merely an objective body of material to be learned, and there is no excitement.

Traditionally, the arts have been taught from master to pupil, individual to individual. The most exciting thing about a dancer-choreographer is that he is burning to express something in dance, and because of that, creates not only a repertoire, but also a point of view about training the dancer's body,

and develops a technique, a way of approaching that training. Immediately, then, the dancer-choreographer becomes a magnet to which aspiring young people are attracted and, right away, we have the age-old scene of the artist and apprentice, and there is nothing more wonderful than that! The student, as apprentice, works in a sort of monolithic way, a very concentrated way, discovering everything his body can do, what dancers' bodies can do, through this particular viewpoint.

In the college dance department precautions must be taken to preserve the excitement and the true meaning of what an art is, the significance of handing the art down from one individual to another through the generations. The dance program must be carefully planned so that individual, excited dancer-teachers are there to inspire the students.

The artist-teacher, to be inspiring, need not always be a professional performer or professional choreographer, for teaching is a creative art with its own kind of ecstasy. But, the artist-teacher must have had a life-transforming experience in dance in some way — an experience that subsumes all information and knowledge about the art, welding it into an organic self-generating creative activity. This is the indispensable requisite if teaching in school curricula is to contribute to the development of the art itself. It is not enough simply to translate ideas and principles of dance into words or books or films, even if this is done intelligently.

This is the main thing: wherever dance is taught it should proceed as a gift-giving situation from one generation to another through personal approaches and contacts. What is taught is secondary because dance is so huge that almost any set of selections of the total possible movement life, if it is taught in this way, will yield the possibility of a contribution to the art of the dance.

Knowing that we must have the artist in the teacher, what about the teacher in the artist? The dancer in his own studio may concentrate on training his students to reproduce as closely as possible his own image, in order that they be useful to him in his choreography. I would describe this as "training bodies" and it is different from "teaching people." The artist in his studio need never develop in himself that spirit of sympathy which makes giving complete. The college dance teacher, on the other hand, may never have developed that spirit of creativity which inspires. We have, then, two distinct qualities that must be found in both the dancing teacher and the teaching dancer. The spirit of creativity, the need to express, is seen in the artist on the stage. In that role he is focused toward one end, and all material goes toward that end. People, objects, everything goes to shape that moment of a statement, and it is a creative, outgoing, aggressive, marvelous thing, rich and overflowing. The other side of that same person can be the spirit of pedagogy, which is a spirit of sympathy, it seems to me, and all the current goes the other way.

Paradoxically, then, the gift-giver must first receive. This "sympathy" enables the artist to open himself to receive from the student what it is the student is trying to express. The artist must be able to shut the doors of his own need to express long enough to open himself to someone else's need and then, out of experience, guide the student toward an expression which is not necessarily the artist's. This is what I mean by the in-going current to the individual teacher-artist, and the other is the outgoing current of the dancer-artist. These two currents are in wonderful flux in any dancer who is also a teacher of dance and I think almost every one of us here knows that feeling.

If the professional dancer-choreographer is going to be involved now in teaching in colleges, a set-up with a broader base than his own individual studio, he will need to develop this spirit of sympathy, for not every student will be slated automatically for his own company as those in his studio might have been. And he has to function in a wider field with varying points of view coexisting. In such an environment it will constantly be apparent that the discoveries of one generation become the sentimentalities of the next. It may be hard for the artist to realize that the things he discovered, those things he shaped and gave form to, are now everybody's property. But the artist who follows, the younger one, is going to have to find a new way.

In organizing the teaching program, there are two things of great importance: first, the inspiring teacher; and second, that the doors must be kept open for a new experience for the student. He must not be told that the answers have all been found; he must not be told that this way or that way of doing a thing is the only way to achieve a statement, an exciting statement in the art.

This seems to open things to a kind of chaos, but the idea that always helps me not to be frightened is that movement itself is made up of the still moment, or the image, the thing you remember, and the moving moments, the part that never stops, which is the energy of the movement. If the dancer is being trained to be able to control and to shape a maximum energy use, he has to appreciate both the clarity of the moment of stillness, and the free flow of continuing motion. In studying a very clearly selected vocabulary of movement, such as ballet, the appreciation for the moment of the still point can be felt physically. On the other hand, in the study of movement in various other approaches to technical training, or in the experience of movement in improvisation techniques, the dynamic of motion is felt as a logical balance to the stillness, thus allaying the dance student's fears of too many things changing too quickly. It is like being afraid to run fast downhill -- the speed is just too much. Or being afraid to do too many turns on your toes because you might fall down — the feeling that motion goes too fast and takes you away with it. Is this something that nobody else ever feels afraid of?

José Limón: "Continually!"

Isn't it scary? You have to dare to do it, right? Well, then, there are all kinds of other things you have to dare to do, to let go, so that you can go on. I think that that is one of the important things in training dancers. It is very easily lost sight of if you are given absolutely fixed patterns in which you learn to feel secure because you do them all the time. That unprepared moment, that moment of a new, unknown, possible movement, is taken too far away from you.

Two things — the flexibility of the mind and the plasticity of the body — should guide the building of a dance program while the student is being trained to appreciate the absolute beauty and clarity of what a statement is, whether the student is to be a professional dancer or not. If one is going to study the art of the dance, there is only one thing to do and that is to get into it, to do it, and to study it for its human value.

If we are thinking about the colleges and universities taking on the training of dancers, making it vital so that it will really contribute to the dance scene, I think the most important thing these institutions have to realize is that the physical entity, the psychosomatic combination of body and mind, which is being educated in the study of dance, is absolutely significant. And it is the education of that psychosomatic entity as an indivisible unit that can point to the answer to all the educational problems of the world! Dance study, because it so obviously includes both body and mind, can reverse the fragmenting process now going on where the mind goes ticking along, finding out this, and finding out that, studying various philosophies, writing them all down from various points of view, and so on, while the body that holds that head up is just as dead as a doornail, because it has never been asked to become integrated into the thought process.

In teaching dance, especially in a college setting, I am sure we have all seen students with very real fears about pushing through to learn something, or pushing through to become more mature human beings. You can always tell where the barriers are in their personalities by what they do when they move. If you can get the student to grapple with that area of movement he has been refusing to deal with, he can make a jump to becoming a new kind of person. This happens over and over again. Thinking of it, not in psychological terms, but purely as dance teachers, as you watch these students turn into dancers you can see where they have had to grow and that they have done it physically.

"Doing it physically" means that they have been able to let themselves grow, and it has affected them mentally and emotionally. This is simply restating the meaning of ritual. We do not have many rituals in our society today, but the ritual of life in process is practiced every time the student goes to dance class. This ritual brings about the possibility of a wholeness in the learning process, so that the student can grow up while he learns.

The combination of theory, movement, analysis, technique, and composition makes the human being grow. I separate these subjects from dance history and other things because I want to express (particularly at this time) that the way the student has to use his mind in working with this combination goes under the heading of research, because he is pushing to the very edges of his own experience, and sometimes to the edge of everybody else's experience, if he comes up with something no one has ever seen before.

My students at New York University School of the Arts, Dance, Theater Program this year — thirty-five of them — range in age from about seventeen to twenty-six. I'll never forget the expression on their faces when I said to them, "I would never presume to tell you what form your dance should take." I thought some of them were going to drop through the floor because they were afraid: "You mean you're not going to tell us how to compose a dance?" Others were so amazed that I then said, "All I want you to do is something absolutely wild — something completely crazy. You're in a safe place; nobody's going to see it but us, so try something."

Not only the artist-teacher, but also the student must produce "inspired" work, i.e., meaningful-to-the-creator. Such an open attitude on the part of the teacher is frightening for the very reason that it forces the student to the edge of his own known world, that is, the place of inspiration. But if the student does produce an honest statement, it is, of course, relatively easy to point out where the statement was unclear and to help find the form that would best express it. The only caution for the teacher is to prevent the students from thinking that anything they dream up, because they dream it up, is great.

The core, the thought that should be in the minds of all of us who want to make a study program, is that nothing should be done to damage the possibility for the courage to be genuine. Then the natural result of attending dance technique classes is the trained performer, providing the student has talent and keeps at it, and the teacher keeps telling him what to do next.

I made an exciting discovery this year at New York University in the program with Nenette Charisse teaching ballet and Gladys Bailin and me teaching contemporary dance, along with guests who came in throughout the year to teach contemporary and ethnic forms. I used to make speeches; I used to harangue about the fact that a dancer didn't need to study ballet to be a dancer. I still know that is true, but the enrichment of the process of learning, and the specific clarity with which one proceeds is remarkable when the student has a chance to work in the traditional, marvelously symmetrical, absolutely secure form that ballet is, while also having a chance to try various forms in other areas, on different days.

Whereas I have always felt it was important to be trained in more than one contemporary style of dance technique, I now realize that that is true of the whole range of dance. As long as all the teachers understand each other and make the student aware of this, working toward the goal of excellence rather than being dominated by any one teacher's personal attitude toward movement, all goes swimmingly.

We must remember and give much thought to that very precious and delicate thing that goes to create an artist. It is so invisible, so subtle, and it depends so much for nourishment and growth on the person teaching. In closing, I can only reiterate my two main points: the students have to be inspired, and they must be allowed to create something new.

Carl Wolz

Allegra Snyder

Valerie Hunt

Alma Hawkins

Alwin Nikolais

I just finished reading Michener's THE SOURCE. This novel describes how someone many thousand years ago became imbued with an insight into a source of Life. The concept was so powerful, caused such fervent devotion that millions of people have endured tragic suffering just to maintain contact with that source. Perhaps it is crass to relate this to the process of art; nevertheless, I think that in some fashion we, too, go through the indignities, the heartaches, and even the massacres — though the last are vicarious. I believe that, in some way, the whole context of our meeting here has to do with this same problem of relating to source.

We are trying to find methods and means by which we can maintain a vista, a route, or some kind of opening, through which students may have a vision into a source — into art. Often, we forget that art is first, dance is second; when we come right down to it, art doesn't give a hang whether it takes place through painting or dance or sculpture, or even some form of multi-media. We are inclined to be too much the specialist. Working in mixed media myself, I can tell a lot of stories about that, because I find that, often, the specialist devoted to dance fails to see the art source. He is like the foot doctor who tries to cure a bad back by prescribing arch supports.

Fundamentally, we are concerned with the mechanics and the environment that we offer to young people so that they, too, may have visions of a source, that is, art. We are awfully afraid of that word "art" now, but I don't believe we can afford the cowardice, despite the fact that we really don't know specifically what it is. If we did know specifically what art is, we wouldn't have to sit here today and think about techniques and methods by which we can practice the fool thing.

I thought that I might best help if I explained somewhat the process I went through, telling my own history in relation to my vision of the source. This probably seems a kooky thing for me to say, because I read, off and on, that I'm supposed to be avant-gardist, and perhaps you wonder what such

a creature has to do with this idea of source. I am also supposed to practice dehumanization. This is a difficult word to contend with in view of my actual passion for what humanity means and what humanism means, and the relation of these to a wellspring out of which all life grows towards some unknown direction, and which the arts explore.

It may seem immodest even to pretend to have seen such a thing as this mysterious source, but I think that an artist operates on faith that he has a constant contact with it. If he doesn't, he can't work. He must have some faith that he has a trunkline to this undercurrent, along which he can pursue his operations to a vision that reveals it. As a choreographer I have the privilege of sitting in an auditorium and watching what I have done. When I watch, I am absolutely terrified every single moment. It doesn't matter if the performance has been done fifty times — the fiftieth time I am just as terrified as the first, because performances change radically. I often wish there was a hole on one side and a throne on the other. Sometimes, I'd love to crawl in that hole, and other times I would like to sit triumphantly on the throne.

Now, in my gathering years, the thing I have learned is to know when I'm good and when I'm bad, and I need no one to tell me. I have to have that faith in myself. Very often, after a performance, people will come back — people whose opinions I respect and whose sensitivities to the arts I greatly admire, and they say unreliable things. I remember one instance, particularly, where I used a large white ball. One person came back and said, "My God, how did you have the bad taste to bring that ball into operation there?" I looked a little bit astonished at this. But hot-foot, right behind him, was another person who said, "That was a stroke of genius to think of bringing that ball in!" Now, each one's opinion I admire. You can take every portion of the thing you have done and, if you listen to everything advised by everybody whose opinion you respect, and alter your work accordingly, you will have nothing left. You have to operate on your own faith in yourself and your own contact with your source.

One day, one of my dancers was out walking with her husband and children in New York City. As they passed a pile of rocks, the baby, who was four years old, pointed and said, "Look, Papa, scoolpture." Children twenty years ago would not have perceived sculpture in that pile of rocks. We know that the peculiarities of history and our rituals of living change constantly. Today they change so quickly that it is hard to keep up with them. It seems to me that although the source remains the same, the physical shape it takes is constantly changing. I call this the socio-dynamics of the time. What made something work for us yesterday is not necessarily the thing that will work for the student today. In reality, what we are talking about now is what techniques, what pedagogical methods and procedures will keep open a path to the source. I don't think we are concerned with any set physical formula sprinkled with vague philosophical mutterings, but the principles are somewhat mystical.

As a young man, I never dreamed of being a dancer, because this was not within the socio-dynamic thinking of the small town from which I came. It was an impossibility. And yet, in the course of events, one day I was taken to see Mary Wigman, and, just as the child said, "Look, Papa, scoolpture," I said, "Look, Nik, dance!" That was it. But what is more, it was my first conscious vision into source.

This was in 1933, and then there was a gap of several years which seems, as I look back, rather short, but I'm sure was painfully long, because I didn't know how to get to the source. There was no information, no way to make a contact with the thing I had seen that was so magnificant, so right - the vision since labeled "modern dance."

In the course of the next couple of years, I found Truda Kashman, who had worked with Wigman in Germany, so I immediately attached myself to her to try to be hammered into something that could manifest or, in some way, make contact with that wonderful thing I had seen.

This led, in 1937, to perhaps the most magnificent experience — Bennington. This was the time when modern dance was at a tremendous pitch. Of course, I came with raw nerve edges, and with a cavity that only the bulldozing process of Bennington, at that time, could fill. In the course of the next three years I saw Martha Graham's LAMENTATION, her IMPERIAL GESTURE and AMERICAN DOCUMENT,

and Doris Humphrey's NEW DANCE with José Limón as that luminous central sun around which the dynamic happening of figures shook every molecule of your life. These were visions that remained in mind, along with Hanya Holm's TREND, where the mass of dancers, just by raising one hand together, blew off the whole top of the universe. These remarkable things fed me.

However, I don't believe I necessarily saw what was intended for me to see. I saw what I wanted to see. For example, in Graham's FRONTIER, of course I saw the magnificence of the pioneer woman, the spirit and all that that meant, but I also saw a manipulation of a spatial environment that was fantastic — that a woman could be a goddess in space, manipulating that mystical substance — and I couldn't help but feel that I wanted to manipulate space; I wanted to explore it, and shape it into my own vision.

With Hanya, who was labelled the teacher of space technique, I didn't see space, really. I saw another kind of dynamic thing. Regarding source here, I was able to make contact with the sight and visions that the performer gave us. There was also the teaching, the actual classroom event, but, curiously, although I was inspired by classes with Graham, with Holm, with Humphrey and Weidman, with Martha Hill, with Bessie Shoenberg, and with Louis Horst, I was much more deeply affected by other things.

I remember most vividly the course in experimental production with Arch Lauterer and Martha Hill. Here, I saw a relation of a dancer with a form in space. Once more, I am not sure that I saw what I was intended to see, but I saw a road toward the visions that I wanted to enter. I look back upon that period and I suddenly think that, from a pedagogical point of view, there was probably a lot wrong in this huge smorgasbord of material. You were fed bouillabaisse, raw onion, cream cheese and sour cream, steaks and what-not, and any ordinary digestive system would have repelled it, being made violently sick. However, you must remember that the socio-dynamic time gave us a digestive acid that penetrated this whole mixture and made it right. I think that if we had taken belly dancing we would still have come out with something, because the spirit of the time was such that we had both the appetite and the juices to absorb it.

I clearly remember the small, intimate classes in dance criticism with John Martin, and recall, too, gaining a real insight into abstraction in, of all classes, those taught by John's wife, Louise Martin. (These were acting classes.)

Someone asked Helen Tamiris, "What do you think is a dancer's most needed requisite?" and she replied, "Chutzpah!" This is a Jewish word that means plain guts, period. You had guts then, but you also had the dynamics. It was that time. I'm not sure that the time exists now. I don't know whether we have the acid to penetrate such a smorgasbord. I do think we can present and adhere to a basic continuity of the art which still allows for things to be born in it.

I come from part Russian and part German background. Once, John Martin said that was a good combination, because the German has the analytical mind and the Russian says "the hell with it," and goes off with wild imagination. I suppose this has served me very well. I know that I have the curiosity, particularly in teaching, to question, question, question all the time the things I do.

During my first year at the Playhouse, Ruth St. Denis called. She said, "I have to make a film, and I need space. Could you possibly let me use the Playhouse, and how much would it be?" I said, "It will certainly be nothing, we would be greatly honored to have you here." She insisted, "No, I want to do something — I must do something. I'll dance for your children there." She didn't know, but at that time we had probably the toughest kids in New York coming to Saturdays at Three. I thought, "Oh God, what's going to happen?" She insisted. I decided, "All right, we'll try to pad it as much as we can. I just don't think it will work." Little did I know about a great performer. That lady came out, and she danced for those kids. They were absolutely still, and they had the vision if they never did before. When the curtain went down at the end, the kids whistled and screamed. They had seen the greatest thing of their lives. Miss Ruth came out afterwards and she just held up her hand. Those kids went right down — zoom — to absolute pin-drop silence. She said, "When I was a little girl I sat in a balcony in Chicago and looked at a dancer performing, and at that moment my life was made. I knew this was it. I only hope that this afternoon I have given some one of you the same experience."

I think that to be able to clear the debris and try to get young people to have these experiences is a wonderful thing about the educational process as we hope it can be.

When I was teaching for Hanya at Colorado College, without a word of warning, two minutes before class time, she said, "Here, Nik, go into this class — there are thirty-five kids — and give them a class lesson." I didn't know what a class lesson was; I hadn't the slightest idea what she was talking about. I knew it wasn't a technique class, so I wasn't supposed to teach technique. In some way, she had the sudden kooky thought that this was what I ought to do next, and I entered the arena thinking, "Now what'll I do?" In a rather frank fashion I said, "We are here to find out something about dance — let's begin." I just put out a simple problem, and before I knew it things were happening in front of my eyes. That whole summer I devoted to a continued exploration, somewhat like the child in "The Emporer's New Clothes," who says, "But look, Mom, he's naked!" Somehow we were able to create an atmosphere out of innocence, out of stupidity, in a way, and then to have something start and, with the most innocent possible eyesight, to really look at it and see what was happening.

A few years ago I was talking in Montreal, and a man from Wesleyan University Press came up to me afterwards and said, "Will you write a book about dance?" I said, "Oh yes, I'd love to do that." Even though I can't write and I don't know why I said I would do it, I was hooked. And this is a wonderful thing, because, in the process of trying to write that darn thing, I had to discover what it was that I knew. This was the job — to bring to the surface one's own experience and one's knowledge.

I started to write, and the first thing I tried to answer was: What is Dance? I spent so many months wrestling with myself about the definition that, ultimately, I ended up writing seven chapters about it. This was a painful process, and still is, and I don't know that I'll ever finish, but I am going to try, because the process of working to get this out of my interior is a very valuable one to me.

In teaching, particularly since the time of that experience at Colorado College, I have been trying to get down to some germinal things. I'd like to provide a basis on which any student could build according to his unique experiences. I don't know if it is possible. We talk about ballet, about Graham technique, about Holm technique, but is there a possible technical basis which rests underneath, and which we can offer to a student, so that he can then be equipped as an instrument to carry out his vision? It seems to me that, fundamentally, we

72

are concerned with culture and education, but that we often emphasize education at the expense of culture, the study of pattern minus sentient evocation, of ritual devoid of magic.

The basis, from our point of view, is sensitivity. We talk about sensitivity, taste, sanity, and all the things that relate to the idea of a person developing his feelings to a point where he achieves such a sensitive reaction to himself, his environment, and his universe, that he is able to perceive and judge with accuracy. This is a matter of training the senses, but, even more, training the perceptions. So we are fundamentally concerned with sensitivity.

To go back a moment, perhaps we would say, "Sensitive to what?" I began to make a definition of dance in which, as a sort of generalized base, I proposed that dance is the art of motion. I like to distinguish motion from movement. It seems to me movement is a term which we apply most frequently to the gross act, or the total act itself. In other words, I move this package of cigarettes from here to there. The nature of the itinerary, the detail that occurs during this transpiration of action, is motion, and that, to me, is the art of dance. It is not the gross movement, it's the detail of the motion which is the fundamental of the art of dance. Therefore, if we are teaching dance, our job is to try to help the student develop his sensitivity to motion to as high a degree as possible.

We are not talking of one thing but, rather, of many things when we think in terms of motion. For example, we have in motion a body of matter. This body of matter has a particular form. We have, secondly, the space in which this matter moves, we have the time in which it moves, and we have the nature of the motion itself. We have the content of the detail, the vista of the itinerary, the realization of that which transpires in between. You take any one of these particular things, and you have the world at your feet, because you deal with the matter itself, that hunk of matter which we call the human body.

Immediately, we have a fantastic thing on hand. When kids stand in front of me and do just a simple plié, I think: What is my responsibility; what is theirs? In the first place, you have this thing you call a human being standing upright in front of you. There is its whole history, right there. What does this creature mean? What does he show? Science

has crazy explanations for man's standing upright — the better to reach a banana, for example, but it would be difficult to stand before a bunch of students and say, "You stand upright now; you have done this because you are reaching for a banana." Another explanation is the phallic image. Again, to me, this is sheer nonsense because as artists we know this is not it. At that moment, man exemplifies the whole desire, the beginning and the end of humanity, the point towards which he goes, and you find that the magnificence of this creature is not being realized. He only has to stand to let you know where his failure is within the scheme of things. We are still talking about the shape of this creature.

Now he begins to move: this is a psycho-neurophysiological action. Out of some compulsion, he begins to move, and the shape changes — it is no longer the same. Is he sensitive to that shape? Does he have the skill, now, to design himself in the shape which speaks?

This is one of the things I have tried to explore. Just look at the arts; look at the new shapes we are contending with today, the meaning of these shapes as contrasted with the more literal shapes we were concerned with earlier. We speak of dance as a kinetic art, and I think this is basically so, but we are concerned not only with kinetics, but with visual things as well. I have many theories about this. For instance, I feel that there is a great difference between what the eye sees and how it introduces what it sees into the brain, as against what the ear hears and how the ear introduces that into the brain. I think the ear has been a more abstract receptive organ than the eye, because we say, "Seeing is believing," but the ear may receive "hearsay," which is not quite as believable. I think this is why music, as an art, is much more highly abstract than the visual arts.

On the other hand, we know that in recent years the eye has become accustomed to abstraction. No longer is it dominated by the literal fact, for the simple reason that, as scientists and artists open up new vistas, we have gone into space and time which are not physically present, and, therefore, we think more metaphorically. The eye has separate ways of introducing things into the brain. When the eye sees color, it goes into the brain by way of another path than when it sees motion. Motion probably goes through organs of kinesthesia, which introduces another kind of psychological itinerary. Shape is probably perceived through still another route.

In my work, I have explored the potential of shape as another kind of vision adding to the kinetic vision, and I have done this with color also. The exploration in this area is vast, and we haven't even begun to talk about time.

The excitements of our new concepts of time are fantastic. Freda Miller has a definition of music. She said it was 2/4, 3/4, fast and slow. There is a certain amount of truth to that. However, we now know that time is a kind of enigma, that it is related to space, and that time and space may even be inseparable. But in handling time, I know I do it quite differently. In 1957 I did a thing called PRISM. One section was devoted to the shattering of time. To do this, I employed some unusual theatrical devices. To me, these devices were not just theatricalities, but, rather, a means by which I could enter a new area of time to break the barrier of "2/4, 3/4, fast and slow." I felt that there were many other things that produce time in a structure, quite different from what we are accustomed to in the normal rhythmic sense.

We have vast new concepts of space. Even motion itself! The other day I got the shock of my life, suddenly realizing that I had become a patterned old greybeard. I was disgusted with myself. Murray had been on tour and, in a zoo in St. Louis, he had taken moving pictures of an eagle. I have never seen motion like that. I have never seen a dancer move that way. And I thought what damn fools we are. There are millions and millions of kinds of motion that we don't bother with, while we pursue our ritual of teaching ballet and this, that, and the other kind of vapid ritualistic movement. What tremendous areas we are leaving untouched! What

vast areas have impressed the young person today with what he sees, that we are not allowing him to explore.

A few summers ago, I was in an audience where five critics were outlining the way they looked at a dance. Four of them had five rules apiece, and each of the four enumerated his rules. As I listened, I thought, "My God, every one of those rules was broken at least fifty years ago. What are they looking at?" Until it came to little Margaret Lloyd. She sat at the end and she turned to the other four and frankly said, "I really don't know what you are talking about. I just go and look." And I thought, "God bless you!"

Let me return to the idea of source. I think there are three areas of source. One is the vision that the performing artist himself gives. Another is the socio-dynamic vision that is happening here and now, and therefore makes things different. The third is the classroom itself. I have always been aware that you people in education are as much responsible for the source as those of us who create and perform. I mean this positively, not negatively. One does not precede the other; it's the old story of which came first, the chicken or the egg? — it doesn't matter. A student may get it in the classroom without ever having seen anything. Someone may see something without ever having taken a class. One may have a natural feeling for the socio-dynamic times and come out with it.

So what do we do to make a situation in which this wonderful thing can occur? I hope we can achieve some success in the direction of a revolutionary outline for dance education.

Drawing by Alwin Nikolais
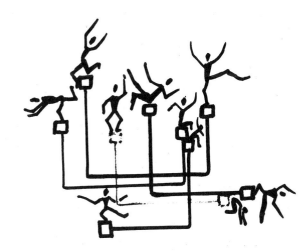

Betty Walberg

Margaret Erlanger

Charlotte Irey

Martha Hill

Patricia Wilde

I would like to start by telling you a little bit about my background in dance, because I think it's very different from all of yours. I joined a professional company when I was fourteen, so I never got into higher education, as you can imagine. The reason that I was able, at such an early age, to go into a company was that I had had very good training in Canada.

Now, I know there are many sides to technique, and it isn't an end in itself, but it is so important in enabling a dancer to become an artist — in freeing him to be a complete artist. My growth in the companies went very quickly, I think, because, being technically capable, I was allowed to work with the great people who were working in the ballet companies at that time, and they used me in every type of ballet. Although I had strictly ballet technique, De Mille used me in RODEO; Massine used me in some slightly neo-classic works; and, of course, Balanchine in a strictly balletic way. Even Valerie Bettis, when she came to the Ballet Russe de Monte Carlo, used me at age eighteen to dance the role of the mother; and I think she was quite pleased with me as a mother!

I was allowed to develop as an artist, because I had come with the technique to back it up. So I cannot stress this area enough — the necessity of becoming completely capable in at least one technique during the early training period. That is not to say that you shouldn't study other techniques. Of course, you must have other techniques, but you must have the assurance, the wonderful feeling of knowing that you can do anything in one area.

I think that it broadens you to go on and do choreography if you have a really fine vocabulary. It is important to work with professionals, people with experience, so that you can grow through the work with them, and then go on to experiment yourselves. It is very hard for the young artist to start off "baring" himself without any background, without any vocabulary to say what he means. I suppose there is a marvelous innocence in not having a vocabulary, but I don't think it remains very interesting for very long. Many choreographers have wonderful ideas, but they don't have dance technique or dance vocabularies with which to sustain the work and to keep it interesting for people.

You are not dancing just for yourselves — a fact which gets lost a lot of the time. People get so involved in what they _feel_ in the dance, but it is also something that you are trying to express to other people. If you can't get it across to them, you should just stay in the studio and enjoy yourself, but you shouldn't be on the stage. What is shown on the stage is often much too personal.

It is most important for a student to be close to a teacher and to believe in him completely, but he then has to go on and learn from many, many different sources — from people he doesn't agree with, often, but he still can learn from them. This will broaden the students as future teachers. They should start their training to be teachers in the universities. Except in rare cases, students in dance in universities will become teachers or people who write about dance — sometimes choreographers — but more often than not they will be teachers, so that the more experience they have under guidance, before they go out on their own, the better. They are going to make mistakes anyway, but it's better if somebody is around to say, "Careful, you're not on the right track," or, "Take it a little slowly in this area."

Working with professionals, experienced in different styles and ideas, can help to form the young artist. This can be done in college and, as a matter of fact, is being done more and more. Masters, such as Mr. Limón, Mr. Nikolais, Miss Erdman, or, in ballet, Mr. Balanchine, can be brought in, even for a brief period, to work with the students in classes and choreographically, so that when they do dances they really have a professional standard, and don't just get out there for experience's sake alone. Such encounters can have an exhilarating effect on dance students. Anyone they are studying with constantly doesn't have quite the same effect. You, as teachers, know that someone can come in and say one word and it changes their whole life. You may have been saying it for ten years.

These are my beliefs: first of all, the technique that they should have to prepare them, and then the opportunity to work with great artists. Together, these experiences will allow the young dancers to go on to become complete artists themselves.

Drawing by Alwin Nikolais

José Limón

A young dancer was speaking to me last week about the dilemma confronting all young people during our present era. He said, "How futile it seems to make the effort to continue to better yourself as an artist, to worry about pliés, stretches and a turn-out, when the world seems to be preparing to blow itself to hell. It is a strong temptation just to give up, grow a beard, stop taking baths, and take to the pills and banana peels."

I found it hard to answer this discouraged and discouraging utterance. One expects disenchantment and disillusionment from older people who have been kicked around for years, and are afflicted by battle fatigue. From the young, one expects the fresh, naïve vigor which innocence and inexperience alone possess. I went back in my remembrance to my own youthful experience, and tried to compare my origins as an artist with those of the present generation of incipient dancers. One can only speculate about the experience of others, but one's own experience is, for better or for worse, the only genuine one. I know that not all young dancers feel this heavy discouragement. There is an abundance of enthusiasm and impetus, fortunately, but the above remarks by a talented and accomplished younger artist are symptomatic of a malaise which exists, often undetected and unexpressed, hidden under many surfaces. How pervasive it is, one can only guess. In any case, it set me to thinking that this is one of the problems that this conference might very well consider and discuss. What can an artist do when confronted by his fellow man's seemingly incurable predilection for violence and brutality; this addiction to savagery and bellicosity? How can he keep from being appalled and paralyzed in all his faculties by the dread phantasm of imminent destruction? How can the arts grow and flourish in the poisoned, embittered ambience of our era? How can they survive?

We are here to speculate on the precept and practice of the art of the dance. We are discussing how to improve the education and training of the tender young plants, which we hope will grow to strong maturity, and what can be done by the artist-educator and the educator-artist to bring this about? In other words, we are here because we have not abandoned our courage, nor our hope, nor our vision: the courage that persists in the face of all adversity, the hope that the human species will come to its senses at the very brink of the abyss, and the vision without which there is no art, and no civilization. Events may well prove us to be wrong; that we are deluded and fatuous. But until that happens, what else can we do but go to the classroom and the studio, and worry about the pliés, the stretches, and the turn-out, the turn-in, the jumps, turns, runs, falls; the design of a movement and a gesture, made beautiful and ineffable in time and space, the ephemeral made as immortal as any man-made thing can be, the power and eloquence and nobility of man the mover, the dancer?

How does one end? How does one begin?

Permit me to cite my own personal experience, which is the only one I know truly.

I attended the sixth, seventh and eighth grades of the Amelia Street School, near East First Street, just this side of the Los Angeles River. Before that, a member of a refugee family from Mexico, I had gone to a convent school in Tucson, Arizona. You see, I am in familiar territory. The nuns saw, instantly, that I could draw and, arming me with colored crayons, paints and brushes, set me to decorating the classroom with strange, fascinating new symbols: for Easter (bunnies and yellow baby chicks), Washington's Birthday (cherries, hatchets, and little boys in three-cornered hats), Thanksgiving Day (Puritans, turkeys, muskets, Indians, bows and arrows), Hallowe'en (witches, brooms, pumpkins, bats, owls, black cats, ghosts), and, of course, most delectable of all, Christmas with you know who and his reindeer and chimneys and bulging stockings on the mantel piece and the heavily loaded tree.

I knew not one word of English. Or rather, I knew two — "yes" and "no." "No" was easy, because it was also the Spanish word meaning precisely the same thing. But the pictures, which the nuns gave me to copy and enlarge on the walls, blackboards, and any other surface available, needed no translation. Very soon, I knew exactly what they meant.

The dear ladies in charge of me at the Amelia Street School recognized the Michelangelo. I had it made. The thrilling adventure at Lincoln High School on North Broadway was four years of art, with algebra, geometry, science, economics and other academics as only incidental and trivial inconveniences, which kept me from taking art classes all day long.

Matriculation at the University of California, Southern Branch (as it was then designated) proved to be a cruel disillusionment. True, I enrolled as an art major. But I discovered to my profound irritation that I was expected to continue the inanities of higher mathematics, and other dreary and cumbersome subjects, and that art was only a small portion of my program. I tried it out for a few desperate months. I was convulsed by an imperious impatience. Nothing mattered but painting and sculpture. The frustration proved insupportable, and one day I severed the umbilical restraint and, using my right thumb, found myself in New York City, Mecca — a drop-out from college.

You will ask, "Very well, what has this to do with dancing?

Let me see: I knew dancing early, in my childhood in Mexico, in the theatres. There was always the Spanish dance, and the Mexican Jarabe (hat dance to you), at all the patriotic and religious festivals — and sometimes mysterious and remote glimpses of the dances of the Indians, seen from a carriage window or a balcony overlooking the square of a small town. And the social dances, of course, the old fashioned ones, waltzes and polkas, mazurkas, etc., to celebrate baptisms, confirmations, birthdays, weddings. Later, across the frontier to the North, I was to see the North American forms, tap dancing, ballet dancing, and, at Lincoln High School, a never-to-be-forgotten moment of the purest magic; at a Christmas pageant in the school auditorium, six girls, all well-known contemporaries of mine from the classes in physics and mathematics, were suddenly transformed, under mysterious multi-colored rays from unseen spotlights, into lithe nymphs, clothed in the shortest, sheerest tunics, their lovely thighs gleaming like alabaster, their arms arching delicately above heads — those of goddesses.

To my entirely unprepared eyes and sensibilities,

the beauty of this vision was almost insupportable. It was only much later that I was able to understand what had happened: the dance was the alchemy which transformed base metal into purest gold. I now see that this was the moment when the seed was planted in my brain, without my knowing it, surely, for, make no mistake, I was, as only an adolescent can be, a male and a man, aggressively so, proud of that manhood which could prove itself among my contemporaries only by a complete scorn and rejection of everything which might be construed as weak or effeminate. I was already on dangerous ground merely by being an art student. Art was bad enough, and just barely admissible. Dancing, especially that which I had seen in the school auditorium, was for girls. No man would be caught dead taking his clothes off and prancing around to music, making sissified movements. Ghastly, unspeakable violation! What I had seen moved me deeply, and I knew that I would rather die ten thousand deaths than confide or confess it. It was to be a wonderful and shameful secret, which I would suppress with all the power of my will: kill it, bury it, forget it.

Now, I was in New York City, and I was going to be Michelangelo and Picasso rolled into one. My destiny was clear as daylight. Then one afternoon, this ignorant provincial was taken to a matinee concert by Harald Kreutzberg and his partner, Yvonne Georgi. There were no transparent Greek tunics; no soft, swooning movements and capricious prancing of young bacchantes. There was a terrible power and beauty and eloquence. There was the compelling drama of the modern dance. I saw, with a searing clarity, something a man could do, because dancing like a proud stallion, or an Angel of Death, or a lover out of a Persian miniature was worthy of a man. There was my destiny.

What has all this personal reminiscence to do with our work here? Now let's see:

I was twenty years old. Too late, I now know, for a dancer to begin his training. Too late, too late. What if I had known about this kind of dance when I was ten years old, or even fifteen or sixteen? What if I had lived in a society and an environment where the dance was not looked upon as unworthy? What if I had known where to go to study? What if the schools, the Convent of the Holy Shepherd at Tucson, Arizona, and Amelia Street School, and Lincoln High School at the end of North Broadway, and the old University of California on North Vermont Avenue had known that there were certain men whose destiny it was to be dancers, and that these fore-ordained ones would go to any lengths to comply with this destiny? What if I, and others like me, had seen not just the shamefully beautiful nymphs, but Nijinsky, Kreutzberg, Shawn, Bill Robinson, Fred Astaire, Ray Bolger, and their many wonderful descendants? You will notice that I am confining myself, for the moment, to the male experience. Girls have had no problem. The parents of the Martha Grahams and Doris Humphries did not feel disgraced that their daughters, after being enchanted by a Pavlova, a Duncan, a Loie Fuller, decided to devote their lives to the dance, and went to serve an apprenticeship with St. Denis and Shawn or Fokine. You can imagine what this eminently respectable pair of middle class parents would have said and done if little Martha or Doris had been, say, little John or Billy. This, as you well know, did happen in other families — this calamity, this disaster — and, when, after all parental pressures, persuasions, diplomacies and threats failed to dissuade the wayward offspring, he was disowned, and told never to darken the paternal portals again. He was as if dead and buried, and his name was never mentioned. The stricken family lived with a shameful secret festering in the remotest corner of its darkest closet.

Much sweat, much perspiration from many dancers has literally covered and soaked many studios and stages, and flowed under the proverbial bridge since those times. The climate has changed. It is much friendlier all around, and young people who are born to be dancers have, if not an ideal present, at least a more hopeful future. There are propitious signs. I know that there are some convent schools that have dance classes. Primary schools concern themselves with the art, to say nothing of high schools and colleges. And I do know that Dance I or Dance II is open to interested boys. And I do know that these boys pay for their temerity by being satirized in the school corridors by their contemporaries. But there is a great difference. The young ones in question are taking dance classes with the knowledge and consent of their parents, and the rest of adult society is not likely to ostracize them as some kind of monster. Parents observe that the world we live in permits a successful dancer as much, or almost as much, status as a successful grocer, banker or lawyer. He has become respectable and, since we live in a conformist, middle class society, our respectability is the "lingua franca" of commerce with our fellow man. Like the dollar bill, it is a fact of life, and try to have a studio and have dancers to work with you, and

compose and produce dances, and perform them anywhere and everywhere without it. Just try!

So Johnny and Billy can go to dance classes: in primary school; later, as an adolescent, in high school; and still later, as a young man, in college or university — or to the local ballet school.

But what classes? Are these good, bad, indifferent, or barely adequate? Who teaches them? What is the caliber of the instructor? What credentials and endowments does this teacher possess? Not academic degrees. Artistic credentials. We are dealing with a performing art — a creative art — one that is every day, every hour, every minute, becoming more demanding, more competitive. And, fortunately, rightly so. Can this teacher give the young aspirant the proper foundation of a successful career, or will this instructor, through ineptness, incompetence and ignorance, endanger, and possibly do permanent and irreparable harm to a vulnerable and unformed instrument?

Alma Hawkins, in asking me to prepare this paper to read to you, mentioned that "dance is in the midst of transition in many of our colleges and universities. There is an opportunity for change and development." She asks, "What do you think is needed? What would you like to see happen?"

I am hoping most fervently that the change is of a radical and drastic nature. Radical in the sense that higher scholastic authority will no longer place the dance under the department of Physical Education. Dance is not gymnastics, nor hockey, nor basketball. It is an art. Some colleges and universities have already done the dance, and themselves, the honor of making this distinction. Drastic in the sense that, implementing this separation from athletics, the ambience for the dance should be frankly aesthetic, that is, having to do with the philosophy of taste, of the critical perception of the beautiful, and, further, fully of the theatre, for dance must be first, and above all, good theatre.

There is no good reason why these two radical and drastic changes should not be realized. Excellence is nothing new to American universities. The faculties of science, economics, mathematics, etc., are often nothing short of brilliant. Already, there exist some first-rate dance departments in the world of higher education. These only point to the need for a proliferation, and (to use an adjective currently of a sinister connotation) an escalation of that excellence.

The attainment of this goal is as simple as it is difficult. First of all, the dance faculty. Ideally, it should be composed of artist-teachers, practicing professionals. This is instantly ruled out. No dance artist in his prime will want to leave New York City and come to some outlying university for a permanent tenure, or even a semi-permanent one. Incidentally, not all first-rate performers are first-rate teachers, but it has been my observation that almost all good dancers know how to teach good dancing. Good dancers are usually the product of good teachers, and in the long process of becoming good products they absorb, whether consciously or not, the methods of their preceptors.

Where does that leave the would-be first-rate dance faculty? There is that category of person who, not being a first-rate performer, has the training and sensibility of one. Here we come again to the aesthetic values, and to the knowledge and the feel of theatre. This person must come as close to the artist-dancer as possible in all respects except that of performance. His aesthetic equipment should be of the highest order, and he must know what makes good theatre. In other words, part of his preparation and training, a good part, should consist of some sort of association and experience with a first-class performing company. If this seems a little too rigorous a requirement, it is well to remember that excellence is possible only when rigorously high standards are demanded and complied with.

With reference to departments of theatre and drama, it is well-known that possibly the best in theatre in this country is being done in the universities. The commercial theatre is either not interested in good drama, both classic and contemporary, or the brutal conditions under which it must function make a venture into good drama a risk it does not dare to take very often.

If such excellence exists in the theatre of the universities, why isn't it possible to achieve it in the dance? Is it because, when you begin your training at seventeen or eighteen years of age, it is possible to become a creditable actor, but not, except in unusual cases, even an adequate dancer?

There is a solution to this, I think. A dancer, to contribute as distinguished an achievement in dance as a young actor contributes to the achievements of drama, should have begun his training at ten years of age or thereabouts. In other words, a deliberately coordinated concatenation of purpose should be established between the universities (and,

ultimately, the professional world) and the primary schools. How fortunate it would have been for me if someone had said, at the Amelia Street School, "Look, there is the dance waiting for you. Come down to Philharmonic Auditorium and see this and that company this week and the next and the next. There are classes you can take. The training is long and arduous. You must begin right now. You can aim at Nijinsky, or Kreutzberg, or Astaire, or all three, if you like. Learn them all, and then decide. Don't be impatient with mathematics, and science, and grammar. A good dancer needs them all. Go on with your drawing. It will not be wasted. A good dancer must be part mathematician, part engineer, part poet. Come, do the pliés, and the stretches, and all the rest. Time is short and there is much to do."

That, friends, was the Age of Innocence, when an artist could look forward merely to the agonies of the artistic struggle. Life and human destiny were predictable. Even the calamity of world wars could be weathered and survived, somehow. You could, if you weren't killed or maimed, return to your work where you left off. I did. But the young dancer, who was telling me about his forebodings and discouragements, has a different situation confronting him. This is no longer an Age of Innocence. We are no longer faced with tanks, submarines, saturation bombing with "block busters," and other such obsolete and primitive weapons. We are faced with nearly total obliteration as a species, nothing less. Man, the perfectionist in all things, is perfecting the means of his perfect annihilation. Those of us who have lived and experienced and accomplished can regard this prospect with an icy, cold, serene fatality, free of the frenzy of fear and panic. Very well, no more Bach, no more Shakespeare, no more Parthenon. If man wants that, surely he should have it; that is what he deserves.

But the young—all the young. And for us here, the young dancer. What do we say to him? How do we answer?

Humankind has been faced with the insoluble predicament before.

I am reminded of a beautiful thing—a theatre—an opera house in Lisbon—the Theatre San Carlos. My company and I played there during our European Tour of 1957. It is an utter jewel of architecture, all white and gold, in the style of the Italian Baroque opera houses. Not too large. Just right. Superb sight lines. Kings, dukes, magnates, and poor men can see equally well what is being done on the stage. The performer feels that he can reach, really reach, the occupants of the nearest stall and the last seats in the highest tier, next to the roof. It is a jewel of communicative theatre. It was built in 1794 A.D. That was at the height of one of the most convulsive moments in human history. The world seemed to be falling apart. There was blood and terror. In Lisbon, they built this lovely edifice, and it has survived to our day.

The violence of 1794 we know, in retrospect, to be mild by comparison with that which confronts us today. And a miracle may come to our salvation. Who knows, man may come to his senses. The possibility does exist. I, for one, hold to it. I have to. Otherwise, I would not be here, looking hopefully for betterment, for progress in our small concern, the dance — small, yet so large, so persistent, so indomitable, so beautiful a component of our nature and our society.

Sanity may yet prevail. That is the answer we can give the young.

Meanwhile, how to improve the dance in education?

I have mentioned the artist-teacher, or his nearest relative, the teacher-artist. Instruct. Instruct expertly and superbly, yes. But more is needed. Inspire. Inspire continually, constantly, and without pause. Bring the artistic experience, raw, immediate and powerful, to the young. They should see, hear, feel, taste and smell the art. To the educators I say, perfect your curricula, get the best available for teaching staffs, get ample studio space, fine theatres for your performances. Yes, all of this. Then bring in your most important ally, the performing artist, so that your best efforts will come to the fruition to which you aspire. You are horticulturists enough to know that the structure, the anatomy of a tree consists of roots, trunk, branches, foliage and fruit. The artist, your ally, is at the creative root of the art which we all serve. You flourish among the foliage, and you bear the fruit which is the new generation of believers. In your concern for this foliage, this flowering and fruit, bear in mind that the roots must not be neglected and starved for lack of irrigation, or, as my good friend Alwin Nikolais put it in his forthright, pungent, Connecticut Yankee manner, don't put manure on the leaves, put it on the roots.

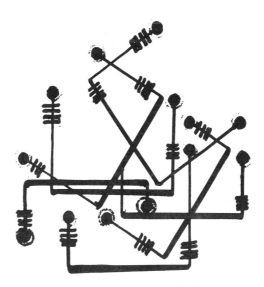

Drawing by Alwin Nikolais

Eleanor Lauer and Helen Alkire

CONFERENCE PHOTOGRAPHS BY NIK KREVITSKY   Greta Brown

Left to right: Betty Walberg, Alma Hawkins, Eugene Loring, Joseph Gifford

Left to right: Helen Alkire, Virginia Freeman Weil, Joseph Gifford, Martha Hill, Bonnie Bird

Virginia Freeman Weil, Carl Wolz, Lucy Venable, Martha Hill, Ruth Murray

Left to right: Charlotte Irey, William Bales, Dorothy Madden, Eugene Loring, Carl Wolz, Martha Hill

Left to right:
Lucy Venable, Vera Embree, Louise Kloepper

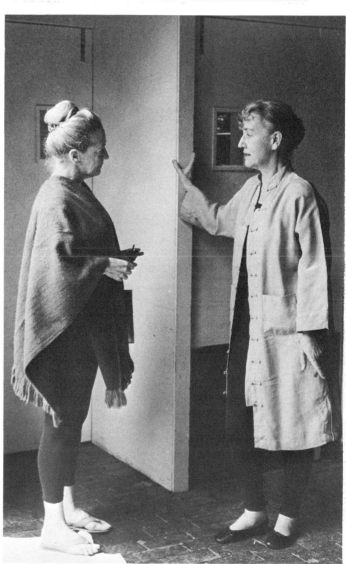

Esther Pease and Marian Van Tuyl

Dance for All Children A Statement of Belief

As the group gave consideration to the farsighted plan for dance in higher education, it became apparent that attention must also be given to what dance experience precedes the college and university levels of study. Foundations should be provided just as in other areas, such as science, English, etc. With the advice and leadership of Ruth Murray, the group made the following formulations with reference to the necessity and the characteristics of movement-dance experience for all children:

> Movement is the core of all art experiences for the child. In fact, it could be said to be the core of all learning.

> With today's knowledge about theories of learning, child growth and development, the necessity in all education to nourish creativity, and the crucial role which movement should play in the developing life of the child, certain guiding principles can be enumerated. These should relate directly to programs of movement and dance for the child from the earliest period, both in and out of the formal school situation, through pre-adolescence and adolescence. In an out-of-school situation, where the child is highly motivated and clearly talented, a more disciplined procedure than is outlined here may be indicated. It should not, however, replace the process of discovery and creativeness inherent in the following guidelines.

Childhood and Pre-Adolescence

> The atmosphere should be permissive.

> The child should discover for himself the potentials of his body movement.

> His adventures in movement should be the kind which do not involve a "right" or "wrong" result.

> Movement tasks should be provided which draw upon the child's imagination and inventiveness, such as those based upon movement itself, obstacles to movement, imagery, imaginary or dramatic situations, sensory experiences — visual, auditory, tactile.

> Initially, the movement expression should be individual. Gradually, however, the child may be involved with a partner or two or three more, who work together to bring about a combined sequential movement form.

> There should be occasional use of simple folk forms so that the child experiences the discipline of working with others, of integrating with a group, of learning to follow a teacher-imposed sequence, of the necessity of moving in unison with others, of enjoying a group movement experience.

> There should be close interrelationships between movement-dance and music, art, and drama in the classrooms. One may initiate another — for example, a learned song may be the accompaniment for the making of a dance; a movement shape may initiate a free-form design in clay; a story or poem may be recreated in movement. Such experiences may relate to each other more naturally under the direction of a classroom teacher who guides the child in all aspects of his learning.

Parenthetically, it is very important that the teacher have movement experience, himself, doing the kinds of things he would expect the children to do, but, at no point is there imposition of any dance "image" by the teacher. It is of utmost importance that the child finds his own way.

Adolescence

As the child moves on into adolescence, he feels the need of and is ready for the development of technical skills and the solving of problems in composition under the expert direction of a teacher of dance, who will bring more specialized instruction to the movement experience.

In addition, some communities may find it desirable to have a school of performing arts, such as the High School of Performing Arts in New York City or the State supported North Carolina School of the Arts.

DANCE IN EDUCATION

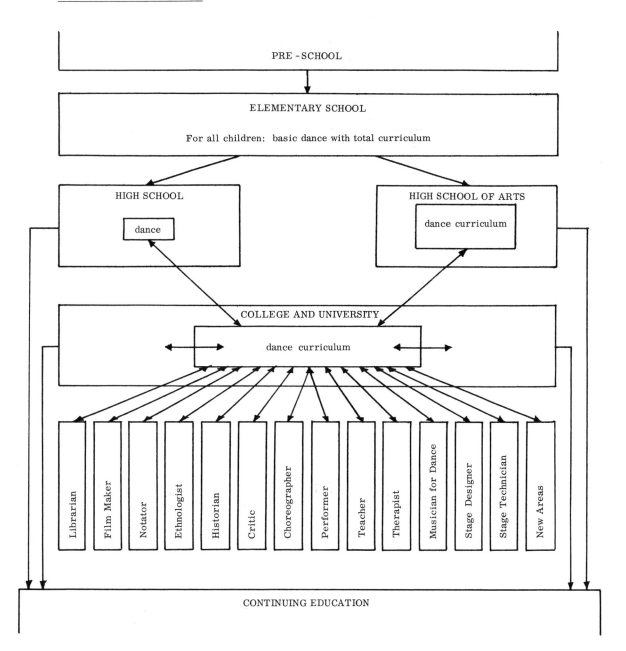

The Place of Men in Dance

What about the place of men in dance? How can we get more men, good male dancers, involved in dance? These questions were considered seriously in various contexts, for the participants knew that the full development of dance requires talented men, as well as women.

The group recognized that our cultural attitude and certain taboos about male dancers have prevented many young men from entering the field of dance. However, it was felt that a factor of even greater significance is the lack of economic security for male dancers. The "problem of men in dance" will not be solved until the talented male dancer can be assured of a career accompanied by financial support that will allow him to take his place in the community along with other artists and professional people.

Recognizing the problem is a first step, but how does one take action that will bring about changes? What can we do? There was unanimous agreement that the conference group should take a strong stand affirming the place of men in dance and the respectability of dance as a profession for men, and should urge individuals and institutions to explore all possible ways of providing some kind of subsidy for them. Financial support could range from scholarships for talented young men to opportunities for a career in a professional dance company subsidized by the university and the community.

William Bales: It is important to have male teachers on the staff of dance departments, and the university should forego academic requirements to get good male teachers.

Nik Krevitsky: I feel that there has been so much resistance to men, that we cannot assume that any general statement or manifesto about dance in education will mean that man will then take his place in dance.

Joseph Gifford: Because of the increasing popularity of dance as a whole, the barrier against boys and men dancing is beginning to crumble. But we have a long way to go. We in education will have to make wise concerted continuing effort to bring men into dance.

Ruth Murray: It is a question not only of changing economic conditions and making positions available, but also a question of changing the cultural image of the male dancer that is held by our society.

William Bales: The point about economics is a legitimate one, because dance has been the least remunerative profession. Because of the economics, male dancers have not survived.

Eugene Loring: We must make some kind of a statement that makes our position clear. For example, "We believe that man has a place in the art of dance, and that dance is a reputable profession." We must spell this out. It is not enough to simply imply our attitude.

Ruth Murray: We should say what we believe.

Eugene Loring: Affirm it.

Nik Krevitsky: Just wanting the situation to change isn't going to make it happen. Creating the conditions that make it natural, make men gravitate to dance, want it more than anything else, is the thing that is important.

John Martin: The financial problem is the main one for male dancers. I think that we will not develop dance in this country until we have some kind of subsidy — provide some security. I don't mean government subsidy, but we have to to have subsidy.

Martha Hill: What can we do about it?

John Martin: Most of the problems can be solved only by money.

Alvin Ailey: I agree with you. Dance companies have to have men, so they just pay them, like athletes. They simply give them scholarships, plus allowance.

Jack Morrison: Physicists do the same thing.

Alvin Ailey: Well, why can't we do that?

Thomas Watson: Then, let's make one of the recommendations from this conference point up the necessity to subsidize young dancers and establish scholarships for men in our schools.

John Martin: I think that you must have subsidized companies where men can go into dance as a career and be sure that they can live decently like other men in the community.

I would like to see professional companies sponsored by universities, so that you can attract the talented boys for a career as dancers. If you want men, you have to have a job for them. You must get them while they are young, perhaps at the age of ten — at least while their bodies are still shapable and their minds too. I don't think that parents will object to their sons going into dance when it is a career.

Joseph Gifford: It seems to me that our effort should be aimed at both the administrators, who are almost all men, and the boys, themselves. In the long run, the way to get boys interested in the dance profession is first of all to see to it that movement is introduced into the school during the kindergarten and first years, and that the child grows up with movement naturally and enjoyably part of his daily living. The administrator must be shown and convinced not only that dance as a profession for men is as worthy as any other, but also that the inclusion of movement in the school curriculum has great potential for the development of the healthy man, emotionally and physically.

In giving master class-demonstrations (basically improvisational in approach) on the teaching of movement and dance to high school boys and college men in this country and in England over the past decade, I have seen over and over again how the students respond first with surprised interest and then with high enthusiasm as they discover physical-emotional resources they were hardly aware of before. The men physical education teachers watching these demonstrations have had all kinds of positive reactions, but repeatedly ask the same question: "How does one go on from this one class? Where can one learn this approach?"

With this in mind, I am formulating a six-week teacher training institute on the teaching of movement for high school boys. The plan would be to invite approximately twenty-five high school physical education teachers and graduate students from various parts of the country to attend the institute to learn basic approaches and methods, both improvisational and technical, of teaching movement and dance to high school boys. Various administrators would be invited to observe the institute. Boys of high school age could be used for demonstration classes. This would afford a practice teaching situation for the institute members. Psychological and physical testing would be made before and after the course, and a documentary film could be made providing a record and demonstration of the methods used and progress gained during the six weeks.

Theoretical Considerations

The ultimate goal of the dance experience is to bring the student into direct contact with the creative and aesthetic aspects of his art. How is this to be achieved? The conference participants were in agreement that the dance student should have the opportunity for choreographic experience, but there was no consensus as to how this experience should be made available. Some participants felt that the creative experience should start early and parallel the technical study. Some felt that the need for choreography in the preparation of the ballet dancer was not as great as for the modern dancer, but others disagreed, and expressed the opinion that there is real need for ballet dancers to have more creative opportunities.

IMPROVISATION

The question of improvisation and its relation to choreography was considered. Participants felt that improvisation is a vital part of the study of dance. The work group on FORM stated:[1]

> Improvisation can be a useful technique for it is an act of finding live connections out of which the individual makes meaningful forms and discovers a new reality. It is a way to get back to the physical reality and allow the form to come from within us.

Joan Woodbury, in her lecture-demonstration, discussed the importance of spontaneity and the idea that improvisation is concerned with "process" rather than product:

> Through improvisation one can discover something about himself and his personal commitment that may be quite different from what he experiences in technique class.

> Art is concerned with making sense out of unrelated moments. Sometimes, through improvisation, you hit upon a moment of movement that has a "wholeness" and feels right.

[1.] See Group Report "Form," p. 143.

You say, "That's it - that's the beginning." Through the spontaneous experience, things may come together in a new way. You recognize that moment and make something of it.

INNER IMPULSE FOR MOVEMENT

The importance of the young dancer's discovery of his own source — inner impulse for movement — was discussed by Mary Whitehouse during her demonstration. She believes that the spontaneous movement response can be a means of bringing together sensation and feeling so that they serve the creative art process.

> An artist's stature, his originality and his uniqueness, depends on his capacity to experience his world. This world has two faces: the outer one, full of objects and events; and the inner one, potentially just as rich, but far less known to most people. Because our culture concentrates so exclusively on the outward orientation, I have been at some pains to explore movement as an inner experience.

> The inner world of the body comes alive in two ways — sensation and feeling. Sensation has to do with the exact feel of body condition and functioning; feeling has to do with the exact sensing of the expressive component, the emotional overtone. If these two are connected only through outer imitation, learned technique, and stereotyped meaning, the imagination which provides and forms material has no depth. The difference between high competence and genuine expressive meaning is imagination. In my work with dancers, I try to get at the individual experiencing of movement sensation and feeling meaning, so that the raw material out of which dance grows is discovered in the body, not preconceived in the head.

FORM

The work group on FORM stressed the need for "ordering" one's experience. They believed that form can grow out of and become an extension of the spontaneous process of improvisation. In other words, the artist's work takes shape out of felt experience:

> Man is a forming organism. He forms by ordering his experience and is thus continuously formed by his experience. His sense of form is innate; it exists because there is form in all life experience, and man is a constant participant in this forming and in forms. Consider the experience of a child's tantrum. It begins with a feeling — genuine and unshaped. It proceeds of its own self-feeding energy, acquiring texture and shape en route. It finds its peak and comes to rest. Another such example is the experience of grief. It is ignited, it builds, it takes over the griever, it spends, it ends. Of course, the shape of the pattern will vary from mourner to mourner. Tracing the history of an idea — from inception through development — will reveal a similar architecture of process.

The completion of forming, occurring through a structuring process, reveals forms which have in the process taken on particular shapes. These are accessible to the perceiver only through performance, past or present. When these shapes are art shapes, they are non-discursive in nature. They are projections of felt life. Although they sometimes are processed through logical ordering (more or less conscious) they must be feeling-based to exist as true extensions of the sentient experience.

Dance forms are particularly clear examples of felt life because of their non-verbal nature and because both the feeling and its resultant form reside in the same location: the human body. The choreographic process could be described, then, as "auto-symbolizing process, occurring through the transforming of fantasy images into metaphor images."[1] The development of a piece of choreography is, therefore, seen to be an evolving pattern of relationships, growing organically, and assuming configuration, texture, and quality. It begins with that initial matrix of feeling which remains the living center or spine of the growing work. In dance this initial matrix never evolves into a discursive or verbal form. It retains its autonomous, non-verbal nature, needing no verbalization and answering only its own demands. To say that the choreographic process is organic and that it evolves from the initial energy of that first feeling is not to say that the choreographer becomes a passive subject taken over by his own work. It seems that way at times, particularly when a piece of choreography is growing rapidly and with apparent ease. Perhaps it is because that primal awareness known as feeling has gathered great momentum and has temporarily outdistanced conscious recognition of the action involved. Forming is an act; it is not passive. It depends ultimately on the will of the form-er, who becomes sensitive to certain potential relationships, heightens some materials, decreases or eliminates what seems to be irrelevant until he has satisfied his completion-seeking self. When the work fails to develop in this organic way, it will often seem contrived because it has been mechanically manipulated, has somehow moved away from the initial matrix, has become a victim of empty formalism.

ARTISTIC GROWTH

From time to time, throughout the conference, the discussion of a specific topic was interrupted in order to talk about the problems of teaching. Participants were concerned not only about the lack of opportunity for dance, expecially among children, but also about the quality of teaching that exists in many situations.

One work group gave serious attention to the question of artistic growth, what it means, and what we should do to facilitate it. The following is an excerpt from its statement:[2]

> In dance, artistic growth consists of the developing awareness and mastery of movement and an understanding of it as an expressive medium of human communication. Since, for each individual, artistic growth is a part of his total development and may proceed quite differently for different persons under different conditions, any attempt to make a definitive statement as to the exact nature of artistic growth would seem to be almost impossible. However, countless teachers are convinced that each of them, and many of their students, have experienced artistic growth, that it is a recognizable phenomenon, and that it is vital to an effective education in dance.

1. Harold Rugg, IMAGINATION (New York: Harper & Row, 1963) p. 305.

2. See Group Report "Artistic Growth," p. 145.

Aesthetic growth for every individual — an ideal in a healthy society — can be nurtured in an atmosphere in which that individual is free to move and encouraged to move (alone and with others) so that human communication can take place on the level of dance. The role of society — the parent, the teacher, the peer — in producing the aesthetic, sentient dance person is that of providing opportunity for the development of the individual movement potential. This requires an atmosphere secure in its permission of uniqueness, comfortable in its recognition of non-conformity, wholesome in its encouragement of physical freedom, and generous in its provision of aesthetic experience.

Thus, conditions favorable to artistic growth in dance are:

Space and time to dance, and acknowledgment that movement is an important activity for all people.

An environment which provides a variety of sensory stimuli to which the person may respond.

A continuing contact and identification with nature.

A teacher who is able to recognize those moments when a student has reached a new

level of development, and can make him aware of his achievement.

An ample opportunity for self-direction.

An atmosphere free from those negative attitudes or taboos which lead to interruption, distortion, or destruction of that artistic tendency which is innate in every individual.

Instructional methods which relate to the varying kinds and rates of artistic growth among different individuals.

As the participants were intent upon what should be done to improve the learning situation, we were reminded by Nik Krevitsky to be cautious about suggesting that we (as educators) can make the artist, because:

The research done to date indicates that artists aren't made and that they aren't born — in other words, the artist makes himself. If the individual has the makings of an artist, he'll develop his potential against all odds. What education can do is assist him in becoming an educated man, so that while he is an artist, his life is enhanced in other ways. I think that we are concerned with art, but, as educators, we are more concerned with dance for everyone.

QUESTIONS FACING THE TEACHER

How do we teach technique effectively, and how do we foster the creative spirit, the imaginative response and discovery, at the same time we achieve the discipline? Technical excellence is certainly one of our goals for the dancer, but how do we achieve it without failing with other goals? How do you keep the two aspects of development in balance?

Alwin Nikolais: I think that they are fundamentally one and the same thing. It is our failure when they don't come together.

This morning I spoke about sensitivity toward the shape of the physical event, the time and space in which it occurs, and the actual emotional content which happens during the occurrence. If a dancer fails in these aspects, to that extent he fails as a dancer. Therefore, the teaching of technique, according to the definition I proposed, shouldn't be the teaching of movement, but, rather, the teaching of motion, which includes the sensation, the sense of the itinerary. To my mind, this should always be a part of technical training. And when it isn't, you are back to movement — the bare outline which makes the hack dancer, as distinguished from the artist.

Jean Erdman: There are certain things which human bodies can do naturally — run, fall, turn, and so on. But if that body is going to be asked to do a pirouette on the toe, or hold its leg up in the air for twenty counts, or turn so many times, the gymnastic things that are expanded from natural movement, don't those require certain periods of practice and doing over and over again in order to teach the body to strengthen the muscles so that the body can go into it naturally?

Alwin Nikolais: But I still think you can have a creative point of view, even in terms of stretches. What's the idea of an extension — a stretch? If you extend the leg without thought in mind, then you just have a leg sticking out there, which is meaningless.

Jean Erdman: Yes, I agree with you.

Alwin Nikolais: This challenge should always be part of the technical development, and then maybe we won't have technique for technique's sake.

Jean Erdman: But then, when you think of the learning process, there has to be a period of time when you practice these things, doesn't there? Even though you think of it as a whole.

Alwin Nikolais: Yes. But the person must have stamina of mind as well as of body.

William Bales: We have to consider the two aspects, the physical and the expressive. We should not separate them in our teaching, but constantly work with the expression of movement as well as the mechanical aspects.

Martha Hill: You do technique so that you can express yourself through movement or through some great repertoire in dance. Technique is to be done so that you can throw it away, rise above it, because, when you really dance, you don't say to the leg, "Lift." The leg lifts itself and is a part of the whole expressiveness of whatever you are doing. I think of technique, no matter what level, as a means not an end.

Alma Hawkins: We have been talking about approaches that are related to two quite different concepts of learning. In one approach, technique would be taught in an isolated fashion. In another approach, the technique, or study of movement or motion, is constantly related to its creative use, so that it becomes an act of discovery — it is seen in a relationship, and is an immediately meaningful experience.

Marian Van Tuyl: In a recent lecture-demonstration, Merce Cunningham brought out the point that every time you do a piece of technique or go into a classroom it should be a discovery, as if doing it for the first time. The moment you find yourself as a student or a dancer just going through the motions, then the thing is valueless.

I think of technique as a tempering process — you are tempering your instrument so that it becomes like a Stradivarius violin, and you can play what you want to play. It is not a matter of what I call the "add-a-pearl" system, or building of a vocabulary. You are working more as a sculptor.

But some of the young dancers who are in the forefront of the avant-garde movement think of technique in a different way. Most of these young people have studied ballet or modern dance, but when they are making dances they feel that everyday movement is more interesting than learned technique. From this point of view, the housewife pushing a broom may be more expressive.

Alwin Nikolais: Their protest. A justified one from the point of view of technique, because it has become meaningless to the student.

Jean Erdman: There is another point here, related to the sociodynamic changes and the fact that every generation has to find a new vision. They think of the generation before as sentimental, but there always has to be something new coming forth from the expression of an art.

The young dancers always feel they are at the beginning — going back to the source. They are discovering a way of creating a vital, live, meaningful relationship. They will strip away every single already selected image in order to allow the living thing to come forth. Therefore, the natural movement does have a validity for them because they really do create a new relationship. Now, you can say that actors were doing that with Stanislavsky long ago, but the young dancers are just discovering this in terms of movement images. When this thing comes out authentically, when it is honest among them, it has great beauty. But when it is dishonest, which it very often is, then it is horrible to watch — it is ghastly. It is the same sort of self-indulgence that followed Isadora. The edges of the art are certainly opening out and we don't have to make a fight about it.

Jack Morrison: We have to recognize what the sciences and humanities talk about — the growing edge, or cutting edge of knowledge. The scientist knows that the important thing in his life is to imagine and then develop the significant, the critical experiment that results in the new solution of a problem. In the arts, I think that we have been remiss in not recognizing the relationship of technique to the artistic end-product. This has been happening, but it has happened in a sort of helter-skelter fashion, instead of as a genuine and recognized part of our teaching.

Robert Lindgren: But there is a point in teaching technique where you have to spend a lot of time learning the technique. You can't just say that you can experiment all along the line. You have to do certain things. You can learn a relevé and a passé and say that's the beginning of a pirouette, but unless you go into a studio and practice pirouettes by the hour, it just is not going to arrive. So there is a point in development when precise and directed teaching is needed day after day. Then you can experiment; people can branch out into whatever they think is another way of doing something. Anyone who wants to be a first-rate ballet dancer has to go through this kind of training period.

Jean Erdman: We have been making a difference between the kind of thing that Bob was describing, which is the necessity to practice the same movement over and over, and the other kind of exploring and building of awareness and sensitivity which does not dictate the outer shape or the specific combination of rhythm and shapes. These seem to be two different projects, but actually they come together in the fact that the expression in the art of the ballet, which is the result of this highly distilled creative moving in a certain way, is just as mystical as the one which is using natural movement but coming at it in another way. You see, I am trying to say that it is possible, even for this new generation, to see the positive in the perfect formed art, the traditional, if they are led to it, and they don't necessarily look at it as something that is nothing but a crust of something that somebody else felt. And that has to do with the way it is taught, that is all.

William Bales: But every dancer has to return to the studio and repeat a movement over and over again in order to master it. I always remember Martha Graham saying, "How many leaps did Nijinsky take before he made the one that startled the world? He took thousands and thousands and thousands."

AESTHETIC EXPERIENCE

What do we mean by the aesthetic experience?
During the discussion various individuals spoke from their own convictions.

Manuel Barkan: The case that we are trying to make is that the arts are special in life — aesthetic experience is something very special. It is not just ordinary experience.

The arts create magic. When you dance, it is not ordinary life, but something special made out of life. The artist transforms something out of life into something that has a particular form and meaning.

William Bales: I think that it is more. The total individual is involved.

Alwin Nikolais: It is an essential within our social life or scheme.

Alma Hawkins: It furnishes a living part that isn't furnished by other facets of living, and without it a part of humanness is missing.

Manuel Barkan: For years we tried to justify art education on the basis of mental health, child development, and all sorts of things. In recent years, we are coming to the realization that the reason for education in art is art itself. Art is experience, an experience of something special which doesn't happen every day. It doesn't happen unless you make it happen.

Virginia Freeman Weil: We can think of art as magic or as a celebration.

Alwin Nikolais: I don't like the idea of celebration. Art is a communication of and participation in a kind of human experience that is possible in no other activity.

Nancy Smith: I think it assists individuals in assessing their place in the scheme of things. A celebration is a kind of participation that assists them.

Alwin Nikolais: Celebration implies a separating event instead of a continuous aspect of living. It suggests the idea of a museum, "a going to" only at a particular time, rather than an enrichment of the whole living process.

Nancy Smith: This continuum is so important; otherwise art is going to seem like an accessory or a museum experience.

William Bales: There is something about the felt experience that is central. Through art the felt experience of living is given meaning. The child expresses and gives meaning to the felt experience through his dancing, his scribbling with color, or making of sounds. I think that art is concerned with the felt experience — that aspect of living that is separated from the conscious and rational aspects.

Martha Hill: I like what Nik said about the continuing aspect and no special point. I remember a friend who said she had a heightened experience as she watched a dancer walk down the street. "It just lifts me to see Doris walking around the corner into Juilliard. She carries her head like a queen." There is that heightened sense of movement which the dancer has.

Alma Hawkins: What is the difference between expressing through movement and forming?

Alwin Nikolais: Well, forming is expressing. Until something has an identity there is no communication. Our manner of forming happens through movement.

Alma Hawkins: Then walking is just as much forming as the making of a dance?

Alwin Nikolais: Yes. Otherwise you couldn't even say the word "walk."

Manuel Barkan: It is the forming which achieves the expressing, in whatever medium one happens to use — words, movement, or paint on a canvas.

Ruth Murray: I am confused by your analogy between expressing and form.

Alwin Nikolais: Well, we can't see an ashtray until the thing has taken shape, and even in terms of abstraction, a circle is not an end product until it assumes the structure of a circle. We don't identify anything until it assumes the gestalt that enables us to sense its presence.

Alma Hawkins: But isn't there a difference in expressing through a run that a child does in the studio and the forming that makes an integrated work, even at the naïve level?

Alwin Nikolais: The run can be a valid part of an art work, as long as it becomes part of a structure which makes a totality, and is communicated. I think that the difficulty in our verbalization is in the fact that art seems to incorporate within the gestalt such a huge portion of non-verbal elements that, until we learn the magic of assembling that which rests underneath, that nine-tenths of the iceberg, we don't assume justly the title of artist. That is a part of the form and structure, just as when a pianist plays the notes on the piano mechanically, he hasn't the right to be called an artist, he has not involved the minute details which need to be there to make the work an art experience.

William Bales: Isn't our concern with the understanding of an extension of some aspect of experience, when one is involved in the art experience?

Alwin Nikolais: It is the recall of perceptions.

William Bales: And the way they are involved at the moment, not just a recall. I wouldn't say the recall is the art experience — it is the extension and what happens in the recall that goes beyond the common, literal experience, and without that you don't have the art experience.

Ruth Murray: I am still pondering this question of expression and form. You say this is an ashtray and it is a form, but before it became a form there were certain raw materials. For instance, if someone just cries out, which we would say is expression, would you also say that is forming?

Alwin Nikolais: Yes, because it is a release of that composite of energies that identifies itself that way.

Ruth Murray: Well, what makes an artistic form?

Alwin Nikolais: To me, it is made by a process of idealization of the event, which means stripping it of all the barnacles, the biases, and the excess stuff.

Ruth Murray: Isn't there a conscious purpose in the artistic form?

Selma Jeanne Cohen: It is not an artistic purpose; though it may be a very beautiful ashtray, the beauty of it has nothing to do with its functional value.

Alwin Nikolais: If the ashtray was so designed that long after we stopped smoking cigarettes, it still remained a thing of such beauty, it would achieve the status of an art object.

Selma Jeanne Cohen: An aesthetic object.

Alwin Nikolais: Just as many of the functional ceremonial objects of Africa and the Church are no longer functional.

Selma Jeanne Cohen: And the dances that were once religious we now look at and enjoy for themselves.

Martha Hill: It all goes back to ritual and observing the rules of form.

Selma Jeanne Cohen: In the theatre, dance becomes a ritual of aesthetic magic. The element of catharsis, of illumination is still there — the Greeks discovered that a long time ago. If the catharsis does not take place, the work has failed artistically.

Alwin Nikolais: Well, I always think of art as a ritual. We want something magical to happen and if we don't do the right thing it won't happen. So the rains don't come. If you intend a thunderstorm and get a leaky faucet — something's wrong!

A Look to Future

ALMA M. HAWKINS

In our discussion we have engaged actively in trying to understand our different points of view and the base from which each of us is working. Now, perhaps, we can begin to evolve some kind of a common vision of dance and its potential in education.

Whether we like it or not, and I think we do like it, dance departments are coming into being at an amazing speed. Dance in education is no longer limited to activity courses; neither are we limited to a dance concentration in the Physical Education Department. The day of the Dance Department is here. Dance is recognized as a significant area of human experience and as a discipline as are History, Language, and English. The fact that dance departments are being established with supporting budgets suggests that administrators are realizing that Dance is worthy of being considered a discipline and having a place in the structure of higher education.

Higher education, in our society, has three primary tasks. One task is to preserve our present knowledge about human experience; the second is to pass this knowledge on to new generations; and the third is to push back the boundaries and expand existing knowledge. If we are to justify our place in higher education, we, too, must assume these responsibilities and make a significant contribution.

We are setting up "models" that will serve as patterns or guides for the next twenty-five years. We dare not limit our thinking to our immediate concern for today and tomorrow. Our great challenge at this time is to think in terms of long-range goals and to establish dance departments that will have the kind of framework that will allow us to take our place within the universities of the future.

The present trend indicates that administrative units for the arts, such as the College of Fine Arts, are expected to assume two roles. One has to do with the performing aspects of the arts, and the other is concerned with the scholarly pursuits related to the arts. In the past, higher education has tended to question the place of activities, or anything that suggested skills. Now, there is a recognition of the value of the performing arts. This means that the heart of our art, dancing and choreographing, has support. I have heard administrators say, "If we are to have dance in the university, then we should develop it at the highest level. "

Several of us who are sitting around this table have met with academic committees responsible for the establishment of a dance department, or the approving of new graduate programs. We know well the kind of questions that they have put to us. "Do you have a body of knowledge?" "Is there an adequate literature in dance to support graduate education?" Because of the greater support for the arts and the establishment of dance as an administrative entity, we can answer in the affirmative as we continue to develop the creative aspects of dance, as well as the research and scholarly studies related to dance. And, I think that we cannot ignore the trend in higher education toward greater emphasis on graduate study.

No longer is higher education limiting its work to the ivory tower. Today, there is a new sense of serving the community in a functional way. This new relationship is most vividly illustrated by what has happened in the sciences. Research funds have been poured into the university so that experts may solve problems and thereby serve society. As a result, we have an input of funds and an outgoing of knowledge such as we have never had before. I think that the reaching out and serving the community, which we have seen in the sciences, suggests the possibility of a parallel development for the performing arts.

Our dance programs, with an emphasis on the performing aspects, could provide one source for the development of talent. The university could provide a kind of home with the security that does not always exist in the professional world. I do not mean that higher education will replace the private studio and the dance company in the development of the young artist. But it is certainly possible that new relationships between colleges and universities and the professional world of dance will evolve.

We should remember that all colleges and universities will not build identical programs. Some institutions will concentrate on selective aspects of the dance programs, while others will have dance departments that provide a broad program and include advanced study in special areas of the discipline. Some institutions will find ways to establish a professional dance company as an integral part of the department's program. Each college or university will contribute to the realization of long-range goals in its own unique way.

Curriculum Model

We turn now to the formulation of a design or plan that can be used as a guide. Here, we present a sample "model" to use as a springboard for our discussion about the Dance Department and the Dance Major.

The center section represents the undergraduate curriculum. The student would proceed through the freshman, sophomore, junior, and senior years and then would receive a baccalaureate degree. He may decide to continue with graduate work which would offer opportunity for specialized study in a specific area of the discipline. He might choose to concentrate on choreography, dance history, notation, ethnology, dance in education (teaching), or dance therapy. (Illustrated in rows above senior year.) After completion of a Master's Degree, some students will wish to pursue advanced study at the doctoral level, and to work for a Ph.D. or a Doctorate of Fine Arts.

On the right side of the diagram, you see another path of study that runs parallel to the central program leading to the box at the top which represents the professional dance company. Some of us have been thinking about the need for an avenue of study that is designed especially for the highly talented young dancer who wants to concentrate on the performing and choreographing aspects of dance. This raises many questions. How should the requirements differ for the students following this path of study? Should they be able to advance according to competence, and not necessarily be held to a four-year sequence? What about the admission requirements? Is the M.F.A. a possible degree for some of these students? What is the relationship between this highly specialized major curriculum and the one for the regular undergraduate dance major? Obviously, there are many problems to consider, but a few of our institutions may be ready to pioneer such a program.

Jean Erdman: I can see how the dancer is going to be able to move up to the professional company, but I don't understand how the dancer can be involved with the doctoral program. If you start to practice your art and choreograph, you have to perform, right?

It seems to me that all those aspects of dance which are not involved primarily with performing and creating can go on logically and quite rightfully as research, but what can you do to assist the art of dance? If you have faculty with Ph.D.'s and artists with the professional company, who will be the leader? The Ph.D. will be top man, right?

Participants: No, not necessarily.

Jean Erdman: I am still trying to see the creative artist with the active professional company functioning with a grand rapport and absolute support from the university if he doesn't have a Ph.D. Degree.

Alma Hawkins: I think we should not be too concerned about degrees. Some of the faculty will need doctoral degrees, in order to work with certain aspects of the graduate program.

DEPARTMENT OF DANCE

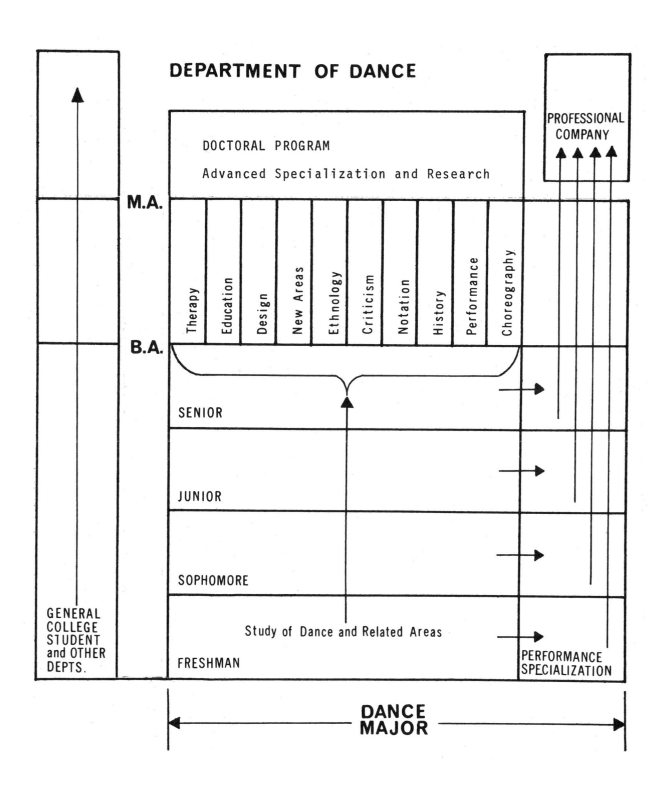

100

Jack Morrison: In thinking of this development in the future, there should be something commensurate with the Ph.D. in science. The important thing for science is to produce the scientist. And it is for us to turn out the artist. There should be some kind of degree that indicates quality of achievement and is as prestigious as the Ph.D. in other fields.

Martha Hill: Getting back to the areas of specialization, I would like to add the dance administrator. We need people who can work with organizations such as the J. F. Kennedy Center in Washington, the State Arts Councils, and the Municipal Arts Centers. Our field will be left behind in these new developments all over the country if we do not have dance people who are fundamentally artists and have artistic judgment as well as a gift for administration.

Alwin Nikolais: Can we expand the specialization to include criticism and design for dance?

Alma Hawkins: I suppose that in that section "other areas" we should provide specialization in any appropriate aspect of dance.

Ruth Murray: There may be new areas that we don't recognize at this time.

Selma Jeanne Cohen: I see marvelous possibilities for relationships between the various areas of study. For instance, the performing company could call on people from the other division for a company manager, or for a historian if the choreographer wants to work on a historical piece. One question, however, do you see this line for the professional company as following the same chronological development as the other division? Wouldn't it be possible, perhaps even necessary, that this path have a highly accelerated program and that students would start earlier? Certainly, you are not going to ask a dancer to go through four years and a Master's Degree before he dances with the company.

Alma Hawkins: This is the kind of question that institutions will have to answer.

Selma Jeanne Cohen: I don't think that it can be answered in too many ways. I think the Russian and Danish schools provide a very good example of how the young student works as an apprentice in small parts at the beginning. If the freshman major is technically accomplished, he certainly ought to be in the company.

Alma Hawkins: I suppose that will be determined by the way we place the emphasis — whether it is on talent in dance, or other phases of education.

Irving Brown: I don't think that we have to equate emphasis with difference of approach. It seems to me that it would be possible for us to have a different approach to the performer within a program of this magnificent scope without saying that the whole program must bow to the performer.

Alma Hawkins: This raises the question of differentiation in program. As we have increased numbers of majors we see a greater spread in interests emerging. Some students wish to start work in their specialization before the graduate year. The question then is: should all majors be held for the same core of undergraduate experience or should we have a broad foundation with possiblity for some differentiation?

Participants: Yes, the latter.

Margaret Erlanger: There must be enough flexibility in the program so that students aren't put in compartments.

The Undergraduate Dance Major Curriculum

MOVEMENT STUDY - <u>What Kind and How Much</u>?

What kind of dance should the dance major study and how much time should he spend in the studio? These questions brought forth many beliefs and vigorous discussion. This was not surprising since participants came from different dance backgrounds and professional orientations, some being associated with private studios and dance companies, others teaching in colleges and universities.

The work group on MOVEMENT set forth the following basic concepts:

Each individual should have a broad range of movement experiences resulting in greater awareness of the total movement possibilities of the body and progress in the mastery of the body.

Basic human movement is the foundation of all dance. The emphasis placed upon it depends upon the stage and level of development and the particular needs of the individual.

In the shaping and clarifying of the expressive qualities of movement with discipline and order, basic movement becomes basic dance. This usually occurs when the individual is able to perceive his involvement. This leads to technical development and the extension of the expressive range of movement through practice and direct learning.

For the dance major, technique, composition, performing, and the viewing of performances are imperative.

The dancer-artist needs the greatest possible range of movement vocabulary resulting from a thorough study of existing techniques and styles, such as: ballet, modern, jazz, folk, ethnic, tap, as well as the differences in style according to historical periods, schools, and regions.

The dancer-artist is one who can respond to all demands of the choreography, intellectually, emotionally, and physically.

The dancer-artist must have an insight and understanding of the choreographic process and must bring an individual, imaginative contribution to the choreography.

This movement training is recommended for choreographers as well as performers. We recognize that a choreographer must have additional training in many other aspects of dance.

There were differences of opinion about the specific kinds of work that should go on in the studio. Some felt that the dance student should spend four hours a day in studio work; others thought it too much and not possible in the academic setting. Some believed that the studio work should emphasize technique; others, that improvisation and choreography should be included along with technique. Some were convinced that the demands in training for ballet were not the same and, therefore, a single standard was not appropriate. And there were different beliefs about how learning in movement takes place, and how you nurture the creative process and further the development of the choreographer.

In spite of the wide range of opinion about the dance program for the major, a kind of consensus evolved:

1. All dance majors must have a strong foundation in movement, although perhaps some differentiation in requirements may be appropriate in the third and fourth years for students who plan to specialize in the non-physical areas of dance, such as history, notation, and therapy.

2. The prospective teacher of dance, as well as the performer, must have a continuous experience in movement and choreography throughout the four-year undergraduate program.

3. All dance majors should have, as a minimum, one and one half hours of technique study each day, and three to four hours work in the studio would be desirable. The development of a dancer with a high quality of performance is dependent on intensive study.

4. More than one approach to technique in addition to improvisation, choreography, and repertory work should be included. Even though the emphasis is on one type, various styles of dance should be studied.

1. See Group Report "Movement," p. 142.

Alma Hawkins: How much time should the dance major spend on dancing in the studio?

Nancy Smith: What kind of dance? Would the time include instruction, rehearsal, etc.?

Eugene Loring: In the report from the last conference we said, "The greatest possible range of movement vocabulary resulting from a thorough study of existing techniques and styles." We listed ballet, modern, jazz, ethnic, and tap. I think that "existing techniques" is the important statement, because in twenty-five years the existing techniques can change.

José Limón: Aren't we talking about moving — the physicality aspect? Can't we go into that before we talk about styles, because styles presuppose physicality? What is the capacity of the human organism?

Eugene Loring: I think that the person has enough physical energy to study techniques four and a half hours a day. He should do no less than three hours as a minimum.

Elizabeth Hayes: Well, I feel that three or four and a half hours a day is more than we can do in a university situation. I think that amount is what the professional company should have — those people who want to go into performing. I don't think it is what one should have in the core for all majors.

Dorothy Madden: Does the four and a half hour time include, perhaps, two periods of one and a half hour classes, plus composing, plus rehearsal time?

Robert Lindgren: No, you mean technical classes, don't you, Gene?

Eugene Loring: Actual physical work. I don't even count choreography in there.

Alwin Nikolais: But you might include improvisation, which can be physically exhausting.

Eugene Loring: If the improvisation class were taught from a purely physical standpoint. I mean three hours of physical work.

William Bales: I don't think that we can make a mandate for all institutions in America. I think that we can suggest a minimum, that there must be a daily technique class of an hour and a half for everyone in the program, and also suggest additional experiences that are desirable, but every college and university will have to set its own specific standards.

Jack Morrison: You can't issue a mandate, but you can issue a challenge.

Nancy Smith: Can't you project an ideal minimum base for active movement spread over technique, improvisation, composing, and exclude rehearsal time?

William Bales: I would like to see time in the curriculum for rehearsals.

Selma Jeanne Cohen: I think that we ought to specify within the minimum that an hour and a half should be a technique class.

Alma Hawkins: Do you really think that the university dance major can be required to spend four hours a day in the studio?

Marian Van Tuyl: I think that we should discuss the relationship of improvisation to technique and improvisation to choreography. I feel very strongly that, along with the technique, the student should have improvisation and choreography. Wouldn't it be possible to have a schedule that would include technique, improvisation and composition?

Robert Lindgren: But that's modern dance. In ballet you wouldn't need that much dance composition. We have many other things that go along including repertory, when people who are doing ballets learn composition.

Selma Jeanne Cohen: How about developing the ballet choreographer? Where is it being done today? In what school are they teaching choreography?

Eugene Loring: I do think that we have got to provide some place — and the university can do it — for the development of creative talent which includes choreography. That is a weakness in dance today. There aren't enough people who compose for dancing.

Robert Lindgren: I don't disagree with the concept of training choreographers. I'm just stating that I believe with a ballet dancer you do not need to spend so much time in teaching people to be choreographers.

Patricia Wilde: They learn to be choreographers by learning about art, music, and design. All of that is related to being a choreographer, and you practice being a choreographer outside of the allotted time for technique.

Alwin Nikolais: I was approached by Ballet Theatre last winter regarding a project which they were thinking about setting up in their school, in which they would ask people to come and help in the creative aspect. They were concerned about the creative process. So I don't think that we are provoking it unnecessarily.

Alma Hawkins: It is obvious that we have different points of view about dance preparation, about the way the dance experience may be organized, and about how a person develops as a dancer. We should not expect to resolve all of our differences, but it is good to be able to hear each other.

CORE OF STUDY FOR THE DANCE MAJOR

Should we consider a four-year program designed for the major as a foundation of experience which should be required of all dance majors, or should we have a "core" of experience that is required, and then allow for differentiation according to the individual's interest and future goals?

Marian Van Tuyl: I think that we have to come to some conclusion about the point below which we will not go in movement.

William Bales: In the group report on "Movement" it was suggested that the movement training of the teacher should have the same breadth as that of the artist-dancer, limited only by other requirements of teacher education.

Jack Morrison: I think that the Bachelor's Degree requirements for the dancers and the dance teachers ought to be the same.

Dorothy Madden: For instance, how much movement should be required of the student who wants to become a historian?

Martha Hill: You might find someone with a physical disability who would like to become an intellectual worker in the field of dance. That could be an exception.

Elizabeth Hayes: Should the person going into dance therapy be expected to have advanced or fourth year ballet?

William Bales: Could we find the norm, instead of talking about exceptions?

Jean Erdman: The person who is going to be a teacher, as well as the dancer, should progress to the advanced level of dancing.

Martha Hill: I would like to see a qualitative standard, rather than a quantitative one. The student should continue to dance through all the four years, but should be placed according to his proficiency.

Elizabeth Hayes: I agree. I feel that it is essential that they dance every quarter or semester, and be placed according to their level of competence. In our situation, we structure the technique classes so that each quarter we cover a different aspect from a different point of view, which leads to a different understanding or concept. People who have been allowed to go ahead into advanced levels discover that they are working with something that they don't understand. They've missed something along the way. We have decided that we will require the entire sequence even though they may be taking the beginning level in their senior year. At the senior level they are willing to go back and look at the beginning work from the standpoint of understanding principles.

Eugene Loring: It seems that the list of specialists could be divided into two groups: those who are concerned with transmitting physical knowledge, and those who work in other areas. In every case, a choreographer or a teacher would need four years of moving experience. Perhaps the ethnologist would not need four years. Let's say the others would need two or more years.

Selma Jeanne Cohen: Perhaps, in addition to saying that the teacher must have a certain amount of training in movement, you would also want to specify some performing experience.

Jean Erdman: They go together. I would go along with Nik that technique and choreography are one study — two kinds of one study in dance.

Alma Hawkins: Our conclusion, then, is that the undergraduate requirements in movement should have a flexibility that would allow a differentiation for certain students, but the major who is interested in specializing as a performer-choreographer or as a teacher should have the "core" experience through the four years. Does this summarize our thinking?

Group: Yes. Agreed.

BALLET AND MODERN DANCE in the Dance Major Curriculum

Participants were in agreement that the dance major curriculum should provide study in modern dance and ballet. It was recognized that most institutions tend to emphasize only one of these forms in their programs. This practice may be unavoidable at the present time when it is difficult to find qualified faculty in either field. The question of when to introduce the secondary form, and how to achieve best integration within the curriculum, was not answered and we need to explore various approaches. There was some feeling that the student should have a foundation experience in the primary emphasis (ballet or modern dance) before the other form was introduced.

The incorporation of modern dance and ballet in the preparation of the major in no way suggests any desire to blend the two styles. On the contrary, there was strong feeling that each form must be presented in its best tradition so that students experience the uniqueness of ballet and of modern dance. Each should be taught by teachers who are specialists in their field. The student's enrichment from the varied study will depend on high quality teaching that assists him in understanding the purpose of the class content, and in achieving, through these experiences, a new level of emotional plasticity that pervades his dancing.

Jean Erdman: Very often, the thought is that, if one is going into ballet and hopes to be a ballerina or dance in a ballet company, one must devote oneself to that technique training absolutely, and the whole point of view that it involves, because, as you say, Pat, unless you have the technique you can't become an artist in the ballet art. I was interested to see that modern dance technique is included in the Harkness School. Is the technique given to the beginning students, or only to the advanced students?

Patricia Wilde: I have only advanced students, so they all have modern dance. But I believe that at eight or nine years, when they start, they should have two years of ballet. Following the two years of good background, you could give them some character dance for freedom of movement, and a feeling for style. Then you could start with modern dance and continue for two or three years, and during the last year include some ethnic dance.

Jean Erdman: Then you don't feel that seeing movement from another viewpoint, and organizing movement slightly differently in the body, destroys the growing dancer working in the ballet style?

Patricia Wilde: No. On the contrary, it broadens their viewpoint.

Eugene Loring: I would like to ask, Pat, how they choose people for the Company; what are they required to know?

Patricia Wilde: Well, finally, we see them not only in ballet, but in modern technique as well.

Eugene Loring: Do they audition people in two types of technique?

Patricia Wilde: Yes.

Alvin Ailey: The dancer must be able to meet demands of different choreographers. This means that technical training must include different approaches and styles. The modern dancer must study ballet also. I think we are moving toward integration, and I do not think that the university can ignore that anymore. You are a "dancer." You must integrate different forms — modern and ballet and ethnic. They have to coexist if you are going to produce fine dancers. This applies to teacher educators as well as performers. (From earlier discussion)

William Bales: I want to make a comment about the prejudice that exists with some ballet dancers, and also some teachers, against modern dance. I feel, now that ballet companies are presenting modern choreography, it will help to dispel the provincialism and encourage ballet dancers to expose themselves to another technique. Once it happens in the profession, the dancer will have no choice.

Eugene Loring: I don't think we should be too complacent about that blending of the techniques. I think that there still is a great deal of prejudice, one side to the other. I have found, in recent work that I have done with ballet companies, some dancers were willing to do something outside the ballet idiom, but they had no equipment. But, by and large, there was still that very stand-offishness and closed mind the moment that movement was not in the ballet idiom. We must not be too complacent.

Jean Erdman: The art of ballet is an art which has a mode of expression of its own, and it is a totally different art from that of the barefoot dancer. It should be celebrated that way. The fact that there are two arts of the dance — it's marvelous. It's better than if there should be only one.

Look at Japan and the way they preserve various arts that have been created at various periods in their cultural history. No one thinks of confusing the Noh Play and Kabuki, or of asking them to amalgamate.

The problem in our country is that because we all love to move, and because we are a mixed people and have mixed all kinds of cultures, it seems perfectly natural to mix everything. But in dance we run up against the problem of prejudice — an innate resistance. It is a pyscho-physical resistance. If you orient yourself and build your world and your relationship to your world around a certain kind of physical organization, then it has deep meaning for you, and it is your life and the way you express yourself. The subtleties and the particular way of feeling about time and space and energy, which are created by the ballet dancer who is trained in ballet technique, are totally different from those which are created by the person growing up in the barefoot dance technique. Naturally, you can't just take your body and reorganize it physically, just like that. So, maybe people shouldn't be expected to do that, providing we want to hold these dances as two unique arts.

Martha Hill: I certainly don't want to see all dance put in one pot so that we all come out with one flavor. We should maintain the tradition of the classic ballet, and we should maintain all traditions. I think the difference lies in the individual. One person will want to hew to the pure classical, and another will want to hew to the pure modern. I don't think that we will have a grown-up art in dance education until we have the whole of it.

Jean Erdman: The dichotomy is only the first half of my story. First you admire the fact that there are two arts. Then, if you want a dancer to be able to function in either one, you must teach in such a way that the details that make ballet unique are not ironed away in favor of a common denominator. The way to make a dancer able to function in either of these quite different ways is to make sure that the young dancer is taught so that each thing has a clarity and is related not only to the physical organization, but to the emotional and mental attitude of the life which it implies. So, in order to get a dancer to evolve into an artist who is plastic, he has to be plastic in his emotional apparatus. It can be done, if each teacher respects the uniqueness of the other, and at the same time explains to the student how he must adjust himself, how he goes from one to the other, and how to see the beauty in each.

William Bales: Jean, aren't you saying that, for our purposes in education (we say that we approve of a variety of styles and techniques), we should find the teacher who is best equipped to teach each particular style? The competent teacher will know the essence of that style and will not betray it. The thing for us to remember, now that we think it is valid to teach a variety of techniques, is that we can't get one teacher who teaches a little bit of ballet, a little modern, a little Spanish, and so on. This would do violence to the thing that we have been talking about.

Selma Jeanne Cohen: I was so pleased with what Jean was saying. I think that this emotional plasticity in the dancer is so important. I think that we must go beyond the physical training of dancers and help them understand why they are moving in the way they are. I find myself watching classes, often with people who have not had a lot of training, and in class they learn exercises, then the exercises are built into sequences, and I never hear one word or one hint as to why they are being taught this way. Why? Why should you move in this way and not in another way?

Alwin Nikolais: I think that this business of generalization is rather dangerous. It seems to me that we have been talking in terms of a way, and it might be better to think in terms of many ways. We know that colleges and universities tend to specialize in certain areas such as psychology or mathematics. Couldn't we think in terms of some colleges and universities being better equipped in certains areas of dance because of the person or group of persons on the faculty? This would be much healthier than to expect every college and university in the country to teach everything — ballet, modern, tap, ethnic, etc.

RELATED ARTS

Should dance majors be required to have experience in the related arts such as music, theatre, and visual arts?

Margaret Erlanger: Music, I think, is a terribly important area. Many of our students are lacking in music. There should be a course for dance majors, especially in theory, taught by someone who understands the needs of dancers.

Betty Walberg: I think there is one area in music which we have not explored enough in our schools. A dancer can know how to look at a score, hear it, analyse it, but that doesn't necessarily mean that he knows how to use it. There is a gap. I think that it would be exciting to have a lab, perhaps at the junior year, where a musician worked with certain dance majors, not just on an improvisational level, but where they worked together spontaneously composing and choreographing. For example, you may do three minutes of material and you improvise, and the next day you start writing it, and the next day you perfect it, or edit it. So the dancer has the experience of working with the musician while he is writing.

Margaret Erlanger: You are suggesting that the musician and students in a choreography class work together.

Betty Walberg: I am talking about not necessarily making a dance that you are going to show even in a workshop, but the actual work experience of doing it — musician-dancer relationship. And I think sight-singing is a valuable learning experience. Through such a course the dancer could learn to read music and to relate to others through singing harmony and counterpoint. In a sense, I would prefer a sight-singing course to a percussion course, because I think it involves more understanding about music.

Martha Hill: We had an experimental project last year in which musicians from the music department teamed up with choreographers in the dance department. They worked together under faculty supervision. Some quite interesting results came out of the project. We presented the finished works in the concert hall to an audience. The musicians had their works heard, the instrumentalists played these works, and the dancers could perform their works. It was most successful.

Betty Walberg: But it should happen more often. One should have a good music program in the dance department in which you could do a project every week in some class. It doesn't have to be a finished dance — just the actual working together, understanding the language and discovering form together.

Marian Van Tuyl: I think that both approaches can be used. All dance departments may not have musicians who are competent in working this way, but most music departments have musicians who want to have their work heard. It seems to me that it would be fruitful for them to work together and it would relate the dance department to the other arts in the college.

Alma Hawkins: Should the dance major have additional music requirements, or should he be limited to those provided by the musician in the dance department?

William Bales: We found that an experience in music not related to dance, which might include such things as ear training, scales, learning to play an instrument, can enhance the dancer's ability to understand the elements of music with which he has to work.

Alma Hawkins: Should this be required, or merely made available?

William Bales: We make it required, because we feel it is an essential.

Betty Walberg: I think that there has to be a strong emphasis on the dance musician in the dance department, and then separate training in the music department. They should experience some classes in the music department because it is another field and location of learning.

Alma Hawkins: Now, let's consider the question of theatre or drama for the major.

Jack Morrison: I wish we wouldn't say theatre, but, instead, would talk in terms of space — three dimensional space. I think that every dance department should have a design technician with dance, who is working with students every day, just as you have a musician. He is responsible for thinking about space in relation to the choreographer's needs.

William Bales: I think that we need two technicians working with dance — one to do costume design and one to do light and stage design. And, in addition, we need something in acting techniques.

Eugene Loring: I think that a dancer must be made aware of qualities, characterization, and so on. We require three quarters in the drama department.

Elizabeth Hayes: I think the amount required depends on what the person intends to do. I think the professional should have it, but I'm not sure that everyone should, at least to that extent.

Thomas Watson: I was asked to this conference, in part, because I represent a very practical theatrical area — the technical side and, specifically, stage lighting for dance. Could many of you light your own dance programs from scratch, from the light plot on to the operation of the switchboard in performance, if you had to do it? There is no reason why all of you should not be able to do these things. In the theatre, we provide the educational base so the student can act, design, dance, and even write the play, if he is so motivated. You need to do that in dance as well, and there are many people who will help you.

In terms of your own production, the more experience you have, the better idea you have of time, money, and energy involved. Learn the technical vocabulary so that you can talk to the stage manager, and so on. Take the classes at the university.

Your concern, first of all with technique, and then choreography, etc., is marvelous, but it can become insular and self-centered. We are all working toward the same goal — the arts — whether dance, theatre, or painting, and I think it is terribly important that we all stay on top of what is going on in all the arts.

Alma Hawkins: We have suggested two kinds of experiences. First, that all dance majors should have the opportunity to work in a functional way with people who are specially trained in theatre — the technical aspects, costume design, stage design; and, secondly, that it is desirable for majors to study acting in the theatre department.

Now, should the dance major be required to have experiences in the visual arts, or courses offered by the art department?

José Limón: We are always speaking about line and design. Dancers need to know about line, style, and design. They need to know about periods; for example, what is meant by baroque. I think this kind of knowledge related to design, sets, and costumes is indispensable.

Jack Morrison: I agree thoroughly, but I do think that the student should be able to elect certain courses from a selected list. If they do it under compulsion, they are going to reject it. They have to discover the need, somehow.

Eugene Loring: May I say that I agree with Betty. You have to correlate the experience with dance. Students do not automatically relate to the study of art or music. One must constantly point out how it will make them better dancers or choreographers.

Alma Hawkins: Gene, do you think that the visual arts should be taught in the dance department and have a functional relationship to dance?

Eugene Loring: At least, art should be taught by someone who knows about dance and how to relate it to dance.

William Bales: I think it is presumptuous of our department to ask another department to apply its art to our needs. That is wrong education for the individual, because he must learn to respect visual arts as art, and music as music. Then he can integrate the experience, and we as teachers can assist in bringing about a synthesis of the various arts.

Alma Hawkins: Since there are so many highly desirable experiences for the student who has a limited amount of time, may it not be best to think in terms of a selective grouping of courses, all of which would be valuable, and then, as Bill said, allow the student to select? If they take the course because they are motivated, they will pursue the work with enthusiasm and make their own associations to dance.

Helen Alkire: That's right. They should have the freedom to make their own connection.

Jack Morrison: I think that this matter of breadth and depth study is a basic curricular problem. We need courses that will do three or four things at one time. We need to know how we can bring areas together. It is possible to have courses that would be technically very solid and, at the same time, meaningful to the dancer. We need research in this area.

Irving Brown: I am worried because we keep talking about courses. The matter of giving the dancer or any of these performers these basic skills we want them to have is dependent on stimulating their motivation. Is there any reason why we should not think in terms of new methods of teaching and of making resources available to students when they encounter a specific need? For example, when the choreographer needs to understand the function of lighting, he could get some acquaintance with lighting techniques through canned instruction.

William Bales: I think that there is another problem. We are taking dance out of the gymnasium and putting it into the theatre. In this transition from the gym to the theatre, there is not enough knowledge, generally, of the necessities of theatre. We are trying, I believe, to establish principles that are needed in order to place the art of movement in the theatre. This includes taking the crafts that are involved, and developing adequate skills. We need to establish principles that will guide us.

Irving Brown: I am not resisting principles, I am resisting conventional answers. Let's keep it open.

Marian Van Tuyl: I think that if a student takes something from a group of electives, for example, a course in History of American Music from the music department, he brings back an awareness of an experience and contributes through his choreography or through his point of view to the dance community of which he is a part.

Ruth Murray: If we allow this selectivity, he will bring back into the community of dancers experiences that would not be possible if we held to rigid requirements.

Elizabeth Hayes: It seems to me that a great deal depends upon the situation in each institution and the outstanding people who are teaching courses related to our needs. I think that it is hopeless to try to categorize a procedure.

Marian Van Tuyl: I still think that we must face the fact that we are dealing with the human body as an instrument, and the basic question is how we take care of that concern, before we start clusters. I feel that when we try to get so many auxiliary experiences, we squeeze the time for the dance experience.

PLAN OF STUDY FOR THE INDIVIDUAL

The study of movement and choreography should be supported by other areas of experience which would enrich the student's understanding of dance as a medium for artistic achievement and human expression and contribute to his intellectual growth and personal development.

Irving Brown made a concise formulation of the purposes of dance education:

Starting with the assumption that one teaches dance because it is an important human activity and should be fostered in the university as an effective path to understanding the nature of human beings (and one's self), there are a couple of purposes in teaching dance. One is

to become capable of dancing, which we have been talking about for a day or so, movement and so on. The other is to understand dance. This is a part, again, of the whole business we are presently concerned with.

Then, in attempting to understand dance there can be three aspects one must be aware of all the time:

The dance instrument: the body elements and their manipulation, rhythm, and so on.

The dance environment — the occasion for dance and the elements that surround it: stage lighting, scenery, dancer-audience relationship, etc.

The dance function in terms of the society: man's needs, habits, entertainment, substitute for violence, rituals, celebration, courtship, etc.

Taking these three aspects, one tends to achieve understanding of dance through three possible studies:

The study of the variety of dance forms and dance functions throughout man's history.

The study of other human activities of similar make-up, elements and/or function, attempting to achieve perspective on dance through seeing how its elements or functions work in other forms (theatre, plastic and graphic arts, writing, etc.).

The study of dance in relation to man's other activities that have different concerns with different elements.

Lastly, we are concerned with pedagogical techniques by which one achieves these ends.

This kind of understanding can best be achieved through individually designed programs of study with courses selected from the related arts, literature, languages, sciences, philosophy, and psychology. The effectiveness of this program planning would depend, in part, on the wise guidance of an advisor. One of the valuable functions of such an advisor would be to bring the student in contact with "great" teachers on the faculty.

Another important consideration related to curriculum requirements and individual student programs is flexibility, allowing time for courses or experiences that prepare for specialized study at the graduate level. The conference participants agreed that the primary purpose of the undergraduate major curriculum is to provide a broad foundation in the art, and that specialization belongs at the graduate level, but they believed that within this overall plan the student should have the opportunity for early contact (at the senior and, perhaps, the junior years) with areas of study that prepare him for his chosen field of specialization. The desirability of some flexibility is apparent as the student becomes aware of his professional goal and he wants to do more study in that field, and, also, certain foundation courses are needed, from a purely practical standpoint, to support graduate specializations.

As graduate programs in dance are firmly established with a five or six year sequence leading eventually to advanced study at the doctoral level, the matter of flexibility and individual patterns of study will become increasingly clear.

The following outline[1] suggests areas of concentration that may be valuable in relation to specific professional goals:

1. Dancer
    a) Understanding the techniques and theories of great dance artists and of different cultures
    b) Experience with a variety of styles and repertory works performed under varied circumstances
    c) Singing and acting

2. Choreographer
    a) The above experiences listed for the dancer
    b) Experience in the craft of composition
    c) Techniques required for films, television, arena stage, and musical theatre

3. Teacher
    a) Child and adolescent development
    b) Psychology of learning
    c) Principles of teaching dance to various age groups
    d) Administration

4. Dance Therapist
    a) Behavioral sciences
    b) Experience working with emotionally handicapped individuals
    c) Experience working with the physically handicapped

5. Film Maker
    a) Still photography, motion picture, and television production
    b) Experience in filming

6. Dance Notator
    a) Advanced notation
    b) Experience in notating dance works

7. Critic and/or Historian
    a) History and literature
    b) History of criticism
    c) Historical method and bibliography
    d) Experience in journalistic and historical writing

8. Musician and Composer for Dance
    a) Music history
    b) Ethnomusicology
    c) Improvisation on various instruments
    d) Experience in composing for dance

[1]. See Group Report "Intellectual Growth," p. 147.

9. Ethnologist
   a) Anthropology, folklore, and mythology
   b) Ethnomusicology
   c) Ethnic dance

10. Theatre Technician for Dance
    a) Staging design
    b) Lighting design
    c) Costume history
    d) Costume design
    e) Stage management
    f) Technical experience in above areas

GENERAL COLLEGE REQUIREMENTS

After extended discussion of the various areas of study that should be included in the dance major experience, the question of college requirements and their relationship to the major program was explored. We recognized that the major purpose of college requirements in most institutions is to ensure breadth in general education. The conference participants were in full agreement about the need for broad experience, but they did have doubts about the number, as well as the nature, of present course requirements.

Since the uniqueness of the needs of students and programs in the arts is a prime factor in the establishment of a separate administrative unit for the arts, frequently identified as the College of Fine Arts, it would seem reasonable to assume that the pattern of requirements for students in the arts might be different from requirements for other sectors of the institution.

The participants felt that we should not accept without question the traditional pattern of requirements held by the College of Letters and Science. Some members felt that the college requirements in general education should be decreased, and that the department of dance and other departments in the College of Fine Arts should be given opportunity to explore and establish new approaches.

THE PROSPECTIVE TEACHER

Throughout the conference there were expressions of concern about teaching and teacher preparation. One of the requirements for a high quality dance program is the artist-teacher. Though the conference group did not work out a detailed curricular plan for teacher education, it did set forth certain beliefs and guidelines.

Teacher preparation should include some kind of an organized learning experience which assists the student in preparing for his new role as teacher. This experience may or may not take the form of courses. But, regardless of organizational pattern, this aspect of his experience should be concerned with helping him to understand his role as one who facilitates the learning of others. Through such experience, dance becomes illuminated in a new way, with the emphasis on "reaching out" rather than "taking in." The student learns the importance of the teacher's sense of commitment and responsibility.

Many students express an interest in teaching when they enter college. Dance educators should recognize the interest and assist the student in relating to experiences that will help him in developing leadership skills. Instead of asking the student to wait until his senior or graduate years for teacher preparation courses, he could be guided toward related experiences such as observation, assisting in dance classes, leadership in community projects and summer camps.

In addition to the academic preparation for teaching, some kind of apprentice experience is highly desirable. Through an apprenticeship the student works closely with a master teacher and is able to observe, explore, and test his own ideas, as well as to develop skills in a "real" situation, and thus grow in competence as a teacher.

Teacher preparation programs must not be concerned exclusively with the college teacher. Preparation of the dance teacher in elementary and secondary schools must be included in the comprehensive teacher education plan.

The trend in higher education toward a recognition of dance as one of the arts, and the development of undergraduate and graduate dance major curricula suggests that the elementary and secondary schools have a new kind of obligation. The student who plans to enter a college major in dance, just as the student in science or the humanities, will be expected to have a foundation in his chosen field of study. Unless the student has this foundation, the dance curriculum in higher education cannot achieve its real potential.

In order to escape from the vicious circle of dancers coming into the dance major program poorly prepared because of lack of opportunity in the early grades, it is up to the university to provide imaginative, responsible dance and movement education for the teachers going into elementary and secondary schools.

The Professional Company in the University

The model for the dance department, as projected in the twenty-five year dream, includes the possibility of a special concentration within the major for the talented student who is interested in performance and choreography. This could lead to participation with the professional company which would be an integral part of the dance department. Such a professional company would provide a "live" model of dance as an active performing art. The association with artists and mature performers would enrich the education of all dance majors, and the company could provide an avenue of professional training — a kind of apprenticeship for selected students.

Since this is a new development in higher education, we will need to explore and have experience with various possibilities. Some institutions may find it desirable to have an artist and his company in residence, while others may envision the company as an outlet for their gifted students, and find it preferable to use several professional choreographers with an artistic director as permanent leader.

Obviously, this kind of specialization for students and the establishment of a professional company could not and should not be undertaken by an institution unless it can be carried out with distinction. Some colleges and universities with well developed major curricula may be ready to pioneer in this direction.

In cases where the professional artist is included in college and university programs, each institution must clarify the exact role he is expected to play. How will the artist contribute to artistic growth of students and enrich the dance program? If there is to be a professional company, should it be directed by a permanent artist choreographer? Is the company to be composed of "imported" dancers, or talented students from the institution? Does the artist work with a broad range of dance majors, with those in the performing program, or with the company members only?

The conference participants did not arrive at answers to these questions, but they did agree that colleges and universities should provide for the highest possible level of artistic development, that the artist can play a vital role in student education, and that talented young dancers should have extensive opportunity for performance experience in a professional environment.

In order for a student to concentrate in performing and choreographing, it will be necessary to provide for some flexibility in the dance major requirements. It was felt that the core experiences should be the same for all dance majors, but that the program should allow the student to enter the concentration at different points in the four-year sequence and to progress through the program according to his own rate of development. For example, it should be possible for a sophomore to dance with the company if he has sufficient competence, but all students should meet the same basic requirements of the major program. To establish two separate patterns would set up a dangerous dichotomy. Adjustments should be made in terms of individual differences, needs, and readiness. A prime consideration at all times should be to relate the student to experiences appropriate to his level of development.

Jean Erdman: Then, with a professional company, it would be possible to picture a situation where all majors would go to school in one place, and those who are particularly talented and learn faster could move ahead in technique and choreography classes. They would all be involved for the same number of hours, but would work at the level appropriate to their development. People who will eventually end up in the professional company may be dancing with the company in their third year, but they would continue to work with other majors at the third year level in areas related to aesthetic understandings and growth as human beings.

Elizabeth Hayes: It seems to me that the major difference is not in subject matter, but, rather, in emphasis. That is, more time will be spent in certain areas according to certain pursuits.

Irving Brown: I understand that the young dancer can be ready to dance at age seventeen. Suppose a student who enters as a major has had a good physical preparation and is ready to dance. There must be a sharp difference between the education for the physically trained seventeen-year-old who is ready to dance, and the entering freshman who is partially trained, or not trained at all.

Martha Hill: It's a big problem.

Jean Erdman: It is a big problem. The only reason that the well trained seventeen-year-old would come would be because of the theatre in the university and the professional company in residence.

Irving Brown: ...except for the intellectual possibilities.

Jean Erdman: I know, if that person of seventeen is ready to go on stage as a professional dancer, he would go, unless he had intellectual curiosity. Then he would find a university that had a theatre and opportunities for performance. So he comes and is ready. He is selected to work with the professional company and would take technique with the company class or the most advanced class. He would not do technique with the freshman class but he would take the "humanizing" part of the curriculum with the freshmen. He may be terribly innocent about some things, while other freshmen may be quite sophisticated in these areas. The only problem is scheduling.

Alwin Nikolais: In talking about the professional company and the high quality of professionalism, the first thing is to consider how to keep such a group intact, so that the quality can be stabilized.

Elizabeth Hayes: I think that the big problem is how to finance it.

Irving Brown: We need to consider the relationship of the aims of the professional artist, his career and artistic goals, to the purposes of the university with its educational and cultural program.

Alwin Nikolais: And then there is the question, particularly in the period of early development, where the interchange between professional companies might be advantageous because of repertoire available.

Virginia Freeman Weil: What about the shape of the company? Is it a single unit built around one artist, or a repertory company that uses works of different artists?

Alwin Nikolais: The shape may vary because of the quality of the personnel.

Irving Brown: You may, for example, not choose, as the head of the professional company, a person who has strength in choreography of any kind. The head might have competence in management and administration of a disciplined company that can respond to the work of guest artists.

Alwin Nikolais: A director who can keep the work at a high level.

Martha Hill: A Diaghilev.

Robert Lindgren: I think there are two separate divisions: one has responsibility for management, and the other is related to the artistic work, with a director who would discuss and choose choreographers and productions.

Shirley Wimmer: What about the relation of the company to the university and students? Will the company be fed constantly by the university, or will there be outside people used as dancers?

114

Martha Hill: If we think of the professional company representing excellence, I expect that it will achieve the excellence in various ways. In one case you may have an established company come in for a short or long period. In other cases the director in the department would be the producer and determine what is done.

Elizabeth Hayes: On the other hand, if you are going to just make a home for professional companies, then the talented students you were talking about will not have a place or, at best, it will be a secondary place. Perhaps, to have a ready-made company is not what the university should be working toward, but, instead, it should give its talented students the opportunity for professional experience under the guidance of an experienced artistic director.

Martha Hill: This depends on the demands of each piece of choreography. If you hold to the standard of excellence, it will be solved in different ways.

Elizabeth Hayes: I think that you can always supplement your talented students with professional people, but if the emphasis is on the professional company, then the students are only used to fill in.

William Bales: I don't agree with Betty, because the growth and maturing of a full-fledged artist is a continuing and long-term thing, and one of the functions of the professional company is to provide a transition into the professional world for the promising student, so that he doesn't leave school and suddenly find himself trying to compete for a place in leading companies. The best possible experience would be to work with professionals in a company, a kind of apprentice relationship, so that there is a gradual transition for the student. This should be a growing experience for the student — an opportunity for continuation of education at the highest level.

Alvin Ailey: You need to give students who are going to become professional some kind of extended professional experience with a variety of choreographers from different parts of the country. They need performing experience, and performing experience with professionals. I think the repertory way is the way modern dance must go. We have passed the period where the dancer is the star of the company, the choreographer, and the costume designer. You have to train dancers with a variety of choreographers, in order to keep their works alive. (From an earlier discussion.)

Alwin Nikolais: Aren't we thinking too strictly, perhaps? I think the professional company will take all sorts of shapes. For example, a university not yet having reached that higher echelon might find it stimulating to have a total professional company there, whereas the university that is functioning in that higher echelon might find it desirable to bring a company in for a period of time as a transitional experience. The visiting company might bring principal dancers who would later be replaced by student professionals.

Martha Hill: I was just thinking of the old days at Bennington College, when the Bennington School of Dance had to close because of the Second World War. During that time, for example, we had Martha Graham with her company in residence at Bennington College for a six-week period at the end of the school year. That's the time that Martha created some of her new works for the next season. Our students sat in, saw rehearsals, and had a marvelous experience seeing a work in progress.

Aren't we identifying two philosophical points of view which a department might wish to consider? One suggests that the institution bring in and give a home to a professional company and make it possible for it to function. In this situation, the students would observe the very best in dance. The other point of view suggests that the company should grow out of and somehow be integrally related to the department's function.

Nancy Smith: There are already existing patterns in the other arts: for example, the theatre group at Sarasota, which is a part of the Florida State University. It exists as a definite company, has its own staff, and resides in Sarasota. During the third tri-mester (spring), our selected students move down to Sarasota, and are there during the company's performance season.

Elizabeth Hayes: The wrong kind of financing can be disastrous. As we move in this direction, we should be clear about what we want, and make sure that there are definite written aggreements with financing bodies. This is necessary in order that you have freedom to operate in the way that you feel is right, educationally.

William Bales: I want to go back to the comment about having a professional company on the campus of a university, but not as an integral part of the curriculum. This would be similar to the way a string quartet is in residence. It might be desirable to have such a company in some institutions, particularly if they teach part-time in the regular program, providing the professional experience for students.

Robert Lindgren: There is a possibility that we could start a reverse trend. The people from major ballet companies or modern dance companies could come to the school and see the talent in performance. They may discover people whom they eventually want to take into their company, and, instead of the raw student having to audition and go through the company's school, he could make the transition as an experienced dancer.

There is another point in regard to scholarships offered by professional companies to the dancer who seems to have potential. Instead of the fifteen or sixteen-year-old girl's parents taking a loan or a mortgage to send the child to New York for the whole learning process, it would be possible for the young dancer to learn in his own community. The professional company set-up would encourage them to stay a little longer. In other words, let them grow a little before they finally go to New York. Such a company would be a marvelous proving ground.

Alma Hawkins: And couldn't it help to spread the arts across the country, instead of having a major concentration in one or two places? This might contribute to a fresh look at the art.

Robert Lindgren: Another point — this word "professional" means two different things to me. Are we thinking of "quality" professional or "financially" professional? Do you think of paying these people, which, in turn, involves unions and so on, or, would it be like our school, where all the performances are free and the money for productions comes out of our budget? Therefore, we have no box-office. In other words, do you have to make money or don't you?

Alma Hawkins: I guess that we have been considering the quality and haven't talked about the economics.

William Bales: When we get to it — it won't be theoretical, but very factual.

Irving Brown: The professional company may cause a sharp reduction in performance and production opportunities for students. There may be a tendency for the educational program to retreat to the classroom because its former function of providing productions for the community has been taken away.

Alma Hawkins: Or we would still have concerts, but at a different level and perhaps a new time, such as four o'clock.

Virginia Freeman Weil: What about noontime concerts? The idea that performances must come at the end of the day has changed.

116

Martha Hill: If there were enough universities which could build professional companies, it could change the whole complexion of the audience for dance in the United States. The companies could tour in areas where it is now very difficult to get major touring companies because of expense.

William Bales: In connection with problems encountered with the professional company, I am reminded of the report of the Theatre Group in which they suggested that the field be realistic about the saturation point and how many professionals they wanted to turn out, and also that one should look very carefully at the number of professional schools and companies that should be organized, where they should be placed, and how many top professionals to turn out. They recommended that extremely high standards for professional achievement be set up.

I think that most of us have no idea of that level and what it takes to achieve it. If we try to set up too many professional companies, we may be in trouble. There aren't that many good teachers and good choreographers.

Alwin Nikolais: I have a slightly ill-at-ease feeling about one aspect of this proposed pattern, and that has to do with the idea of creativity itself. It seems to me that creativity is the basic substance upon which everything else rests. The central factor isn't technique, or even the talented dancer, it is the creative fact itself. Choreography is a weak link in what we have been discussing, and yet choreography is affected by the creative drive and impulse, as are the other experiences such as history, notation, criticism.

Alma Hawkins: I have always believed that the foundation of our program should be concerned with releasing and developing the creative ability of the individual. All the other experiences should support this aim.

Alwin Nikolais: I think so. There seems to be an academic development which aims to include the professional artist to a greater degree, but we still exist primarily in New York, in a life that is quite different. I have this other feeling that the college and university hope to be the begin-all and end-all of aesthetic life, and, therefore, we will have no need for the kind of loft operation that we engage in now.

Alma Hawkins: I did not intend to give that impression.

Alwin Nikolais: I am just concerned. For instance, we are getting many invitations to come and be in residence. This seriously affects our own continuity of work. Someone says, "Will you come for seven weeks?" That is fine for the seven weeks, but what about the other forty-odd? It affects a way of life. But the colleges and universities are getting money, so the artists have to conform more or less to their standards and their budgets.

Alma Hawkins: I don't believe that any institution thinks that what develops in that environment will ever replace or do away with the highly talented artist in the community.

José Limón: I don't think the university is trying to pre-empt the activity or the function of what we call the creative artist, who, unfortunately, is in a loft in New York City. Perhaps a possible solution would be to invite the entire company to be in residence for seven weeks, not just detach you and emasculate your company.

I think that perhaps it is time that we have a decentralization, or at least a temporary or seasonal decentralization, away from the horrors of the loft.

Irving Brown: The first function of the university is to further the art as a per-forming art. One of the research functions, then, is to investigate the frontiers of the art with your company and with your talent. A part of the function of the professional company is to present new works.

Jean Erdman: I have the feeling that if the dance departments in the universities really want to involve artists creatively, then the whole department has to revolve around that peak. If the artist is the center with a professional company, then the freshman and the other students always have this level of work before them. If the artist really were the center of the department, then it would be clear why all the other activities exist.

Alma Hawkins: I would hope that, in addition to the potential for students to observe and relate to the artist and company, there would be functional means of relating the artists to areas of study for all majors.

Alwin Nikolais: No scheme has come up, as yet, which really is practical — economically, psychologically, and emotionally. I think that the problem is, partly, how does the artistic temperament fit into the "cookie mold."

Jean Erdman: Obviously, we are not thinking in terms of twenty-five years, we are thinking of now. If a dancer who has evolved a company and a repertoire, like Nik, can't bring his whole company and all the things he works with, how can he come? He can't — even for a short time — because he is separated from what he has built. So what you actually need are new artists who would not have roots already put down in a loft in New York City.

Alma Hawkins: And eventually some young artists would emerge through the university program and then feed back into it.

Jean Erdman: Yes, exactly. Then the only concern is related to climate for the development of the creative artist. Sometimes you can't work in the most beautiful set-up.

Irving Brown: Are we confusing the problem of making the transition from the present state of affairs to a possible state of affairs with the problem of a possible state of affairs being a negating and limiting factor? It would seem to me that such a university structure would employ a resident artistic director who would be in charge of the company and the school of performers.

Alwin Nikolais: You are also faced with the fact that you don't necessarily want to be identified with one individual over such a long period of time. So there has to be some interchange going on.

William Bales: Perhaps our job is to find and encourage the promising young artists. Nik is one of the artists who could come around on tours and make another kind of contribution.

Alwin Nikolais: Actually, I've avoided an academic and grading system because we didn't want to be hamstrung.

Marian Van Tuyl: Exactly, but if we had our ideal situation you would be an independent and non-academic entity under the university umbrella, with money provided.

Robert Lindgren: Is this set-up we are talking about two different things: a resident choreographer and a resident company? What about the student structure? And are we saying a company? Is this a modern dance company with a modern dance choreographer, or a ballet company with a ballet choreographer, or what? We have been speaking of Nik. Would you have him come with his whole company, or would you have him come in to train your students in the university?

William Bales: It would depend on the institution and what it wished to do.

Graduate Education

Graduate education in dance is offered in a limited number of colleges and universities at the present time, but we can expect the number of institutions with Master's Degree work to increase as more dance departments are established and the undergraduate major programs improve in quality. Therefore, we are in a strategic position now to shape the development of advanced study in dance in the way that seems most desirable.

The graduate program is designed to provide advanced study in the discipline. The master's program should offer opportunity to concentrate or specialize in one aspect of the field, and to include independent research or creative work as an integral part of the total program of study.

Today, there is an ever-increasing emphasis on the doctoral program, particularly in the universities. Even though we are concerned at this time with the undergraduate and master's programs, we must begin to consider the advanced graduate education in dance, because eventually this too must be developed.

The trend in many of our universities is toward greater emphasis on graduate education. In some institutions sixty percent of the university's work is at the graduate level. In other institutions it is seventy-five percent in the graduate field. The pattern of graduate education is shifting rapidly because of the great expansion of knowledge.

In a recent meeting in Washington, D.C., Dr. Gustave Arlt from the Council of Graduate Schools in the United States, talked about what is happening in graduate education and projected what seems to be inevitable for the future.[1] Let me quote one paragraph from his speech:

> And what of the future role of the graduate school? First of all, there will be a continued increase in the number of graduate schools and the number of students attending them. There are today 190 schools offering work leading to

the Ph. D. By 1975 there will be at least 250. In 1965 there were 16,467 doctoral degree awards. According to the Office of Education's projection in 1975 there will be at least 36,900, and I think that number is very conservative. According to the best informed guess of the U.S. Office of Education, there are today about 455 schools offering work leading to Master's Degrees. By my own informed guess, most of the 792 four-year colleges that will survive until 1975 — and a good many will not — will by that time award Master's Degrees. In other words, there will be virtually no more four-year liberal arts colleges. If this guess is correct, and I am confident that it is, we can see another trend developing, and that is the gradual abandonment of the Bachelor's Degree. We have already seen the disappearance of Associate in Arts or Sciences; the Bachelor's Degree is next in line. The first harbinger of this trend has already appeared on the scene — the three-year Master's Degree. The award of the baccalaureate in this program is already a mere formality and formalities have a tendency to disappear.

One of the major responsibilities of graduate education is to further the development of artists, teachers, and researchers, who, in turn, will be able to give leadership to the depth study in special areas of the discipline. Some "generalists" are needed in our dance programs, but "specialists" are an essential prerequisite for graduate study, research, and professional production. At the present time, we have a serious shortage of competent faculty in specialized fields.

The very real need for graduate education does not imply that all institutions should try to have a Master's Degree program. On the contrary, it is important that institutions not offer advanced study unless they can provide graduate curricular offerings and creative and research programs under the leadership of an adequate number of competent faculty.

1. Gustave O. Arlt, "Graduate Education in the United States," lecture delivered in General Session of Conference on Graduate Education sponsored by AAHPER.

PATTERNS OF STUDY

The graduate program, in contrast to the under-graduate program, should be characterized by a high degree of flexibility. The student, with the advice and approval of his graduate advisor, should be able to design a program of study that is uniquely suited to his needs and talents. He should keep close contact with the moving and creative aspects of dance, even though the specific focus of his study may be in areas other than performance and chore-ography. Courses from other disciplines which support and enrich his program of study and re-search should be utilized.[1]

The discipline of dance embraces a body of know-ledge comprising:

The psychological, physiological, and kinesio-logical principles of human movement.

Movement basic to expression and communi-cation; choreography; history and philosophy of dance.

The art of sound as related to dance; principles of theatre as related to dance; and

Dance ethnology, i.e. social, ritual, and art forms in various cultures.[2]

Based on the core knowledges of the discipline of dance, the following areas of study and research should be available to graduate students:

Movement
Choreography
Music
Repertory — Reconstruction and Performance
Production and Direction
Theatre and Design
Notation
History
Aesthetics
Criticism
Writing
Ethnology
Biological Sciences
Teaching
Therapy
Film and Television
Research Techniques

THESIS REQUIREMENTS

The student should complete, as a part of the Master's Degree requirements, a major piece of independent work. This work, an integral part of his program of study, may take one of four forms:

A thesis based on experimental, historical, or other research methods;

A major choreographic work presented in concert.

The creative performance of a major role in a repertory work; or

A comprehensive project related to the indi-vidual's focus of study.

The exact nature of the thesis or creative project will need to be determined by each institution in relation to its graduate policies and curricular offerings.

Alma Hawkins: We have two aspects of the graduate program to keep in mind: the areas of study, and the thesis plan. For example, a student might be very interested in performing, but might do his independent project (thesis) in one of the other areas open to him.

William Bales: Or he might do performing as his thesis.

Margaret Erlanger: Or in lieu of a thesis — a concert.

Marian Van Tuyl: Some institutions have two types of theses, one of which can be a concert.

Nancy Smith: What about the student who is interested in performance, not choreography?

Ruth Murray: In other words, he would do a concert performance without having any responsibility for the choreography.

[1] "Programs of Study in Dance — Report," from the proceedings of the AAHPER Conference on Graduate Education, Washington, D.C., January 1967, was used in the discussion on graduate curricula.
[2] Ibid., p.2.

Alma Hawkins: Then that would mean that student A could do the choreography, make the dances, and student B, who is a fine performer, could assume a major role and perform throughout the concert.

Nancy Smith: If student B were doing his master's work in performing, it would be repertory. He would be investigating, learning, and performing.

William Bales: Not every graduate student is able to choreograph a master's concert. Then there are students who can choreograph, but cannot succeed as performers.

Alma Hawkins: Perhaps we should think about the different patterns for theses. Usually, we have experimental or research oriented theses which could include the choreographic and performance theses. Then there is the comprehensive thesis, which is an independent project that contributes to application of knowledge and learning for the individual. Are we saying that the student who is an excellent performer can meet the "original criteria" as expected of the experimental thesis?

Nancy Smith: I think that this is tricky. But perhaps we can say that, if our expectation and demand goes beyond technical facility to perform just any work. It should be a selected piece of repertory, and the performer's success would depend on what he does with the role — how he transforms the work through his performance. I know that musicians are allowed to present a selected piece of musical literature, but the performance must go beyond a mere technical presentation.

William Bales: I think that drama is even closer to dance.
The actor does not write his play — he is the performer.

Virginia Freeman Weil: Nor does the director on the master's level have to write the play or be in it. His creative work comes through his direction.

Nancy Smith: We spoke of the comprehensive, non-thesis program. I don't know exactly where I stand, but I know I have serious reservations about it.

Alma Hawkins: What is your reservation?

Nancy Smith: I guess I feel that it doesn't necessarily advance the body of knowledge — maybe it extends the individual doing it, but I'm not sure it is an original endeavor, nor that it advances the body of knowledge — the two criteria which the other theses require.

Ruth Murray: You are saying, Nancy, that even though a university does not require a thesis, the dance department should? Some institutions substitute credits for the thesis; of course, what then happens is that most students follow the non-thesis plan.

Helen Alkire: But you are in a position to recommend and guide. We had a student under this plan who made quite a study of notation systems. It could have been a thesis, but she chose to do it as a project. But it did extend the body of knowledge.

Nancy Smith: It sounds to me like a thesis.

Ruth Murray: Or original study.

Selma Jeanne Cohen: As I understand it, the doctoral dissertation is expected to make an original contribution to knowledge, but that is not expected of the master's thesis. I should think that the master's would serve the individual and not necessarily contribute to the field. But institutions would hope that the master's thesis is original work that helps the individual to move in a way that would make it possible for him to do something at the doctoral level that would have real effect on the field.

Alma Hawkins: Perhaps all we can say at this time is that we feel that some kind of an individual project or depth study should be a part of the graduate education.

CERTIFICATION OF TEACHERS
FOR SECONDARY SCHOOLS

Universities, colleges, and state credential boards should give consideration to the need for new certification standards for dance teachers in the secondary schools. Since the desirable standard for teacher preparation includes the dance major or equivalent experience, it would seem reasonable to assume that state certification requirements should reflect similar standards.

At the present time, credential standards in most states require the teacher of dance to have a major in Physical Education. This practice, though historically understandable, does not ensure adequate preparation of dance teachers for today's schools. Because of the changing pattern of education, many secondary schools in urban and suburban areas are seeking teachers who are specialists in dance. In order for the secondary school to establish dance as one of the arts along with music, art, and theatre, and to offer the student opportunity for serious study of dance, including choreography and production, it is essential that the dance teacher have special competence gained through the dance major or equivalent experience.

The small school system presents a different problem and will require teachers who can teach more than one subject. Obviously, many communities cannot appoint a special teacher in dance or any of the arts. But the demands or limitations of these schools should not set the pattern for schools where teacher specialization is possible.

The need to review state credential practices and to establish new standards that ensure adequate preparation of teachers of dance is a critical one. New criteria related to the dance major preparation should replace present criteria. However, in this period of transition, we should not assume that all dance major curricula would or should automatically meet credential requirements.

The conference participants felt that the standard for teachers of dance in the private schools should be the same as for public schools. Even though the private schools do not require a state credential, it seems desirable that the teacher of dance in any secondary school have a dance major or equivalent experience.

Drawing by José Limón

Faculty

In the near future, departments of dance in some of the major institutions will have increased numbers of people, perhaps ten to thirty, on their faculties. This size faculty seems large when we think of the one-teacher dance programs that we have known for so many years. But if the department is to offer a comprehensive undergraduate program, and depth study in special areas at the graduate level, it will be essential for the dance department, as for all other departments on campus, to have faculty who have special preparation in various fields. For example, it will not be possible to offer high quality education in areas such as choreography, history, notation, ethnology, and therapy without specialists in each field.

The conference participants felt that the dance department should have a group of permanent faculty who could give stability to the ongoing program. This core group could be supplemented by full and part-time faculty who have special competence in particular fields.

It was agreed that the musician must be one of the highly competent people working with the dance program, should work closely with the dance teachers, and contribute to the class experience. No longer should we use the title "accompanist" for the talented musician who teaches classes, composes for choreography, and directs music for concerts. Academic appointments should be made when the musician's professional preparation and role in the department is comparable to that of dance faculty.

Participants agreed that faculty appointments should be made on the basis of competence. Academic degrees are an important factor in the preparation of faculty for some aspects of teaching, but degrees should not be the only criteria for selection. It should be possible to make academic appointments on the basis of professional and creative achievements, as well as academic preparation. Both kinds of preparation are needed in the department that is concerned with creative and scholarly achievements.

Jack Morrison: There are a couple of patterns that we might think about. For instance, there is the adjunct professor of medicine who carries on a private practice and also works in a hospital, doing research and teaching. Another is the research associate who doesn't teach at all. He comes into the institution on a research project, which may be his own or one for the institution. He may work for six months, a year, or ten years, depending on the project.

Martha Hill: We will have to be concerned with conserving the energy of our artist-teachers who will teach and direct choreography. How much can the artist teach and still have energy for creative work? This is a real problem.

Jean Erdman: You can't teach full-time and do it.

Robert Lindgren: Do you have teaching assistants, or student fellowships? For instance, on our faculty we have people who teach every day, but when these people are choreographing a work, they are relieved of their regular teaching assignment. An assistant will take over the classes until the work is finished and the regular faculty resumes teaching.

In addition, we have one swing salary that is used for visiting artists who come for various periods of time.

Irving Brown: It might be worthwhile for us to say that, whenever possible, advanced and qualified students become assistants to resident performers or guest faculty. It seems to me that this would be a part of their learning experience and one of the principal reasons to have a producing company related to the academic structure.

Jack Morrison: About the professional relationships, I think that we should say that the professionals are a regular part of the faculty.

Alma Hawkins: And, in addition, would you say that we should have a core faculty that is stable — not a shifting population? Wouldn't we need a faculty who could give continuity to the program, work as specialists at the graduate level, and assume responsibility for on-going services such as advising?

Jack Morrison: Without a stable core, the students just go crazy. But if there is a good stable core, the visiting person can bring something exciting and fresh.

William Bales: With the visiting artists, do we look for degrees?

Participants: No.

William Bales: With the core faculty, do we look for degrees?

Participants: No.

Martha Hill: Competency is the primary concern.

Irving Brown: Couldn't we say that in some of the fields competency is indicated by degrees, but in other fields the degree is not the criterion for competency?

Alma Hawkins: Yes. It seems to me that we need both kinds of faculty — some whose competence is achieved through artistic development and work in the professional world, and others whose competence comes through intellectual pursuits. I guess that we are trying to say that the professional artist has a place in our world, with or without a degree, that competency is our primary concern, and that in some areas competency will come or may come through a degree program.

William Bales: I think that the size of classes is germaine to the question of number of faculty. This is particularly true for classes such as composition, which are tutorial in nature. You have to be able to work with the individual, so the size of the faculty in relation to the size of our student body influences our efficiency.

Robert Lindgren: In our state, the number of teachers goes up in direct ratio to the number of students who come to the school. We figure something like twelve students to one teacher.

Margaret Erlanger: This matter of size of faculty is so relevant to our situation. Our present system of determining F.T.E. ratio (Full Time Equivalent) is not relevant to what we are doing in dance. We are being denied increase in number of faculty because, according to the standard, we do not have enough students to justify an increase. The criteria seem to have nothing to do with the work that we do. We talk about time for choreography and all the other things we have been discussing — nothing is done about increasing faculty.

Alma Hawkins: We know that many of us, who are in the process of developing a new department, find it necessary to carry heavier loads than faculty in other departments. However, one of our goals should be to build an adequate faculty as fast as possible, so that our loads are proportionate to faculty in other departments. This is important in order that we have time for creative work, be fresh for teaching, and also have time for other individual achievements that are used as criteria for promotion.

Jack Morrison: We have to state our needs, for instance, the F.T.E. ratio for the school of medicine is not the same as the ratio used for the department of history, and it shouldn't be.

Alma Hawkins: What about the position of the musician in the dance department? Today, many departments have full-time musicians who assume responsibility for a variety of work including composing and directing music for concerts. In spite of the fact that we must have highly qualified musicians, many institutions still employ them as non-academic staff and pay salaries that are not commensurate with their professional preparation. Shouldn't we try to establish a more appropriate basis for appointment — either a professional or an academic classification?

<u>Participants</u>: Yes.

<u>William Bales</u>: I am very concerned about musicians for dance. We have suggested that we need a crash program to train teachers. I think we need a crash program to train musicians for dance.

<u>Martha Hill</u>: I think that it is not a matter of training. The big problem in our field is to make an interesting situation for the musician, by having him teach music courses for dancers, or maybe even teach in the music department and share his time with the dance department. Too frequently, the musician feels that he uses his art to serve another art, and he feels like a second-class citizen.

<u>Alma Hawkins</u>: Then are we saying that we should strive to relate musicians to the dance department in some academic fashion, either by having them teach music courses or by working with the dance classes in some functional way, such as Betty Walberg talked about?

<u>Participants</u>: Yes.

Drawing by José Limón

Standards

ADMISSION TO THE DANCE MAJOR

New methods of determining the capacity of the prospective dance student for success in university work need to be established. Artistic competence and intellectual achievement should be considered. Both of these measurements need to be brought into balance, so that the talented young person will not be refused admission because of poor achievement in certain academic requirements.

Institutions may find it desirable to make exceptions for a small percentage of applicants who show special talent but are deficient in certain areas. Experience suggests that some students who have been deeply involved in dance have not been motivated in other areas of study. The student's past record does not always provide an accurate index of future academic work in a different learning environment which allows him to advance in his special field.

ADMISSION TO GRADUATE STUDY

A student must have an undergraduate major in dance, or equivalent competence, in order to be admitted to graduate study. A desirable candidate, who has met most of the requirements, may be admitted with the understanding that designated deficiencies will be overcome. Institutions may require assessment of the student's competence in dance (technique and composition) as well as his knowledge of the field.

TRANSFER STUDENTS

Each institution should establish standards at appropriate levels of proficiency for the Bachelor's and Master's Degrees.

Students who transfer to graduate programs in dance from other fields of study should be required to meet the standards held by the institution for undergraduate dance majors in movement and choreography, as well as a broad range of understanding in the field of dance. Provision should be made for deficiencies to be made up through proficiency examinations or regular course work. Since the undergraduate work provides the foundation for depth study at the graduate level, it is important that the department require competence equivalent to the undergraduate work. Where such standards are not maintained, the value of the Master's Degree is vitiated, and persons holding that degree would not necessarily be as qualified as those holding the Bachelor's Degree.

Robert Lindgren: Because of the college student's level of maturity and growth, you can immediately tell something about him physically, which you cannot do with the student in the elementary school. For instance, a child who was thin and well proportioned at adolescence suddenly changes completely and becomes heavy or disproportionate.

There is no use taking a girl, today, who is "turned in," relatively stiff, and with poor insteps, and saying, "You can be a good ballet dancer with hard work." There are too many people who are "turned out," who are loose limbed, who have good insteps. On the other hand, you can't say that they won't be able to perform or do something on the theatrical stage, but you couldn't encourage those people to be classical ballet dancers. Today, you can't cover up or fool anyone. You can't get by with those heavy legs or strange proportions.

Elizabeth Hayes: For what kind of profession? You might have someone with fat legs who would make a fine choreographer or dance therapist. We have all kinds of needs. For what you are speaking about, it is true, but there are many other areas where perfect body proportions may not be so necessary.

Alwin Nikolais: Thinking from a psychological point of view, there are some kids who are avidly interested in contemporary dance. I think the qualifications are different.

William Bales: You have to say competence for what. If it's competence for the professional ballet field, that is one thing. For this top level of professional performer, then, we have a way of looking at the body instrument, but there is another point that I wouldn't like to lose. Students go to universities to get an education. Every student who takes literature is not going to be a writer, a poet, or a dramatist. Some of our majors at Bennington will not be performers, but we feel that they can get an education through dance. It is legitimate to accept them as majors in dance. Education is a very broad spectrum of experience.

Martha Hill: I am concerned about what I call physicality. I don't know how you get at it. You know, the person who moves with some joy in his muscles, some liveliness or vitality. Sometimes we find students who move nicely but they have no physicality.

José Limón: They move, but they can't move you.

William Bales: But you may take a person like that in the liberal arts department and not take them in as professionals.

José Limón: I think the word is magic. Does he or she have magic? That is exactly what it is.

Marian Van Tuyl: Magic, but I think the physicality Martha speaks of is what causes the magic.

José Limón: Yes, it is built out of the muscles, but the result is enchantment.

Eugene Loring: I think that when you begin to set a physical standard you are on very bad ground. It would mean that you would never have some important dancers who had big legs, or a short neck, or too big a nose, or arms that were too long. I could name a thousand people like that.

José Limón: It goes back to magic — long nose, short legs, long arms, but magic.

Eugene Loring: It is very dangerous to cut out people who do not fit into the cookie cutter, and who have something very important to give to dance — something very strong.

William Bales: I agree with you one hundred percent. But there is a kinesthetic understanding that the dancer for the top level should have.

Selma Jeanne Cohen: I wonder if we are not saying that the standard physical requirements are one thing that we look for, and we can list some others, but we are going to take other factors into consideration. So the applicant who has short legs might have something else that compensates.

Eugene Loring: There is a little Japanese girl whose legs really are too short for her body, and they are too heavy, but when she dances she is just transformed — the whole figure is something else. Also, I don't think you can always tell at the beginning. Sometimes, people develop. I've seen whole physiques change.

Jean Erdman: It seems to me if we name just one more requirement, we have all we need as a collection — the other one being the rhythmic sense. You can see that, whether they have had any training, good training or bad training, as soon as you see a person move, you see whether he has a real sense of rhythm or not.

Patricia Wilde: I am wondering what kind of a basis you have technically, as far as taking them in. They can't be beginners, as you all agree. Can you set some kind of standard either in modern or ballet, so that they really have some basis in a technique?

Elizabeth Hayes: Doesn't that go back to the kind of a school it is? It seems to me that the level of technical qualifications must be geared to the school.

Alwin Nikolais: Are we really so poverty stricken as a profession that we can't afford to take a broader chance? I think that, from the point of view of education, if you deny anyone who has the desire, despite the knock-knees, to test himself and make the decisions himself, it is wrong. I think that we can be much more generous on this point and perhaps still get a raised standard.

Jack Morrison: I think that there is our trouble. We don't have strong elementary and secondary work, like other fields, and we must have. We ought to state that there must be growth at the elementary and secondary school levels. We cannot take on the responsibility of introducing everybody to dance; they should have had that earlier. On the other hand, since dance isn't developed, we have to take a little wider look at those who do want to start later. We have to maintain a flexibility, but then have a certain cut-off point.

Selma Jeanne Cohen: Nik mentioned earlier the idea of schools that specialize. I think that this is a possibility. You should be able to say in certain cases, "We are not the right school for you, but there is school X or school Y that would be right for you."

Alwin Nikolais: It would seem to me that it is impossible for us to set up a formula to supplant the intelligence of the person handling the selection. I would say that it would be rather difficult for us to present teachers across the country with a sort of dogmatic outline.

William Bales: It is impossible. We are not setting up a dogma, we are only making suggestions to the top level — suggestions to look at the instrument for some physicality, some kind of body magic, and talent. And that's going to be difficult for everyone looking — everyone sees it differently.

Elizabeth Hayes: This is why I think that the system of having a probationary period works very well. If in two years' time a student doesn't show some promise in the development of magic through the experience of freeing himself, or in the rhythm training that is necessary for the dancer, and the kind of body that makes him able to perform, then we encourage him to go in some other direction. Either he can find some other area in the total field of dance, or perhaps he may find that another profession would be advisable.

Robert Lindgren: But that is selectivity. You are saying that either they are good enough to continue or they are not.

Elizabeth Hayes: Yes, but not right at the beginning.

Jean Erdman: Do you take everybody?

Elizabeth Hayes: Yes, as freshmen.

Martha Hill: What is the purpose of the curriculum, Betty?

Elizabeth Hayes: It has various purposes. Teacher training, performance, choreography, or it might be basic preparation for therapy. There are many areas that they can go into. We can't pigeonhole people in one kind of mold, because there are so many different needs.

Jack Morrison: What we are really trying to get at is not a screening device, but criteria for selection — the criteria that we feel are necessary. We have suggested body build, physicality, magic, performing ability, and rhythm.

Dorothy Madden: Another one is staying with it.

Robert Lindgren: I would say dance personality — the drive and energy that gives you the personality to be a dancer.

Jack Morrison: Commitment.

Marian Van Tuyl: But the commitment doesn't necessarily show the first day.

Alma Hawkins: Let me try to summarize the main points of our discussion. We are saying that we might be in real danger in education if we don't give people a chance, that we can't always predict what a person can do by his physical build, but there are certain basic capabilities that are important if the student is to progress in various paths. As we work with students we need to assess their potential development, and, if they do not seem to meet the criteria set by the institution, we talk with them and advise appropriate directions. They may qualify for some other area of dance, even though they do not meet criteria for performance, or they may need to be advised out of the major.

Alwin Nikolais: I think the probationary idea is what we should work toward.

Elizabeth Hayes: I think a lot of the elimination of those who do not qualify would come about in a natural way. If you are teaching professional people, you certainly aren't going to teach the same way that you teach a class for the general public. If you teach according to a certain level, the people who can't keep up are going to eliminate themselves. I don't think that you become soft-hearted and feel that you must come down to their level. I think you have to say, "This is a class for this purpose, and if you can't keep up you'll have to find your level in some other class."

Jean Erdman: Could we say that even at the beginning levels, a class must progress at a certain rate? Even the students in the classes for the liberal arts students should meet a certain technical standard by the end of the first year. We shouldn't have people who are unable to do technique at all go on and do something else. No matter what the school is set up to do, you can't let people go on to a teaching program in dance, or a dance therapy program or anything, if they can't manage a particular level of training.

GRADE POINT REQUIREMENTS FOR ADMISSION TO GRADUATE STUDY

Margaret Erlanger: I'd like to talk about the grade point average required for admission. There are a number of people highly qualified in terms of their choreographic and performance ability, as well as general knowledge, who do not meet the "B" requirement. Scholarships and fellowships usually require a grade-point average of "A" or at least "B." In our institution it is now possible for the creative performing artist-student to be considered with a grade point average between "C" and "B" if he can demonstrate competence in choreography or performance. I think that "B" is too high for the performing arts.

Elizabeth Hayes: Can't you have students on a probationary basis, until they prove their ability to maintain the "B" average?

Margaret Erlanger: Yes, but the graduate assistantship requires a "B" average. This eliminates people who should be considered.

William Bales: The objection I have about the probation idea is that it places a penalty on achievement in performing and choreography. I think the dance competence should be equated in some way.

Nancy Smith: Could we say that the competent student who does not meet the grade point average could be accepted on probation?

William Bales: That would still penalize the student for achievement in choreography and performance.

Elizabeth Hayes: But those things are being graded also.

Ruth Murray: This may be different in the future. If we are thinking in terms that, let's say, fifty percent of the work on the undergraduate level is done in dance so that the student can bring to his graduate study an excellent reputation as a performer or a choreographer, then he will have the advantages of a high grade point in the dance area. He will be able to achieve the "B" average.

Helen Alkire: I don't think that we should accept a student at the graduate level in dance and make him a second-class citizen. If we accept him on a probationary basis or as a special student, that is exactly what we are doing. As we think about the twenty-five years ahead, this is the moment to convince administrators that students coming in as dancers and choreographers have to be recognized for that achievement. I don't know how we will do it, but I think that is what we must do now.

Virginia Freeman Weil: In the future, no one will be in the graduate program without the equivalent of the undergraduate dance major. In the meantime we have to make some exceptions.

William Bales: Then, do we admit an "A" student with a chemistry background into graduate study in dance?

Alma Hawkins: If he makes up deficiencies.

Martha Hill: Equivalence of the undergraduate major.

Alma Hawkins: Our experience suggests that it is feasible, sometimes, to make an exception, but generally we have found that, when we have allowed a person to go ahead without the equivalent experience, they lack the insight and understanding we want in the dance at the graduate level. Now we feel strongly that students should be held to our standards and exceptions should be screened very carefully. I think that we must have flexibility that takes care of the exceptional student, but at the same time we must protect our standards and the quality of our work.

Dance Department—Minimum Standards

The conference participants felt that it was important that professional and educational leaders in dance give consideration to standards of quality that should be used as a guide in the establishment of new dance major curricula. They recognized that all major programs will not be the same. In fact, curricula will vary markedly because of the uniqueness of each situation. For example, one would not expect the dance major in a small liberal arts college to be the same as the program in a large university. Also, one would assume that the graduate program in each institution would be built around the special resources and faculty strengths available. Some universities with large faculties will be able to offer a variety of specializations, while other institutions will decide to give emphasis to a certain area of specialization. Diversity among our institutions will give strength to the total effort in dance. But undergirding all of the differences should exist a certain standard of quality.

Before an institution attempts to establish a new dance major, it should consider its ability to provide a comprehensive curriculum, a competent faculty, appropriate facilities, and a supporting budget. Unless certain minimum standards can be met, the institution may be most effective by concentrating on the dance program for general college students. Those institutions with existing dance majors which do not meet minimum standards should be encouraged to bring about appropriate changes that would improve their programs.

The following statements reflect the point of view held by conference participants and identify standards which they believed should be considered as minimum criteria for a dance major.

FACULTY

The dance faculty should include two full-time teachers, plus adequate faculty resources in areas such as music, theatre, production, kinesiology, and other theoretical foundations. These additional resources may be available through joint departmental appointments or part-time specialists.

All studio classes should have a competent musician working with the dance teacher.

A musical director should be available for all productions.

The dance faculty should have a broad experience in dance which includes technique, choreography, and theoretical foundations. This preparation requires a dance major background or equivalent study.

The dance teachers should be qualified to teach advanced technique and choreography.

Faculty should have an understanding of several dance forms, but the emphasis should be on art dance.

The student-faculty ratio should be comparable to the institution's standard for other majors such as visual arts and theatre. A ratio of 15 students per faculty would seem to be a desirable standard for dance.

MAJOR CURRICULUM

The dance major courses should comprise approximately 50% of the student's total course work, including studio experience and non-studio classes such as dance history and kinesiology.

Requirements outside the dance department should ensure a breadth of study.

The standard for courses and quality of work should be such that students will be able to meet admission requirements for graduate study in other institutions. The student who has completed an undergraduate dance major should not be confronted with the situation where his work is not acceptable in another institution.

FACILITIES AND EQUIPMENT

Adequate space for classes and rehearsals should be available.

Two large studios with resilient floors and outdoor windows should be provided.

Studios should be equipped with mirrors, barres, piano, percussion instruments, record player, and tape recorder.

Dance major students should have access to a well equipped theatre that can be used as a class laboratory and as a performance center.

Adequate storage space for costumes, sets, and equipment should be adjacent to teaching spaces.

Appropriate dressing and shower facilities should be provided for students and faculty.

BUDGET AND SUPPORTING FUNDS

The dance major curriculum must be supported by an adequate budget that will make possible the appointment of competent faculty, and the implementation of a high quality program.

Research

Dance as a human experience has a long and vital history, but the concept of dance as a discipline in higher education is of recent origin. The amount of research produced to date in the discipline of dance has been meager. The literature representing the body of knowledge in dance appears limited when compared to the literature in other fields. In order for dance to mature as a field of study, a comprehensive literature, including film, tape, notation scores, and written works must be made available.

Graduate study and the education of competent specialists in various areas of dance, as well as the aesthetic growth in the art, are dependent, in part, on the creative work and research that are produced in the field. Since research in dance is a pressing need, the conference participants felt strongly that dance departments, graduate programs, dance educators, and artists should assume responsibility for increasing awareness about the areas in dance that need study, and for establishing research projects.

The arts, in contrast to other disciplines, make use of two types of original work: creative work and research. Each type is concerned with "bringing forth something new," and is guided by recognized criteria. While there are similarities in process of the two methods, there are also significant differences. "Creative work" refers to an aesthetic achievement that is qualitative in nature, while "research" implies the acquisition of new information through the use of appropriate research methods, such as the historical, the experimental, and the field study. Both types of original work are essential to the development of dance as an art and as a discipline in higher education.

Since dance leaders, teachers, and performing artists are more familiar with the process used in choreography than with traditional research methods, there is need for immediate in-service, short-term courses of institutes directed toward the problems of design, gathering data, and evaluating data, which would assist the inexperienced researcher to take hold of this essential area of work.

Certain questions arose. What kind of new knowledge is needed in dance? In what areas do we seek new information in order to expand existing knowledge, to improve the teaching-learning process, and to further the aesthetic development in the art of dance?

The following list summarizes areas of study that were suggested by the conference participants. The listing represents a first step, namely, the identification of research needs in dance. It was the hope of participants that these suggestions, which grew out of considerable discussion, would act as a stimulus for future work. The next step, of course, calls for the translation of suggested ideas into specific research projects. This task can be undertaken by individuals and institutions.

SUGGESTED AREAS OF RESEARCH

Basic Research

1. Factors affecting communication — sensory awareness, perception, abstraction, expression, projection

2. Consideration of new concepts of space-time

3. The role of the senses in the teaching-learning process. Sensory response and sensory perception related to technique and creative work

4. Discovery of a valid means of testing rhythmic acuity

5. Technological resources to serve the dancers' needs

History

6. Development of a film archive which will protect the dance heritage of the past and of the present. Gathering of materials; making films of contemporary dance; cataloguing film resources

7. Taped oral history records preserving significant information about artists, dance leaders, and unique dance developments at certain periods

8. Field study recording dance of primitive cultures while it still exists. Use film, tape,

notation, and the resources of anthropology relating dance to the culture

9. Recording of American dance as a part of our culture — American Indian, early fold forms found in different sections of the country, and social dance forms both current and historical

10. Historical studies of attitudes towards dance

11. Historical studies contributing to expansion of dance literature, including contemporary period as well as the past

12. Studies of attitude changes about dance in dance education.

Choreography

13. Tape and film as a means of getting at the nature of the creative process. Work with artists, using sound and film recordings for "getting inside of the process — a kind of sensory travelogue"

14. Current trends in choreography

15. Computer choreography

16. Choreography for different media: film, TV, and different stage spaces, such as thrust and arena stages

Theatre

17. Lyric theatre form (where movement is central) and the integration of light and design with movement

18. Technical aspects of theatre related to dance — consideration of new lighting instruments, new ways of using lights, and programmed lighting

Teaching-Learning

19. Comparative study of results obtained from two methods of teaching technique: one approach based on the understanding of movement principles, the other approach using teacher directed, demonstration, and drill methods of teaching

20. Determination of the most effective and economical method for developing range of movement (flexibility) in dancers

21. TV as a tool for learning:

   a) Self-appraisal of technique through the use of monitors
   b) Video tape as a means of self-observation of technique and choreography

22. Instructional media as contributors to creative learning

23. Programmed learning in dance

24. Development of graphic notation illustrative materials

25. Notation as an adjunctive technique in teaching, compared with other methods.

26. Experimental studies in methods of teaching dance history. Consider the use of methods and materials in various approaches. For example:

   a) Dance history correlated with history of other arts
   b) History class taught in the laboratory and classroom where students learn dances and discuss them in relation to the culture of the period, including political and religious thought, as well as the other arts
   c) Non-chronological approaches to history which do not necessarily progress from primitive to contemporary, but might progress through these periods several times in the process of tracing various aspects of the study, such as style.

27. Ethnic dance as means of enlarging dancer's understanding of his art

28. Work done in other countries on movement and dance education for children

29. Electronic research — to find if individual movement habit patterns can be computed in order to round out an individual's movement experience

30. Determine if choreographic form can be computed (for facilitating learning)

Therapy

31. Theoretical basis for the use of movement as an adjunctive therapy

32. Movement characteristics of the malfunctioning personality and of the normally functioning personality

Notation

33. Comparative study of notation systems

34. Electronic recording of notation

Terminology

35. Development of a vocabulary of common terminology

Philosophy

36. Aesthetics of dance

37. Nature of the critical function as a part of the study of aesthetics

Sociology

38. Movement characteristics of sub-cultures in urban societies related to acting and dance

Additional Suggestions for Consideration

1. Educating the dance audience

2. New ways of extending the university into the community

3. Survey of the field to gather information about:

   a) Existing dance programs and dance teachers in the high schools
   b) Status of dance in elementary and secondary schools
   c) Administrative location of dance today in higher education (physical education, dance department, or related to other arts)

4. Studies in the field of economics of dance

NOTE:

A great part of the research and development proposals listed here qualify for financial support under programs established at the Office of Education, the National Endowment for the Arts, the National Endowment for the Humanities, State and local Arts Councils, and a number of other Federal, State, and local agencies. During the past few years the Office of Education, and, lately, the National Foundation on the Arts and the Humanities, have offered for the asking one or another kind of directory of Federal aid to the arts and to education in the arts. To obtain guides to their activities, inquiries should be addressed to these Washington, D.C. agencies. In addition, the Office of Education operates a storage and retrieval system for reports of educational research. A subscription fee will bring monthly indexes of the system's ingestions. The program ERIC (EDUCATIONAL RESOURCES INFORMATION CENTER) will then provide microcard or 3/4 size process copies of research documents at modest prices. For information on ERIC and other educational projects write to the U.S. Office of Education, Washington, D.C. 20202.

Shirley Wimmer

Summary Last Session

As the conference drew to a close it was possible to make some formulations which reflect the hopes, concerns, and beliefs of this group of dedicated and distinguished individuals. The total conference time, seventeen days in two phases separated by six months, allowed a gestation period for the ideas presented and discussed in the first meeting to grow and form a base for the later curricular planning session.

The conference interchange emphasized the need for a strong working relationship between persons in both the professional world and in the academic world who are concerned with dance in our society. Putting the blueprint on paper is only one step. It will come to reality only through personal commitment and individual action to assist in developing the art of dance to its greatest potential.

Platform for Dance in Higher Education

The creative experience is always at the core of the total dance major or area of dance study.

All dance majors should have a continuing contact with the studio for direct participation in dance.

All dance majors should have the opportunity for some differentiation and some specialization in keeping with their personal commitments and future goals.

The highly gifted person should have the opportunity to develop his talents to the fullest.

There is a place for professional dance companies within the academic structure.

Graduate programs should be developed to provide advanced specialization and research in various aspects of the field.

Different degree patterns may be appropriate in the education of the dance major.

COMMENTS

From someone's remark that the conference meant a great deal to him, the dialogue shifted spontaneously to further personal responses to the conference.

"I have come out of my insular bailiwick and feel that for the first time I have been a part of something that was moving into a common center and a common goal."

"It is fascinating to be with people involved with dance, because there is such a commitment and dedication. I feel charged as an individual and strengthened to continue with my work. "

"This conference has broadened me and also has given me a sense of humility with the awareness of how much needs to be done. "

"It has made me think about my own situation and to evaluate it in terms of the general thinking around the country. "

"The atmosphere has been very permissive. I felt I could say anything I pleased. "

"And I did. "

"For the professionals and the educators to exchange thoughts has led to an understanding of each other. "

"We have become more aware of the scale of our problem — of how much has to be done — and we know it must be done so soon, so fast, so hard, so often, and so everywhere. "

"Almost magically our time together has brought our different orientations, regional problems, points of view into a common concern which should give us faith that we can work together for the development of dance. "

Appendix A   Short-Term Projects

Many problems confronting dance education need attention now. In the long view, the undergraduate and graduate major programs have the responsibility for the improvement of dance education in our schools. But, in the meantime, short term courses and workshops could be an effective means of bringing about immediate changes and improving the present level of teaching and planning.

Perhaps one of the primary needs in the field is a seminar to study research methods. As suggested earlier, many people in dance are not knowledgeable in the area of research design and procedures for collecting and evaluating data.

The projects listed below illustrate the kinds of courses or workshops that could make a valuable contribution to in-service education in dance.

MOVEMENT AND DANCE FOR THE ELEMENTARY CLASSROOM TEACHER

A short course should be offered in the various areas of the United States.

Length   The course, which may take the form of a seminar or institute, should be two or three weeks in length. This short period of time will be more attractive to teachers than the usual six-week summer session. However, the course should be long enough so that teachers have time to experience movement and break down their own inhibitions. They must feel secure in the work if they are to give effective leadership.

Credit   Credit should be available for those who wish to have it, and for those teachers who are required to work for promotion.

Sponsorship   This short-term course might be scheduled as:

A regular departmental curricular offering.

An extension workshop or institute.

A cooperative institute sponsored by the city board of education and the university.

Support   The budget may be provided in various ways, according to the planning in the local institution. For example, the course could be funded through:

The institution's usual procedure of charging fees for institutes and summer programs.

Full or partial support of the city or state board of education.

Grants made available by the Office of Education. Some projects may qualify for Title III funds.

When   The need for in-service education is now. Courses should be initiated by leaders in dance as soon as possible.

Program   The course should be planned as a movement-dance oriented experience. The purpose would be to acquaint classroom teachers with ways to present and guide the movement experiences of children. Another approach could be through an integrated learning experience in the arts. Such a plan would utilize leadership from music, drama, art, and movement. This latter approach has been used successfully with elementary teachers in Detroit, Michigan.

IN-SERVICE EDUCATION IN SECONDARY SCHOOLS

Short courses, seminars, and institutes for dance teachers.

For Whom   The emphasis in the re-education program should be for physical education teachers and others who have had limited experience in dance. The focus should be on beginning work. If it is not made clear that the focus is on beginning dance (not intermediate or advanced) the less experienced teachers may be hesitant about participating because they feel inhibited and fearful.

There could be value in workshops for more advanced work, but the imperative need at first would seem to be for improvement of the foundation level of teaching.

Purpose   The purpose would be to acquaint teachers with the materials of dance and approaches to teaching, and thus to improve the quality of dance in the secondary schools. The major goal should be to reach these teachers and assist them in becoming better teachers.

Program   Perhaps the active participation in movement should be optional. Teachers could gain a great deal through observation of teaching and performance that is expertly done. In some instances, there may be value in using a demonstration group in order to make clear certain materials, principles, and approaches to teaching.

Where   In-service education should happen in all parts of the country. Leaders and institutions in cities, states, and regional areas should take steps to provide offerings that are appropriate to the situation.

Some re-education programs of short-term duration could be presented in certain institutions or cities in such a way that they draw teachers from all over the country. For example, if such a course were offered in New York City, teachers could combine a "junket" to New York with a study program.

A MODEL DANCE PROGRAM IN THE COMMUNITY

A sample of the "best" in dance education, starting in the elementary school and continuing through junior and senior high school.

Value   A model program in the community could provide a sample of what is possible, as well as demonstrate high quality teaching and a preview of a sequentially planned curriculum. The model would serve as a resource for other schools and as a vital influence in upgrading teaching.

Models should be established in several communities, as well as urban centers.

MUSIC FOR DANCE

A three-week workshop or institute.

Focus   Playing for dance technique and composing for choreography.

Method   Use of dance film and tape as a means of relating music to dance.

1. Make a film of dance technique. Use film with a class of musicians.

   Using tape for recording, have them play to the film.

   Have them look at the film and listen to tape.

   Use film and tape as basis for discussion and learning.

2. Make a film of short dance compositions. Use film with class of composers.

   Have them improvise to film of dance compositions.

   Tape the music.

   Look and listen to play-back tape and film.

   Discussion of work.

3. Film a dance work already set to music.

   See what different musicians compose.

   See effect upon choreography of different music compositions.

Value   The hearing and seeing at the same time would contribute to awareness and learning on the part of the musician. The use of film and tape could shorten the teaching-learning period. The presence of music and dance on tape and film would provide a "real" situation as a basis for discussion which would be more effective than verbal discussion about composing.

Such a class could be valuable for the young, inexperienced composer and also for the experienced composer who is looking for new ideas.

This kind of exploration could lead to the development of a sound film that could be very useful in classes for composers.

Sponsorship   This kind of workshop or course should be offered in the music department of the university with the cooperative support of the dance department. Such an experience should be available to musicians who wish to work with dance or theatre.

SCIENTIFIC FOUNDATION FOR MOVEMENT RELATED TO THE DANCER

A proposed seminar.

Purpose

1. Understanding of basic and new scientific information that is applicable to dancers and their mechanical problems.

2. Awareness of principles that would contribute to better teaching and development of dancers.

3. Knowledge about body use and development that would prevent injuries.

Method   Presentation of information accompanied by laboratory demonstration.

SUMMER COURSE FOR MEN

A six-week institute.

A class for men taught by a man. The purpose of such a course would be to stimulate interest in dance among men. The emphasis would be on dance as a masculine activity with provisions made for classes for younger boys as well as college age students.

TEACHING METHODS

A comparative study of methods used for developing movement skills and performance.

LECTURE-DEMONSTRATIONS

A conference to organize, advise, and construct a variety of lecture-demonstrations of dance, and to disseminate them.

RELATIONSHIP OF MUSIC TO DANCE

A conference to improve the relationship of music with the film, the class, the concert, the lecture-demonstration.

THEATRE TECHNICIANS FOR DANCE

A short training course in which dancer and technicians explore the specific nature of the dancer's needs in the theatre.

DANCE WRITING AND CRITICISM

A workshop or seminar concerned with aesthetic education and the preparation of the audience for the dancer and choreographer. Such a seminar could help to establish a working relationship between leaders and artists with writers and critics who are associated with papers and magazines.

FILM SEMINAR

A four-week summer seminar to encourage those people having particular interest in the special problems of dance film making. See Appendix B, page 141.

LISTING OF DANCE FILMS

Compile an annotated list of foreign and domestic films of dance with information about sources and how they may be obtained.

MANAGEMENT AND PUBLIC RELATIONS

A conference on management and public relations for dance.

Note:

Many of these projects are as eligible for government or foundation support as those listed in the Chapter on RESEARCH. See page 133.

Left to right: Eugene Loring, Carl Wolz, Martha Hill, Lucy Venable, Joseph Gifford, Esther Pease

Appendix B   Work-Group Reports

To provide a setting for the Work Group Reports, excerpts from the invitation to the conference are included.

"The conference is planned as a working conference. The general pattern of the opening days will include a presentation by a consultant, a discussion period for the total group, and one or two work sessions for small groups. In our general meetings we will have an opportunity to pursue ideas presented by a consultant, and to explore other ideas or problems that come from the work groups or individuals.

"The task of the small work group will be to pursue its specific area and to produce a statement at the close of the conference. Each participant will be related to one of five groups as outlined. The descriptive phrases are intended as suggestions which should not restrict the natural development of the group. Please indicate your choice of work groups."

I. DANCE AS A FOUR-DIMENSIONAL ART

The broad context of dance including music, theatre crafts, production; theatre and stage as a working laboratory; aesthetic climate; the professional company; position of dance in education.

II. MOVEMENT

Movement considered from various approaches including motivation and inner experiencing (non-mechanical), the learning experience, search for movement, discovery of movement potential; movement style, varieties of style; movement principles for the efficient instrument, for performance.

III. FORM

The architecture of a work, choreographic process, innate sense of form; form as an object, shape of content; organic structuring, changing forms; perception of environment, and of dance.

IV. ARTISTIC GROWTH

Various aspects of and influences on growth including aesthetic awareness, taste, education of feelings, imaginative responses; the artistic encounter, creative environment, 'daring to risk' and 'right to fail,' psychological safety and freedom; perceptual and creative growth, developmental nature of growth; interplay of the arts.

V. INTELLECTUAL GROWTH

The legacy of dance, body of knowledge, critical viewing of dance, recording of dance, music related to dance; contact with the 'best' in dance, environment that supports growth; liberalizing experiences through non-dance, humanities, arts, social sciences, science.

On the basis of their choices the participants formed the work groups which met for approximately thirty hours during Phase I of the conference brainstorming their way through the designated assignments. Even though excerpts from the Group Reports have been incorporated into the body of this publication, it is appropriate that they be presented in their original form. It should be recognized that these reports represent a tremendous amount of work-in-progress arriving at a kind of consensus. In some cases, however, there were serious disagreements, as well as problems arising from attempts to clarify vocabulary. It was a situation in which any one of the group members had sufficient experience and conviction to attack the subject and write an individual report. Hammering out a group report was comparable to having five or six choreographers for one dance. So, of course, there were "minority reports," but, in the end, a graceful acceptance of the group effort.

Chairman, Charlotte Irey
Margaret Erlanger
Martha Hill
Dorothy Madden
Allegra Snyder
Betty Walberg
Thomas Watson

Dance—A Four-Dimensional Art

EXPLORING AND EXPANDING THE CLIMATE AND ENVIRONMENT FOR DANCE

Favorable elements in the climate of dance:

> Dissolving taboos concerning the body.
>
> Freedom in contemporary dress.
>
> Freedom in physical activity, especially in popular dancing.
>
> Wider acceptance of the active and applied forms of the arts in education.
>
> Increase in good dance education.
>
> Increase in private and governmental support of the arts, local, State, and Federal.
>
> We live in a verbal world and in an electronic age which contemporary man can accept as his natural environment. Acceptance may create a favorable element.

Unfavorable elements in the climate of dance:

> We live in a verbal world and in an electronic age which contemporary man has accepted as his natural environment. This acceptance creates an unfavorable element.
>
> Economic insecurity in the field of dance, and, therefore, the choice and continuation of dance as a precarious profession.
>
> Some of the current unimaginative treatments of dance through the mass medium — television.

I. THE THEATRE AND STAGE AS A WORKING LABORATORY

The following is a construction for expanding the environment of dance:

A. The bringing together of the theatre experience:

    1. For working
    2. For observing

B. Experience in this aesthetic environment:

    1. Exploration of all styles of dance (ethnic, ballet, modern, jazz)

    2. The building of an awareness of sources — such as ethnic forms

    3. Experimentation with light, sound, space, props, costumes, visual and tactile stimuli

C. The staff for the Working Laboratory:
  1. Director-administrator
  2. Artistic director
  3. Music director
  4. Teaching staff
     a) Dance
     b) Music
     c) Theatre Arts
     d) Art
     e) Film
     f) Notator
     g) Physical therapist
     h) Apprentices to the various areas of
        dance, music, theatre, art, and film:

On salary
On scholarship
  5. Secretarial help
  6. Designer
     a) Technician
     b) Stage manager
     c) Crew
  7. Costume designer
     a) Wardrobe mistress
     b) Seamstress
  8. Business manager
     a) Public relations director
     b) Tour manager
  9. Visiting and resident artists from America
     and other countries*

* Why is the artist in the university?

  a) Students need and want closer relationship with the performing artist and
     opportunity of being in works by an experienced choreographer so that through
     constant performance they grow in their art.

  b) The artist is there to teach repertory class and to do productions
     on whatever level is appropriate.

  c) Students will have the benefit of performing if expert enough. Others can
     serve as production apprentices.

  d) Students will learn:

        The wholeness of dance and not to divide the craft from the art

        Commitment

        The paradox of freedom and discipline

        That a work has to try for excellence and cannot be hurried

What does the performing artist mean to the university?

  a) He contributes a first hand view of his art.

  b) He expands the audience.

What does the residency mean to the artist?

  a) Freedom and time to compose new works and to rework old ones.

  b) Opportunity for performances not only in the university but also concerts and
     demonstrations in the community and environs with consequent prestige and
     financial support.

D. Laboratory with proper and resilient floors throughout. A plant for teaching and research is a necessity and demands extensive study by experts. The
   following are only guidelines:

   1. Stage
   2. Rehearsal space somewhat larger than the
      stage (sound insulated)
   3. Small experimental working laboratory
   4. Green room
   5. Rehearsal studios (with windows, sound
      insulated)

      a) Ethnic
      b) Ballet
      c) Modern
   6. Practice studios (piano, built-in phonograph,

and tape recorder)
  7. Choreographers' studio
  8. Meditation room
  9. Lecture and projection rooms
 10. Library and reference room (books, music,
     records, tapes, and films)
 11. Recording studio
 12. Observation balcony (to facilitate uninter-
     rupted rehearsals)
 13. Storage space (easily accessible to stage,
     experimental laboratory, and rehearsal
     areas) for:
     a) Props
     b) Musical instruments
     c) Lighting equipment
     d) Costumes

14. Construction rooms for:
    a) Music (making tapes, recording)
    b) Sets
    c) Costumes
        (1) Designing and sewing
        (2) Dyeing
        (3) Washing, drying, cleaning
15. Office-conference room
16. Toilet and shower facilities
17. Restroom (remote from toilet and showers)
18. Therapy room
19. Snack bar

E. Equipment:

1. Lighting equipment
2. Sound system
3. Provision for musicians, including properly designed music stands
4. Pianos (one with damper arrangement to facilitate working without disturbing others)
5. Other instruments such as:
    a) Harpsichord
    b) Percussion instruments
6. Music literature, records, tapes, dance notation scores, and films
7. Video tape equipment
8. Movie projector and screen

II. PROJECTS FOR EXPLORING AND EXPANDING THE CLIMATE OF DANCE

A. Summer Film Seminar

While the need for more filmed material on the dance has been stressed, it has also been demonstrated that the filming of dance must satisfy needs unique to the area of dance and therefore requires a special point of view in the making of such films. A precedent has been set in the fields of medicine and science where a large body of films, special to their particular needs, has been created. The dance film-maker requires at best a thorough knowledge of both dance and film — the eye of the trained dancer-choreographer implemented by a basic knowledge of the potentials, dichotomies and limitations of film in specific relation to the particular needs of dance. Since this kind of specialist is now rare, as are the educational facilities to foster the skill, it is proposed that a four-week summer seminar be set up to encourage those people in the dance area who show some particular interest or concern for the special problems of dance film-making. Experts in various universities having adequate film facilities should be present.

The seminar would be divided into two two-week sessions. The first section would emphasize intensive analysis of films by viewing, thus building towards a theoretical understanding of the film aesthetic, particularly in relation to space, time, and movement.

The second two weeks would be devoted to actual filming and working in the cutting room. The aim would not be technical competence, which should remain with trained film personnel, but the gaining of a working feel of the two parts of filming.

The end result would be that through such an experience the dance-film director would emerge.

B. Economics of Documentary Films

It is necessary to investigate union regulations in relation to the making of documentary films of performances by dance professionals in a professional setting.

Up to now we have been unable to meet the growing demand for a filmed literature of dance, since fees for dancers, musicians, and film personnel raise the cost of making this type of film far above the expectation in monetary returns. These films are educationally rather than commercially based. They are materials for the classroom, library, research center, and adult education program, and in no way take the place of live performance.

C. Annotated List of Films

An annotated list of foreign and domestic sources of films should be compiled, together with information as to how they may be obtained.

D. Conferences

1. To organize and construct a variety of lecture-demonstrations of dance and to disseminate them
2. To improve the relationship of music with the film, the class, the concert, the lecture-demonstration
3. On training theatre technicians and designers for dance
4. On management and public relations for dance

E. Additional Projects

1. To gain support for the placement of young trained musicians in schools to compose for dance.

2. To gain support for cultural exchange at home with a selection of choreographers, with or without companies, willing to spend a year in a geographic area

3. To investigate possibility of gaining economic security for dance artists through union or other means

Recommendation

The addition of a Dance Education Specialist for the U.S. Office of Education.

Chairman, William Bales
Joseph Gifford
Valerie Hunt
Louise Kloepper
Eugene Loring
Ruth Murray
Lucy Venable

Movement

I. Human Movement

Movement is organized energy. Human movement is the response of the human organism to its environment. As it responds it becomes aware of the interacting processes (internal and external). It is a continuing, dynamic process involving change and development, first through the response, second through the awareness. The process is the core of all movement. It is the heart of dance.

The physical environment is a fact of reality. The individual must interact in this environmental reality with the sequence of events, which is time. There is a pull of gravity which is weight. The handling and the understanding of this weight is our force component. The most encompassing element is space. It involves recognizing and defining the differences of human and non-human objects in space with the space reality of one's own body. The latter is always the point of reference.

II. Basic Movement Experience

Each individual should have a broad range of movement experiences resulting in greater awareness of the total movement possibilities of the body, progress in the mastery of the body, and the development of perceptions and concepts relating to these movement experiences.

Basic human movement is the foundation of all dance. The emphasis placed upon it depends upon the stage and level of development, and the particular needs of the individual.

III. Basic Dance Experience

In the shaping and clarifying of the expressive qualities of movement with discipline and order, basic movement becomes basic dance. This usually occurs when the individual is able to perceive his involvement as a total experience. This leads to technical development and the extension of the expressive range of movement through practice and directed learning.

A broad range of experiences is desirable, including technique, improvisation, composition, performing, and the viewing of performances.

IV. Dancer-Artist

Also called the Ideal Dancer
Also called the Professional
The criterion is the highest standard of excellence

A dancer-artist is one who can respond to all demands of the choreography, intellectually, emotionally, and physically, in order to bring "truth" to his performance.

The dancer-artist must have an insight and understanding of the choreographic process, and must bring an individual, imaginative contribution to the choreography.

The dancer-artist needs the greatest possible range of movement vocabulary resulting from a thorough study of existing techniques and styles, such as: ballet, modern, jazz, folk, ethnic, tap, as well as the differences in style according to historical periods, schools and regions.

This movement training is recommended for choreographers as well as performers. We recognize that a choreographer must have additional training in many other aspects of dance.

We also recognize the importance of the experience in dance that does not have the amount of training and involvement required of the artist-dancer, but which can be a rewarding personal experience.

V. Teacher training

The movement training of a teacher should be of a breadth and scope that follows the direction of the movement training of the artist-dancer to a depth limited only by other goals and requirements of the profession of teaching.

Chairman, Virginia Freeman Weil
Helen Alkire
Vera Embree
Nancy Smith
Joan Woodbury

Form

I.

Man is a forming organism. He forms by ordering his experience and is thus continuously formed by his experience. His sense of form is innate; it exists because there is form in all life experience, and man is a constant participant in this forming and in forms. Consider the experience of a child's tantrum. It begins with a feeling — genuine and unshaped. It proceeds of its own self-feeding energy, acquiring texture and shape en route. It finds its peak and comes to rest. Another such example is the experience of grief. It is ignited, it builds, it takes over the griever, it spends, it ends. Of course, the shape of the pattern will vary from mourner to mourner. Tracing the history of an idea — from inception through development — will reveal a similar architecture of process.

The completion of forming, occurring through a structuring process, reveals forms which have in the process taken on particular shapes. These are accessible to the perceiver only through performance, past or present. When these shapes are art shapes, they are non-discursive in nature. They are projections of felt life. Although they sometimes are processed through logical ordering (more or less conscious), they must be feeling-based to exist as true extensions of the sentient experience.

Dance forms are particularly clear examples of extensions of felt life because of their non-verbal nature and because both the feeling and its resultant form reside in the same location — the human body. The choreographic process could be described, then, as "an auto-symbolizing process, occurring through the transforming of fantasy images into metaphor images."[1] The development of a piece of choreography is, therefore, seen to be an evolving pattern of relationships, growing organically, and assuming configuration, texture, and quality. It begins with that initial matrix of feeling which remains the living center or spine of the growing work. In dance, this initial matrix never evolves into a discursive or verbal form. It retains its autonomous non-verbal nature, needing no verbalization and answering only to its own demands. To say that the choreographic process is organic and that it evolves from the initial energy of that first feeling is not to say that the choreographer becomes a passive subject taken over by his own work. At times it seems that way, particularly when a piece of choreography is growing rapidly and with apparent ease. Perhaps it is because that primal awareness, known as feeling, has gathered great momentum and has temporarily outdistanced conscious recognition of the action involved. Forming is an act; it is not passive. It depends ultimately on the will of the form-er, who becomes sensitive to certain potential relationships, heightens some materials, decreases or eliminates what seems to be irrelevant until he has satisfied his completion-seeking self. When the work fails to develop in this organic way, it often will seem contrived because it has been mechanically manipulated, has somehow moved away from the initial matrix, has become a victim of empty formalism.

The choreography is the elaborated, articulated extension of the choreographer's first sentient experience. It has been termed a "living, autonomous model of consciousness."[2] The choreographer has exercised his

will, has made decisions all along the way, although many of these acts have been born of intuition.[3]

As in all creation, there are phases of what seems to be destruction. But the actual energy of the work is not destroyed. It is transformed; that is, it has moved from form into form, until the ultimate shape has been achieved. This process involves labor and effort, as does all birth. It can be encouraged, induced, but, if forced too soon, it can result in a de-forming. The choreographic process is forming from felt life. It is sentient experience transformed.

II.

What, then, does all this mean for the potential dancer-artist and for the artist-teacher? What are the responsibilities to the young, questioning, would-be artist whose life will be so touched by what the teacher feels, thinks, does, is? How can the teacher provide an atmosphere which will foster the creative spirit — the life force?

Movement is the "stuff" of dance; it is shaped to be a projection of a dance idea. It is the actual content, in that it is the movement itself that speaks. The dance idea is carried in the movement. It springs from the choreographer's intuition, and is given over to the intuition of the perceiver. The act of forming has its genesis in the silent space of the individual's inner world. But, at the same time, it bears the imprint of experience that is socially constituted in objects, events, conditions, and qualities of his total environment.

Freedom is essential in the act of discovery and image making. Improvisation can be a useful technique in the forming process, and has validity as a way for the student to find "live" connections out of which he may discover forms, instead of superimposing them on the movement, and get back to the physical reality of what he is doing in time-space, letting the form come from within. This allows the dancer to bring from the subconscious those elements which are not determined by the intellect.

For the dancer-choreographer, there is the necessity for the fullest possible use of our historical legacy through the study of past and current dance repertoire, through the study of traditional forms in music, dance and the other arts, and through the study of new, emerging forms.

1. Harold Rugg, IMAGINATION (New York: Harper & Row, 1963) p. 305.
2. Susan Sontag, AGAINST INTERPRETATION (New York: Farrar, Straus & Giroux, 1966), p. 31.

3. "Style is the principle of decision in a work of art, the signature of the artist's will. And as the human will is capable of an indefinite number of stances, there are an indefinite number of possible styles for works of art. (Ibid., p. 32.)

144

The teacher can serve as facilitator, as catalyst, in the process of discovery. He senses when to offer resistance in the choreographic process, when to provide a kind of abrasion that will result in creative tonicity.

The teacher serves as critic by being the objective eye which aids the student in dilating his own vision. He tells the student what he (the teacher) perceives the piece to be, not what it means. He does not translate the piece in terms of meaning, for the piece is non-discursive in nature and autonomously so. The teacher-critic should receive it experientially. In this way, the student-choreographer may learn to carry his own criteria.

III.

There is a need in man to find, hold, and manipulate forms that take him out of the ordinary and provide for him a kind of transformation and immortality, a visa from present to future. This need finds ample stimulation in today's new technology. At times, the new technological age intimidates and frightens us, but we must learn to utilize and exalt its constructive influences, as well as cope with its destructive forces. The computer age is with us, and often mechanistic power seems a hostile aspect of contemporary life. We are accustomed to regard the machine as anti-humanistic, but perhaps we will learn to think of the new technology, not just as an extension of human intelligence, but as an indication that the scope of humanity — of what we have considered to be human — is far more vast than we have ever conceived. The new humanism may embrace an enormously increased spectrum of human abilities and sensibilities. We are already operating on drastically revised and enlarged concepts of space and time; yesterday's mysteries are today's science. If art enhances reality, as Camus suggests, and if art shapes are projections of experience, then the artist will discover and develop new forms, utilize them expressively, giving them the luminosity of his expanded imagination, thereby retaining the relevance of his art.

There are increasing possibilities of perception, and with new percepts, new concepts will emerge. The one thing today's artist cannot afford is to remain insulated by preconceptions. Rilke described the artist as someone who works "toward an extension of the regions of the individual senses"; McLuhan calls artists "experts in sensory awareness." Not only does today's artist find himself in rapidly evolving new worlds, but also he finds that he has increasingly sensitive antennae with which to perceive them. New worlds create new forms. Dance today will become today's dance as it discovers its new forms. It will become a relevant manifestation of the new humanitas as it casts its changing sensory materials into new expressive shapes.

Suggested research

1. Electronic research — to find if individual movement habit patterns can be computed in order to round out an individual's movement experience.

2. To determine if choreographic form can be computed (for facilitating learning).

3. To determine if notation can be recorded electronically.

Chairman, Eleanor Lauer
Bonnie Bird
Greta Brown
Nik Krevitsky
Jack Morrison
Esther Pease

Artistic Growth

The artistic growth of an individual occurs in his pursuit of one or more art forms as a participant and/or audience member. The experience provides the opportunity for the artistic encounter, out of which artistic growth may proceed. All creation is a mystery, but the creation of art is a uniquely human experience. The use of art is to fulfill man's life. Without it, he exists — and merely exists, rather than lives — in a "bread-alone" world.

That man must have "more than bread" to live becomes increasingly evident on all sides. When he is deprived of some means of expression, distortions of his potential for health occur, moving him toward conditions of illness. When he is unfettered and encouraged, he unfolds, he creates; his products satisfy him, enrich his world, and society benefits. Dance, as one of the arts, provides a profound means through which man can fulfill himself. From the earliest moments of life, man lives in his body, he is continuously in action, from states of stillness, of no apparent motion, to the explosive totality of a great leap. The quality of human health is inextricably bound up with the amount and kind of movement the body can make. The empirical data of skilled teachers and observers in the field of dance, and the greatly increased information derived from numerous scientific studies, indicate that dance, in all its aspects as an expressive medium, has an as yet untapped contribution to make to the education of the whole person in our society.

In dance, artistic growth consists of the developing awareness and mastery of movement and an understanding of it as an expressive medium of human communication. Since, for each individual, artistic growth is a part of his total development and may proceed quite differently for different persons under varying conditions, any attempt to make a definitive statement as to the exact nature of artistic growth would be almost impossible. However, countless teachers are convinced that they, and many of their students, have experienced artistic growth, that it is a recognizable phenomenon, and that it is vital to an effective education in dance.

Society, the Teacher, the Student

Aesthetic growth for every individual — an ideal in a healthy society — can be nurtured in an atmosphere in which that individual is free to move and encouraged to move (alone and with others) so that human communication may take place — on the level of dance. The role of society in producing the aesthetic, sentient, dance-man is that of providing opportunity for the development of individual movement potential in an atmosphere secure in its permission of uniqueness, comfortable in its recognition of non-conformity, wholesome in its encouragement of physical freedom, and generous in its provision of aesthetic experiences in all fields, disciplines, and environments.

For teachers, the chief concern is to provide conditions offering the greatest opportunity for artistic growth, to be on the alert for its appearance and to recognize it appropriately when it does appear. Though skills and techniques have an important place in the curriculum, though information about dance and dancers is meaningful and adds a level to the experience, it is only in the involvement with art as a direct experience or encounter that full aesthetic growth can occur and the individual can reach that level of human-ness we refer to as the "educated (whole) man."

The teacher must be guide, catalyst, perceptive leader — understanding and encouraging. He must provide security (love) as well as challenge. He must avoid being mechanistic, a drill coach, merely a disseminator of information.

The student must learn to think and to feel rather than merely to memorize and repeat. He must be free to observe fully with his total responsive mechanism — to respect the poetic level of expression as meaningful and important and more vital than the mundane, the factual, the computerized, and the processed, which constitute the present emphasis in "education."

Encouragement of Artistic Growth

Conditions favorable to artistic growth in dance are:

1. Space and time to dance, and acknowledgment that movement is an important activity for all people.

2. An environment which provides a variety of sensory stimuli to which the person may respond.

3. A climate of acceptance of the person by himself and by those around him.

4. A continuing contact and identification with nature.

5. A teacher who is able to recognize those moments when a student has reached a new level of development and can make him aware of his achievement.

6. An ample opportunity for self-direction.

7. An atmosphere free from those negative attitudes or taboos which lead to interruption, distortion, or destruction of that artistic tendency which is innate in every individual.

8. Instructional methods which relate to the varying kinds and rates of artistic growth in different individuals.

Evidence of Artistic Growth

Each art has unique properties that distinguish it from all others. Dance exists within the dancing body — and exists only as it is being performed. Components of the kinesthetic aesthetic exist in each of the other arts, but it is the aesthetic of dance.

There are observable clues to artistic growth which a responsive teacher can recognize in a student of any age or any level of ability. They are:

1. The ability to incorporate increasing complexity into a unified whole.

2. The increase in responses to stimuli — sensitivity.

3. The heightening of an ability to see, hear, and feel relationships between forms, verbal and non-verbal, and visual, auditory, and kinesthetic.

4. Evidence of greater confidence as the individual becomes self-actualized — motivated from within.

Essential Experiences

In the fostering of artistic growth, certain experiences should be provided for all students. Application and understanding will, of course, vary in accordance with the physical, emotional and intellectual growth of the individual, but the concepts seem consistent throughout. They derive from the fact that man is constantly moving — taking in and responding to sensory stimuli, and "forming" from the backlog of experience which he has had. This process of sensing, responding, and forming, has been recognized as part of the creative process and is of particular importance in dance education.

If conditions are favorable for artistic growth, the student will use his body as a structural whole. He will discover the movement potential of his body and will move in a variety of ways within an exploratory framework. He will understand and apply the principles of movement in relation to body alignment, flexibility, strength, endurance, locomotion, elevation, descent, and revolution.

He will discover his own movement potential through improvisation and exploratory movement in relation to the concepts of time, space, and force. He will respond in a variety of ways (through participation, observation, conceptualization and evaluation) to a variety of stimuli. He will bring order to this storehouse of experiences and form something uniquely his own. He will make his contribution to his environment and will discover his creative potential. He will observe, participate in, and evaluate his own work in relation to the work of his peers and the total artistic world. He will understand and apply the principles of form and will create through traditional as well as experimental processes.

Within the educational systems in which dance is taught, opportunity will be provided for the development of kinesthetic awareness, increased sensory responsiveness and forming. Differentiation at the various levels of sophistication will be only a matter of emphasis. In the elementary levels, the emphasis will be on the kinesthetic awareness, with some experience in the areas of response and forming. The focal point will shift gradually so that, at more advanced levels, the emphasis will be on forming and performing, based on a rich experience of movement from a feeling base.

Past, Present, Future

There is a continuum of that which is meaningful and beautiful in dance. Each historical period has contributed to it. While we cannot directly experience its past, since dance by nature is of the instant, many of the elements of expressiveness can be reconstructed with the assistance of the other arts and disciplines such as music, painting, philosophy, anthropology.

The "truths" of dance which have been revealed throughout successive stages in the past are brought into the light of today to be used and reshaped within a context of the present. Dance mirrors man the dancer at this moment, in this place. It can never be otherwise, since dance lives in the physical body of the man.

Even while we realize the deeper significance of dance and add a segment to that continuum which began when man first danced, we begin to observe evidences of change. These trends, though vague and not completely intelligible, might provide the key to new directions of the dance art. We have discovered the dance of the 20th century. Perhaps, among our present-day artists, but more likely within the ranks of the young, are those who will begin to envision the dance of the next century. The shape and significance of the evolving dance forms will be directly related to the nature of the development of the individual within society. It is the responsibility of society, the teacher, the parent, to provide for each person opportunities for the realization of his dance potential and, thereby, for maximum artistic growth.

Chairman, Selma Jeanne Cohen
Elizabeth Hayes
Marian Van Tuyl
Shirley Wimmer
Carl Wolz

Intellectual Growth

I. A PROGRAM FOR INTELLECTUAL GROWTH ENVISIONED THROUGH A DANCE CURRICULUM

A. Intellectual growth can be gained by all students through general dance class experiences which include the following:

1. A concept of man as a total human organism, and recognition of the need for total body awareness

2. An understanding of kinesthesis as a basis for dance expression and communication

3. Knowledge of body structure and its movement possibilities

4. Knowledge of how body movement is controlled — how certain techniques are achieved, how certain movement qualities are attained

5. Recognition of time, space, and energy as factors that can be manipulated to create expressive movement

6. Skill in analyzing dance movement and ability to read its notation

7. Skill in analyzing rhythm as it relates to the dance movement and to the musical structure

8. Awareness of the need for form, and understanding of concepts of dance structure

B. Intellectual growth for the dance educated person (as distinguished from the dance major) can be further extended by a humanities course in dance and related arts to include introductory explorations into the following areas:

1. The interrelation and interaction of the arts

2. The functions and purposes of dance in human living

3. The historical development of dance

4. The concept of art as a creative process

5. Knowledge about theories and practices of individual artists. Ideally, this classroom approach should be supplemented whenever possible by laboratory experiences with movement to give added meaning to these intellectual explorations.

C. Intellectual growth for the dance major needs to be reinforced in the following basic areas of knowledge. (This section would include a study in increased depth of the areas listed in I-B.)

1. Anatomy and kinesiology (preferably combined and directed to the dancer's needs)

2. Application of the above knowledges to the study of human movement (Valerie Hunt's approach)

3. Evaluation of dance improvisation and composition

4. Rhythmic analysis and advanced practice

5. Resources in dance accompaniment (Music, percussion, use and making of electronic tapes, etc.)

6. Advanced dance notation

7. Dance history with compositional application

8. Dance aesthetics and criticism

9. Form and function of the lecture-demonstration with practical application

10. Stagecraft, lighting and costuming with practical application

D. Intellectual growth for the dance major can be further extended in the direction of related art fields selected on the basis of individual interest and need.

1. English Composition
2. Literature
3. Foreign languages
4. Practice in visual design (art, architecture)
5. History of other arts
6. Anthropology
7. History of ideas — various fields
8. Philosophy
9. Psychology
10. Physiology

Most of all, importance should be given to encouraging study with great teachers, regardless of subject matter areas.

E. Intellectual growth can be provided for the dance major (particularly at the graduate level) to fulfill his needs in special areas of competence. (For many people, more than one area of competence will be desirable.)

1. Dancer
 a) Understanding the techniques and theories of great dance artists and of different cultures
 b) Experience with a variety of styles and repertory works performed under varied circumstances
 c) Singing and acting

2. Choreographer
 a) The above experiences listed for the dancer
 b) Experience in the craft of composition
 c) Techniques required for TV, films, arena stage, and musical theatre

3. Teacher
 a) Child and adolescent development
 b) Psychology of learning
 c) Principles of teaching dance to various age groups
 d) Administration

4. Dance Therapist
 a) Behavioral sciences
 b) Experience working with emotionally disturbed individuals
 c) Experience working with the physically handicapped

5. Film Maker
 a) Still photography, motion picture, and TV production
 b) Experience in filming

6. Dance Notator
 a) Advanced notation
 b) Experience in notating dance works

7. Critic and/or Historian
 a) History and literature
 b) History of criticism
 c) Historical method and bibliography
 d) Experience in journalistic and historical writing

8. Musician and Composer for Dance
 a) Music history
 b) Ethnomusicology
 c) Improvisation on various instruments
 d) Experience in composing for dance

9. Ethnologist
    a) Anthropology, folklore, and mythology
    b) Ethnomusicology
    c) Ethnic dance

10. Theatre-Technician for Dance
    a) Staging design
    b) Lighting design
    c) Costume history
    d) Costume design
    e) Stage management
    f) Technical experience in above areas

II. LEVELS OF INSTRUCTION IN RELATED FIELDS

A. Elementary School

Music, theatre, and dance history experienced in projects correlated with the total curriculum. Science of human movement, movement notation, and critical viewing of dance integrated with the dance experience.

B. High School

1. General High School: Study to continue in the manner outlined above

2. High School of Arts: In recognition of the talent and interest of dance students in these specialized high schools, more intensive work in music resources and analysis, anatomy and human movement, movement notation, and history of the arts

C. College and University

To meet the needs of varied abilities and purposes work to be offered in:

1. A continuing contact with dance for the general student
2. An intensive program for students educated in the general high schools who now wish to major in dance
3. An intensive program for students coming from the high schools of art

III. REQUIREMENTS FOR IMPLEMENTING THE PROGRAM

A. Need for well trained teachers

B. Need for materials:

1. Tapes:
    a) Music
    b) Oral history

2. Scores:
    a) Dance repertory
    b) Music repertory

3. Visual Resources:
    a) Photographs and slides:
        (1) Performers and performances
        (2) Relevant visual arts and environments
    b) Films:
        (1) Records of repertory
        (2) Imaginative documentary of repertory
        (3) Filmic dance
        (4) Demonstration
        (5) Biographical and historical

4. Publications:
    a) Books, all types, for all age levels
    b) Continuing bibliographies
    c) Encyclopedia with annual supplements
    d) Journals

5. Live dance, touring companies:
    a) As models of excellence
    b) As subjects for critical evaluation

C. Need for undertaking projects:

1. To train teachers:
    a) Immediate: summer institutes
    b) Future: regular program will provide

2. To make materials adequate and accessible

    a) Regional information centers at colleges and universities, with broad geographical spread
        (1) Library
        (2) Research training
        (3) Distribution
        (4) Publication
    b) Work with available material
        (1) Survey of material
        (2) Editing of material
        (3) Cataloguing

    c) Provision of new material as needed

3. To utilize modern technological resources

Note:

Chart "Dance in Education" on page 87 was designed in this work group.

Appendix C Participants

ALVIN AILEY, dancer, choreographer, teacher, director, had his early dance training with Lester Horton. Mr. Ailey's own company, the American Dance Theatre, has toured the Far East and Europe under the sponsorship of the U.S. Department of State. He has choreographed for the Joffrey Ballet, the Harkness Ballet, and the Metropolitan Opera.

HELEN P. ALKIRE, Professor and Director of the Department of Dance at Ohio State University, is the founder, director, and choreographer of the Ohio State University Dance Company and "Choral Dance Theatre" with which she has toured in this country and Europe. She has an extensive background of professional study in dance, has taught at Sweet Brier College, Teacher's College of Columbia University, and the Cape Cod Theatre School. She has held offices in the Dance Division of AAHPER, and is a board member of the Dance Notation Bureau.

WILLIAM BALES, Dean of the Dance Division of the State University of New York, College at Purchase, N.Y., was formerly chairman of the Dance Department at Bennington College, and has taught and performed at Connecticut College School of Dance. Mr. Bales was a member of the Humphrey-Weidman Company and the Dudley-Maslow-Bales Company. He is on the Board of Directors of the New Dance Group Studio and the Advisory Dance Panels of the Cultural Exchange Program, U.S. Department of State, and National Foundation on the Arts and Humanities.

MANUEL BARKAN is Professor and Chairman, Art Education Area, School of Art, at Ohio State University. He is also Director, Aesthetic Education Curriculum Program, Central Midwestern Regional Educational Laboratory.

FRANK BARRON, Associate Research Psychologist, Institute of Personality Assessment and Research, University of California, Berkeley, is currently in Rome, Italy on a Guggenheim Fellowship. Mr. Barron has taught at Bryn Mawr College, Wesleyan University, Harvard University, and was a Fellow at the Center for Advanced Study in the Behavioral Sciences. He is the author of CREATIVITY AND PSYCHOLOGICAL HEALTH.

BONNIE BIRD trained at the Cornish School in Seattle and, after working, teaching, and performing with Martha Graham in New York, she became head of the Dance Department of the Cornish School. Upon her return to New York, she directed the Dance Department of the YMHA and the Merry-Go-Rounders, has directed the Dance Educators' Workshop at Connecticut College School of Dance, and was Chairman of the National Dance Guild. Under the auspices of the Board of Education of Hastings-on-Hudson, N.Y. she is conducting workshops for elementary teachers, "The Use of Expressive Movement in the Classroom."

GRETA BROWN teaches modern dance at Culver City Junior High School "to every girl within the physical education department." She has studied and performed with Gloria Newman, and is currently at work on a Master's thesis, "Negro Dance in America," at the University of California, Los Angeles.

IRVING M. BROWN is Theatre Education Specialist and Acting Dance Education Specialist for the Arts and Humanities Program of the U.S. Office of Education. He came to the Office from Lake Erie College where he was Director of the Theatre Arts Program as well as of the Lake Erie College-Community Theatre. He has been active in theatre, film, and dance production here and abroad as director, actor, administrator, teacher, lecturer, and consultant.

SELMA JEANNE COHEN, Editor of DANCE PERSPECTIVES, has taught dance history at the High School of Performing Arts, Connecticut College School of Dance, and University of California, Riverside. She has published articles in many periodicals, has served on the boards of the American Society for Aesthetics, National Association for Regional Ballet, and Committee on Research in dance. She is currently a member of the Advisory Dance Panel for National Council on the Arts, and of the executive committee of the American Society for Theatre Research. Miss Cohen is author of THE MODERN DANCE: SEVEN STATEMENTS OF BELIEF.

VERA LEWIS EMBREE, teacher-director of Central High School and the Contemporary Dance Group in Detroit, was educated at the Hampton Institute, Virginia. She has written, choreographed, and produced for both commercial and educational television, notably the special program, "The Odd Breed." She serves on the Dance Committee of the Michigan State Council for the Arts, and is Board Vice-President of Metropolitan Educational Cultural Activities Association.

JEAN ERDMAN, dancer-choreographer and founder-director of The Jean Erdman Theater of Dance, was for seven years artist-in-residence with her company at University of Colorado and for three at the Vancouver International Summer Festival. Touring seasons have included Canada, Europe, India, and Japan. Her work for total theater, THE COACH WITH THE SIX INSIDES, received the Vernon Rice and Obie Awards in 1963, then for four years toured the world. She is now Head of the Dance Theater at New York University's new School of the Arts.

MARGARET ERLANGER, Director of the Dance Division, University of Illinois, studied at the Bennington School of Dance and the Wigman School. In 1953 she was Fulbright Lecturer in Dance at University of Otago, Dunedin, New Zealand, and in 1961 she studied Japanese Drama at Waseda University, Tokyo. She is Chairman-Elect of the National Dance Division of AAHPER and author of numerous articles on dance.

JOSEPH GIFFORD, Assistant Professor of Theatre Arts, School of Fine and Applied Arts, Boston University, is also in charge of dance activity for Boston University at Tanglewood. He was a member of the Humphrey-Weidman Company, faculty member and director of the New Dance Group Studio, and director-choreographer of the Joseph Gifford Dance Theatre. He was delegate to the International Theatre Institute Congress in Vienna (1961) and Warsaw (1963), and has given numerous master classes and workshops in this country and in Europe. He is a member of the Board of Directors of the Dance Notation Bureau, and the Executive Committee, National Dance Guild.

ELIZABETH R. HAYES, Director of Modern Dance, Department of Ballet and Modern Dance, University of Utah, studied with Margaret H'Doubler at the University of Wisconsin. She is former chairman of the National Dance Section and the Dance Education Section of AAHPER, and the author of INTRODUCTION TO THE TEACHING OF DANCE and DANCE COMPOSITION AND PRODUCTION.

ALMA M. HAWKINS, Chairman of the Developmental Conference on Dance, is Professor and Chairman of the Dance Department, University of California, Los Angeles. She is Dance Substantive Specialist in the Aesthetic Education Program sponsored by Central Midwestern Regional Educational Laboratory. She is the author of CREATING THROUGH DANCE and MODERN DANCE IN HIGHER EDUCATION.

MARTHA HILL, Director of the Dance Department, Juilliard School of Music, has been director of the Bennington School of Dance, the Bennington School of the Arts, was chairman of Dance and choreographer, Bennington College, and the director of Dance, New York University. She is also a Director of the Connecticut College School of Dance and the American Dance Festival. She was a member of the Martha Graham Company. Miss Hill has been awarded the Degree of Doctor of Humane Letters, Adelphi University, and the Doctor of Fine Arts, Mount Holyoke College.

VALERIE V. HUNT, Professor of Physical Education and Director of the newly established Movement Behavior Laboratory, University of California, Los Angeles, is consultant in Federal, State, and local agencies on education in the arts and the effects of perceptual motor limitations upon learning. She is author of RECREATION FOR THE HANDICAPPED and co-author of CORRECTIVE PHYSICAL EDUCATION.

CHARLOTTE IREY, Assistant Professor, University of Colorado, and Chairman of the University Dance Program, is past chairman of the National Section on Dance AAHPER, and was director of the conference on DANCE AS A DISCIPLINE in 1965. She has danced in the summer companies of Jean Erdman and Pearl Lang, has choreographed and performed extensively in Colorado, and recently was guest lecturer at a Modern Dance Workshop at the University of Alberta, Canada.

C. BERNARD JACKSON, musician, composer, and resource consultant for mental health programs, has been musical director of the Alvin Ailey Dance Company, the Al Huang Dance Company, and of Graduate Concerts at University of California, Los Angeles, where he has lectured in the Dance Department. He is Executive Director of the Los Angeles Inner City Cultural Center. Mr. Jackson has composed music for film, plays, and dance, including scores for FLY BLACKBIRD and SCUDORAMA. He received the Obie Award (Best Musical 1961-62) and was a John Hay Whitney Fellow in 1963-64.

BYRON R. KELLEY is Executive Director of the New Jersey State Council on the Arts. Previously, he has held positions as Director of Professional Entertainment, U.S. Army Headquarters, Europe; Director Performing Arts, Brooklyn Academy of Music; and Executive Director, Harkness House for Ballet Arts, New York.

LOUISE KLOEPPER, Associate Professor and Chairman of the Dance Division, University of Wisconsin, studied at the Wigman School, and was teacher and performer at the Hanya Holm School of Dance. She was a fellow at the Bennington School of Dance, and has taught in the summer sessions at Bennington at Mills College, Colorado College, and University of California, Los Angeles.

NIK KREVITSKY, painter and designer-craftsman, Director of Art, Tucson Public Schools, has a background of study in dance. He was associate editor of DANCE OBSERVER, and is a member of the editorial board of IMPULSE. In 1962 he was U.S. representative to the UNESCO Institute for Education in Hamburg, and in 1964 a panel member of the Fifth International Congress on Aesthetics in Amsterdam. He is author of BATIK — Art and Craft, STITCHERY — Art and Craft, and APPLIQUE — Art and Craft.

JUANA DE LABAN, Associate Professor of Dance at the University of California, Los Angeles, is lecturer, writer, and researcher on dance. She is a member of the Council of the Society for Ethnomusicology, the Committee on Research in Dance, and member and former chairman of the American Educational Theatre Association.

SUSANNE K. LANGER, Professor Emeritus of Philosophy, is research scholar at Connecticut College. Dr. Langer is the author of PHILOSOPHY IN A NEW KEY, FEELING AND FORM, and PHILOSOPHICAL SKETCHES. The first volume of her new work, MIND: AN ESSAY ON HUMAN FEELING, has recently been published.

ELEANOR LAUER, Professor and Chairman of the Dance Department, Mills College, Oakland, California, has had extensive experience in choreography and performing. She taught at the Actors' Company School of the Theatre in Chicago, and travelled and taught in the Far East on a Ford Foundation grant. She is director of the childrens' arts program at Mills College, and has been associated for the past two years with Upward Bound, the Federally sponsored anti-poverty education program for high school students.

JOSÉ LIMÓN, dancer, choreographer, and teacher, is on the faculties of the Juilliard School of Music and the Connecticut College School of Dance. He is director of his own company which has toured extensively in this country, Europe, South America, and Asia. His was the first dance company to be sent abroad under the International Cultural Exchange Program of the U.S. State Department. Mr. Limón received an Honorary Doctorate from Wesleyan University and the Capezio Dance Award.

ROBERT LINDGREN is Dean of the North Carolina School of the Arts and a teacher of ballet. With his wife, Sonja Tyven, Mr. Lindgren established the Lindgren School of Ballet in Phoenix, Arizona after having performed as featured artist in the Ballet Russe de Monte Carlo, New York City Ballet, and Ballet Theatre. He has appeared in Broadway productions and over 100 television shows, and has choreographed for the North Shore Music Theater, the Phoenix Musical Theatre, the Phoenix Art Festival, and the Sombrero Playhouse.

EUGENE LORING is Chairman of Dance and Senior Lecturer at University of California, Irvine Campus, and Director of the American School of Dance, Los Angeles. As a choreographer his credits include numerous ballets (BILLY THE KID), motion pictures (FUNNY FACE), television shows (OMNIBUS), Broadway shows (SILK STOCKINGS), opera and Ice Capade productions. Mr. Loring has been a dancer and choreographer with the Metropolitan Opera Company, Ballet Caravan, The National Theatre, and The Dance Players.

DOROTHY MADDEN, Chairman of the Department of Dance, University of Maryland, was a member of the Nirenska and Butler Dance Theatre Companies. She was a visiting lecturer at Dartington College of Arts, Totnes, England, I. M. Marsh College, Liverpool, England, and at the Universities of Ottawa and Iowa, as well as guest teacher, Ministry of Education, Paris. She also served as vice-president of the National Council of Arts in Education 1965-67.

PORTIA MANSFIELD, Co-Director of the Perry Mansfield School and Camps, taught dance in many private schools, made a series of color-sound films on dance, and produced, with Louis Horst, six volumes of exercises in basic movement. With Charlotte Perry she organized the Perry-Mansfield dancers, and toured with them in this country for six years.

JOHN MARTIN was dance critic for THE NEW YORK TIMES from 1927 to 1962. He served on the faculty of the New School for Social Research and Bennington School of the Dance. He is now on the faculty of University of California, Los Angeles. Mr. Martin is the author of THE MODERN DANCE, AMERICA DANCING, INTRODUCTION TO THE DANCE, THE DANCE, WORLD BOOK OF MODERN BALLET, BOOK OF THE DANCE.

JACK MORRISON, Dean of the College of Fine Arts and Professor of Theatre, Ohio University, Athens, Ohio, was formerly an associate professor and a director in the Theatre Arts Department, University of California, Los Angeles. He has served as Theatre and Dance Consultant to the Arts and Humanities Program of the U.S. Office of Education, and president of both the American Educational Theatre Association and the National Council of the Arts in Education.

RUTH L. MURRAY, Professor and Coordinator of Dance Activities and Chairman of the Women's Staff of the Division of Health and Physical Education, Wayne State University, Detroit, has been chairman and advisory member of the Dance Section of AAHPER and editor of DESIGNS FOR DANCE for the journal of that association. Currently, she serves as chairman of the Dance Committee of the Michigan Council of the Arts. Miss Murray is author of DANCE IN ELEMENTARY EDUCATION.

ALWIN NIKOLAIS, choreographer and composer, is Director of the Henry Street Playhouse and his own dance company. In addition to regular seasons of dance-theatre in New York City, he has toured the United States, presented commissioned works for art festivals in Montreal, New London, Illinois, and Utah, and has worked extensively in television. He has been the recipient of two Guggenheim Fellowships and a grant from the National Council on the Arts. His group has participated in the Spoleto Festival and the program of the New York State Arts Council. Mr. Nikolais is President of the American Association of Dance Companies.

ESTHER E. PEASE is Chairman for Dance at the University of Michigan and Director of the Theatre Dance Touring Company. She has taught at Whittier College, San Diego State College, and Purdue University, and co-authored MODERN DANCE: Building and Teaching Lessons. She is the author of MODERN DANCE in the William C. Brown series on physical education activities, is past chairman of the Dance Division of AAHPER, and serves as consultant to the Bureau of Research, U.S. Department of Health, Education and Welfare.

NANCY W. SMITH, Associate Professor and Chairman of Dance at Florida State University, was formerly a member of the dance faculty at Sam Houston State College. She is Chairman of the Dance Division of AAHPER, and has served as national editor for the Dance Division as well as editor of FOCUS ON DANCE IV: Dance as a Discipline.

ALLEGRA FULLER SNYDER has a comprehensive concern for dance, which she feels can best be expressed and implemented through film. She is now on the faculty of University of California, Los Angeles, and has performed with Ballet Society, and choreographed for the Robert Joffrey Ballet. She is dance-film editor of FILM NEWS and a recent contributor to DANCE MAGAZINE, DANCE PERSPECTIVES, and IMPULSE. Her documentary film on Phillipine dance, BAYANIHAN, won a Golden Eagle Award.

MARIAN VAN TUYL, editor of Impulse Publications since 1951, former dancer and choreographer, was chairman of the Dance Department at Mills College, and also taught at the University of Chicago for ten years. She toured extensively with her dance group, and was one of the first fellows in choreography at Bennington School of Dance. Recently, she has been a member of the faculty at Connecticut College School of Dance.

LUCY VENABLE, Certified Labanotation Teacher and Notator, is President of the Dance Notation Bureau. She has danced with the companies of José Limón, Pauline Koner, and Ruth Currier, taught dance at the Limón studio, dance and Labanotation at Juilliard School, Connecticut College School of Dance, and the YM-YWHA. She was a founder and company director of the Merry-Go-Rounders. Miss Venable has notated PASSACAGLIA and NEGRO SPIRITUALS, and is co-author with Fred Berk of "Dances from Israel" and "Ten Folk Dances in Labanotation."

BETTY WALBERG composes and arranges music for dance for theatre, films, and television. She has been on the faculties of New York University, Connecticut College School of Dance, and Juilliard School, and has been associated with Martha Graham, Anna Sokolow, José Limón, and other leading figures in the dance. She was piano soloist with Jerome Robbins' BALLETS: U.S.A. Her credits include WEST SIDE STORY, GYPSY, FIDDLER ON THE ROOF, FUNNY GIRL, DR. DOOLITTLE, and a current television special, THE FRED ASTAIRE SHOW.

THOMAS S. WATSON is Chairman of the Department of Dramatic Arts and Speech, University of Delaware. He has been director of the Theatre of the State University of New York at Buffalo, and instructor in Stagecraft and Lighting at Connecticut College School of Dance. He counts among his skills those of director, designer, theatre consultant, and administrator.

VIRGINIA FREEMAN WEIL, Assistant Professor, American University, teaches at the National Ballet School and the Arena Stage in Washington, D.C. She has directed the Washington Dance Repertory Company since 1964, and was a founding director of the Dance Quartet. Mrs. Weil has taught at the University of Illinois, University of California, Los Angeles, Sarah Lawrence College, and assisted Louis Horst at Connecticut College School of Dance. She was a recipient of a grant from the National Endowment for the Arts.

MARY WHITEHOUSE is a charter member of the American Dance Therapy Association, and is engaged in the development of a movement approach to the integration of personality, based on studies in Analytical Psychology at C. G. Jung Institute, Zurich, and in Los Angeles. Her dance training includes study at the Wigman Central Institute, the Jooss Ballet School, and the Martha Graham School. She is on the dance faculty of University of California, Los Angeles.

PATRICIA WILDE is well known as a ballerina with the New York City Ballet here and in Europe, Russia, and the Orient where the company toured. She has appeared as guest soloist and choreographer for the New York Philharmonic Promenade Concerts. She has taught master classes for the Ford Foundation, and acted as consultant to the New York State Council of the Arts. She was director of the School of Ballet and Dance of Harkness House where she had set up choreographers' workshops and programs of lecture-demonstrations.

SHIRLEY WIMMER, Director of the Dance Program, College of Fine Arts, Ohio University, Athens, Ohio, was formerly on the faculty at University of California, Los Angeles, chairman of the Dance Department, Mills College, and assistant director at Connecticut College School of Dance. She has had extensive experience in performance and choreography, and received a Ford Foundation Fellowship to investigate the relationship between Folk and Classical styles of dance in India. She was chairman of "Programs of Study in Dance," AAHPER Conference on Graduate Education, and is Field Reader and Consultant: Arts and Humanities Program, U.S. Office of Education.

CARL WOLZ, Assistant Professor, University of Hawaii, teaches dance and related subjects in the Drama and Music Departments. His field of specialization has been in Art History and Asian Studies, and he has a background of study in ballet, modern dance, and ethnic dance. He has taught Labanotation at the Dance Notation Bureau, Juilliard School, Connecticut College School of Dance, the University of California, Los Angeles, and in Tokyo, and is President of the Hawaii State Dance Council.

JOAN J. WOODBURY, Assistant Professor of Dance at the University of Utah, is Artistic Director of the University of Utah Repertory Dance Theatre. In 1955-56 she received a Fulbright Scholarship to study with Mary Wigman. She has been guest lecturer and performer at the University of Wisconsin, Utah State University, University of Rhode Island, University of Arizona, and at the Walker Art Center.